GLOBAL TRADE
and
POOR NATIONS

GLOBAL TRADE
— *and* —
POOR NATIONS

The Poverty Impacts and
Policy Implications of Liberalization

BERNARD HOEKMAN

MARCELO OLARREAGA

editors

CENTER FOR THE STUDY OF GLOBALIZATION
Yale University

GROUPE D'ECONOMIE MONDIALE
SCIENCES PO
Paris

BROOKINGS INSTITUTION PRESS
Washington, D.C.

Library of Congress Cataloging-in-Publication data

Global trade and poor nations : the poverty impacts and policy implications of liberalization / Bernard Hoekman and Marcelo Olarreaga, editors ; foreword by Ernesto Zedillo.
    p.   cm.
Summary: "Assesses the impact of reformed trade policies on the poorest of the poor
from a spectrum of poor nations across different regions. Provides guidelines regarding
the likely impacts of a global trade reform, utilizing a methodology that combines information to capture effects at the macro level and in individual households"—Provided
by publisher.
Includes index.
ISBN-13: 978-0-8157-3671-4 (pbk. : alk. paper)
ISBN-10: 0-8157-3671-1 (pbk. : alk. paper)
1. International trade. 2. Commercial policy. 3. Poverty—Developing countries.
4. Developing countries—Commerce. I. Hoekman, Bernard, 1959– II. Olarreaga,
M. (Marcelo) III. Title.
HF1379.G586 2007
339.4'6091724—dc22   2007016124

Contents

Foreword

This book grew from what was originally conceived as a much smaller project to supplement the work of the United Nations Millennium Project Task Force on Trade, for which we had the pleasure to serve as co-coordinators. In its initial form, four research papers were commissioned to assess the impact of potential trade reforms on poverty reduction in specific low-income countries: Cambodia, Ethiopia, Madagascar, and Zambia. What were the potential economic gains these countries might experience from improved access to global markets and their own trade reforms required by the Doha Round? And what would be the impact of both types of reforms on the welfare of their poor populations? To answer questions such as these, the studies identified the poor in terms of their consumption and production patterns and investigated the effects of both the status quo set of trade policies and possible changes in these policies. Our overall goal was to quantify the likely impact of global reforms agreed under World Trade Organization (WTO) auspices as part of a Doha Round outcome on individual developing countries. And we also wanted to identify specific policies and interventions needed to expand and broaden the supply response to reforms and to address adjustment costs.

Ultimately, the initial four country studies were expanded to seven. The authors reviewed and analyzed an enormous amount of information representing the latest research and country-level experiences on trade. They discovered over and over that research supports the findings of the Task Force on Trade: trade openness can be a powerful driver of economic growth, which is, in turn, indispensable to reducing poverty and fostering development.

The project was a joint venture of the Groupe d'Economie Mondiale, Sciences Po (Paris), the Yale Center for the Study of Globalization, and the Development Research Group of the World Bank. The main findings of the first papers on Cambodia, Ethiopia, Madagascar, and Zambia were incorporated in the task force report, *Trade for Development: Achieving the Millennium Development Goals* (www.unmillenniumproject.org/reports/tf_trade.htm). Subsequently, all of the papers were revised, and three more were completed on Bolivia, Nicaragua, and Vietnam.

Financial support is gratefully acknowledged and came from the Groupe d'Economie Mondiale, where the manuscript was completed while Bernard Hoekman was a visiting professor during the 2004–05 academic year, as well as from the John D. and Catherine T. MacArthur Foundation, the Yale Center for the Study of Globalization, and the governments of the United Kingdom (Department for International Development–DFID) and the Netherlands (through the World Bank–Netherlands Partnership Program). Many of the ideas contained in the concluding chapter draw on research that was commissioned as part of the Global Trade and Financial Architecture Project, which was supported by DFID and chaired by Ernesto Zedillo.

The editors are indebted to Alan Winters for his support and guidance; to all the authors for their willingness to prepare background papers at short notice under a tight deadline and to revise their papers extensively to ensure the use of a common methodology; and to Barbara Bender, Rebecca Martin, and Haynie Wheeler for help with the logistics.

As with all volumes such as this, all views expressed in this book are those of the authors and should not be attributed to the institutions with which they are or have been affiliated.

PATRICK MESSERLIN   ERNESTO ZEDILLO
Groupe d'Economie Mondiale   *Center for the Study of Globalization*
Sciences Po, Paris   *Yale University, New Haven*

Introduction

ERNESTO ZEDILLO

The biggest problem confronting the World Trade Organization (WTO) at the time of writing this—end 2006—is surviving the Doha Round. The Doha Round negotiating process generated some positive developments for the trading system, one of which is the focus of this book: a better understanding of the linkages between trade and poverty and the need for complementary measures to assist the poorest countries to benefit from global trade opportunities, including "aid for trade." But this positive aspect of the process is greatly outweighed by the negatives. It is still not known whether the Doha Round will eventually be brought to closure, but whatever the outcome deep concerns are warranted about the consequences of the Doha Round for the future of the multilateral trading system.

It is useful to recall how difficult it was to launch the round. The road from the disastrous Seattle ministerial to the approval of the Doha declaration was a relentlessly rocky one. The odds of holding a successful ministerial gathering at Doha that could initiate a new round were very small even as late as the summer of 2001. After all, the two biggest players—the United States and the European Union (EU)—had hesitated until June to endorse formally and jointly the idea of a new round. Even after this endorsement, suspense and drama continued to pave the road to Doha.

In his late July 2001 gloomy reality check, Mike Moore, the WTO director general, concluded, "A large number of players are not yet convinced," and

"The situation is fragile, and without generosity, good manners, and goodwill, the process could implode and become unmanageable."[1] He was right to be worried. Based on the purely mercantilist logic that had driven previous rounds, some of the key players seemed to think that they had little reason to support a new round. Some feared that they would end up yielding more "concessions" than the ones they would probably receive from others. In the case of the United States, a possible reason for not pushing strongly for the new round was that it saw more promise in extracting "concessions" through the expedient of preferential trade agreements (PTAs). Many developing countries were rejecting the idea of a new round on the grounds either that developed countries had failed to deliver on commitments they had made under the previous Uruguay Round or that certain WTO provisions had, in practice, proved to be counter-productive. Then there were those, like the European Union, that agreed to the round but in the end would do the utmost to resist a firm commitment to undertake serious reforms in the key area of agriculture.

Given the much larger and diverse country composition of the WTO as compared to the composition of the previous General Agreement on Tariffs and Trade (GATT) rounds, it should have been evident that the pure logic of mer-cantilist negotiations—based on reciprocal concessions—could not be the driv-ing force that would launch the new round and make it succeed. This approach could hardly do the job of achieving further trade liberalization given the varia-tion in priorities and interests of the WTO membership.

The challenge of deepening global trade liberalization had become much less of a traditional mercantilist undertaking and more a task of providing a global public good, with all the sovereignty issues and free-rider complications that such an endeavor entails. In the absence of an otherwise undesirable global government with the capacity to coerce countries into international agree-ments, creating the conditions for the adequate provision of global public goods critically depends, not on sheer authority, but on effective leadership. Certainly leadership stems from power, but another crucial element is legiti-macy grounded in clarity of purpose and the willingness to move toward that purpose without waiting for others to do so. Sometimes it also depends on the willingness to contribute incentives that will entice others to follow.

Sadly it took the 9/11 tragedy to bring together the ingredients demanded by Mike Moore in his mid-summer reality check and to inspire the leadership required to launch the new round. The atrocity energized not only the military but also the soft power of the United States, although, unfortunately, only briefly. Because of the latter, a vision different from the mercantilist one preva-lent until then came into play. This vision, novel at that point in the Bush gov-ernment, was best put forward by U.S. Trade Representative Robert Zoellick in

1. WTO (2001).

a series of articles and speeches he started to deliver less than ten days after 9/11. They were part of a strategy to convince the U.S. Congress of the need to pass the Trade Promotion Authority (TPA) and the need to launch a new round of trade liberalization. Zoellick kept repeating,

> The international market economy, of which trade and the WTO are vital parts, offers an antidote to this violent rejectionism. Trade is about more than economic efficiency; it reflects a system of values: openness, peaceful exchange, opportunity, inclusiveness and integration, mutual gains through interchange, freedom of choice, appreciation of differences, governance through agreed rules, and a hope for betterment for all peoples and lands.[2]

Curiously, these concepts earned Mr. Zoellick quite a few bitter and unjust attacks. For example, a usually circumspect member of Congress said that Zoellick's claim would be laughable if it weren't serious. Others accused him of melding principle with opportunism and of cynical exploitation of widespread misfortune. An aggressive commentator went so far as to accuse Mr. Zoellick of using tactics reminiscent of those applied by the infamous senator Joe McCarthy in the 1950s. That opinionated commentator should have known better. By linking trade with the pursuit of peace and democracy, Zoellick was not using McCarthy's tactics, but rather evoking old ideas, advocated and put to good use before by statesmen like American presidents Truman, Roosevelt, and Wilson. In fact, Zoellick was relying on concepts that go back to Kant's *Perpetual Peace*, published in the late eighteenth century and, to some extent, as far back as the early seventeenth century, when Eméric Crucé first claimed that trade would prevent war.

At any rate, the new sense of urgency gave rise to a strong acceleration of trade diplomacy that, in less than two months, culminated—not without much wrangling—in the adoption of the Doha Ministerial Declaration on November 14, 2001. The leadership, generosity, good manners, and goodwill that converged at Doha were enough to launch the new round, but not enough to prevent an overloaded agenda that, in the rush to avoid another Seattle, had to accommodate all kinds of requests from the member countries. At Doha I became particularly concerned when EU representatives substantially hardened their demand to have nontrade, even environmental, issues included in the agenda precisely when it became clear that they were alone in opposing the commitment to undertake negotiations on agriculture as expressed in paragraph 13 of the declaration. At the time, I wondered whether the inclusion of nontrade issues could be better characterized as a Trojan horse or a time bomb.

---

2. Zoellick (2006).

All this indicates that the Doha Round encompassed a hazardous paradox: it was launched mainly because of geopolitical factors and global public good considerations; however, since the very beginning both the agenda and negotiation dynamics have obeyed essentially a mercantilist logic. As a global public good endeavor framed in a broader strategy of international cooperation, Doha had a powerful *raison d'être*. As an enterprise of 149 countries in which each, with no exceptions, acts on a strictly mercantilist logic and holds veto power under a single-undertaking framework, it had a very weak one.

The vision and logic that propelled the round's launching seemed to vanish as soon as the lights were turned off in the big conference room where the Doha closing ceremony took place. Once this fact is acknowledged, the story of missed deadlines and lack of substantive agreements that the round has produced so far is not surprising. To paraphrase Gabriel García Márquez, the story is a chronicle of a failure foretold.

July 31, 2004, was a rare moment of potential optimism. The adoption of the framework constituted progress. Afterward, however, and for well over a year the negotiations produced nothing significant. Only the specter of another failure compelled trade ministers to agree to a declaration at the Hong Kong ministerial meeting in December 2005. The fact that an outcome similar to the one of the ill-fated Cancún meeting was avoided made some commentators confident that the round might have turned the corner at last. This assessment was at best premature, if not outright unwarranted, given the scant substance contained in the Hong Kong declaration.

The end date for agricultural export subsidies (2013) agreed to at the Hong Kong meeting not only covers only a small percentage of total farm support but also is later than the date that serious analysts consider to be a balanced compromise (2010); indeed, 2013 was already the date implicit in the current European agricultural policy for phasing out export subsidies. Likewise, the elimination of cotton export subsidies by developed countries by 2006 was not a very impressive achievement. The major offender, the United States, was due to effectuate something similar anyway because of the WTO dispute won by Brazil. The decision to give duty-free, quota-free market access for 97 percent of the exports of least developed countries is not very meaningful given that the excluded 3 percent of tariff lines would allow developed countries to continue protecting products of great export potential for the poorest countries.

The most important subjects—agriculture, manufactures, and services—made no progress whatsoever beyond an understanding on a raft of new deadlines for the modalities for market access on both agricultural and non-agricultural products (end April). Given the round's perfect track record of missing every single deadline before then, it was not a great surprise that all the Hong Kong deadlines were missed and that the round was put into a state of suspension at the end of July 2006 by Pascal Lamy, the new WTO director general.

A sensible way to explore whether a good outcome is feasible is to imagine the sequence of conditions and events that must occur to produce a happy ending before the expiry of TPA in mid-2007 and to subject this scenario to a reality check, à la Mike Moore. Simply for illustrative purposes, let me sketch such a sequence.

There cannot be a sound Doha result if rich countries do not apply substantial reductions in agricultural tariffs and subsidies. These countries should also be forthcoming with further cuts in their industrial tariffs, including on textiles and clothing. The biggest opposition to meaningful agricultural liberalization all along has been from the European Union, followed closely by the G-10 countries with high levels of protection of agriculture (Japan, Switzerland, Korea, Norway). So far, the European Union has stuck to its guns on this issue. The trade and agricultural European commissioners had their hands tied by the French-German pact on the EU agricultural budget agreed in the fall of 2002 and the 2003 EU Common Agricultural Policy (CAP) reforms. Every time a pertinent commissioner has tried to deviate from the CAP straitjacket, a scolding has been delivered, either directly from Paris or via Brussels, achieving instantaneous results.

The dearth of latitude given to the EU trade commissioner was confirmed, once again, by the European response to the U.S. agricultural proposal in October 2005 and by what happened in Hong Kong. Ceteris paribus, the European Union will continue to resist major cuts in agricultural tariffs and will continue asking for a large number of products to be designated sensitive and therefore exempt from the general rules to reduce protection. Considering the present political situation in France and other European countries, I do not see how the EU position on agriculture could go through the required and indispensable changes any time soon.

Even if the EU negotiators miraculously were granted a reasonable margin of action on agriculture, this would not be accomplished without getting meaningful concessions from others. Assume that the U.S. Trade Representative can put on the table what it takes to get the deal done, a heroic assumption in light of current American politics, with the Democrats having obtained the majority in both houses of Congress and the fact that the inability to offer a relatively small increase in subsidy disciplines led to the suspension of the round. Assume also that the G-10 is brought on board. After that, it would be the turn of the majors in the G-20 to pay. Are Brazil and India ready to slash industrial and agricultural tariffs? Are they ready to make more ambitious offers in services? To give some preferences to least developed countries? Even if Brazil did all these things, for India to do so would be no small enterprise, considering how slowly the processes of reform tend to proceed in the Indian democracy. At the very least, some additional incentives would be needed to get India to do its part. Binding free entry of electronic delivery of cross-border services and a gesture in mode four of the General Agreement on Trade in Services (GATS) might be required as a bonus by the Indian officials to move. Are these conditions feasible?

Were all of the above to be solved, plus the rest of the G-20 problems as well as the pertinent issues on rules, dispute settlement, and PTA disciplines, still remaining would be the question of how to deal with the concerns of the least developed and other developing countries. Many of these countries have yet to acquire the capacity to export agricultural and industrial products and would have their trade preferences and fiscal revenues eroded if a truly liberalizing Doha outcome were to come about.

In addition to getting a *complete* duty-free, quota-free market access system, those countries, which should commit to freer trade for their own sake, although with greater flexibility than that accorded to the others, would need support to compensate for fiscal revenue losses incurred as a result of lowering import duties, to build the human capital and physical infrastructure they need to benefit from increased market opportunities, and to adjust to erosion of existing trade preferences that result from multilateral negotiations.

As argued in the *Trade for Development* report of the Millennium Project, greatly increased international technical and financial support for reform and adjustment by developing countries is needed to achieve sensible liberalization targets.[3] A temporary "aid-for-trade" fund commensurate with the size of the task or significantly ramped-up contributions through existing channels are needed to support poor countries in addressing adjustment costs associated with the implementation of a truly reformist Doha Round. The Hong Kong aid-for-trade pledge, the progress that is being made to create an enhanced integrated framework secretariat in Geneva to bolster trade assistance for least developed countries, and the report of the Task Force on Aid for Trade are all positive steps. However, they do not constitute credible steps to address this issue. A solid political will to pay the price for preventing the least developed countries from blocking a good deal is yet to be detected among the key players.

In short, my modest reality check is not favorable at all to the possibility that a good package of agreements can be concluded in time to avoid the expiration of the U.S. TPA on June 30, 2007. Therefore, it is imperative to start openly entertaining scenarios of what must be done in the face of this reality. Governments have a serious responsibility to look ahead and consider how to handle the situation. It is unlikely that the enlightenment that was absent for five years will appear at last. It is better to accept that countries will continue to be driven by a purely mercantilist logic. But even if they remain faithful to this logic, governments should realize that it is in nobody's interest to undermine the existing multilateral trading system further. I cannot think of any WTO member that would win, now or in the foreseeable future, from a weakened WTO. Assuming that it becomes evident that the goal of reform in the Doha Round is missed, the goal of at least preserving the WTO should become the priority for all concerned.

---

3. UN Millennium Project (2005).

Basically, there are three options. The first is to extend formally, either with a fixed term or without it, the time horizon to conclude the round. The second is to adopt a package of light or minimum agreements and proceed to close the round on time for ratification by members in 2007. The third is to declare the round dead. It is not easy to decide which would be the least damaging to the system. Considerable risks are associated with all three options.

In reference to the first, I do not see how any progress in the negotiations could be made at all within the next two or three years, particularly in the absence of the U.S. TPA and given the intensification of electoral politics in key places like the United States and France. Meanwhile, two bad things will be happening. On the one hand, the WTO will continue to be under the tremendous stress of running the existing system and the round talks simultaneously. One activity complicates the other. Furthermore, countries that have an urgent need to liberalize their foreign trade will continue delaying action on that front so that they can keep their negotiating chips for the unclosed round. Both circumstances conspire in favor of global protectionism.

The second route of a "Doha lite" is also full of downsides. Nothing guarantees that the pending big issues will be solved when put back into the built-in agenda. Besides, in the absence of a truly overhauled system, increasing protectionist pressures and trade conflicts, which sooner or later will be brought to the WTO, will inevitably tax its institutional resources. The risk of inefficiency by fatigue is a serious one for the WTO.

The third scenario implies writing off five years of investment by governments and the private sector, a likely increase in disputes on contentious policies, with rising stress on the multilateral trading system, and even greater incentives than exist today for governments to turn inward and approach trade policy reform through a bilateral or regional track. This can only be to the detriment of small countries and the poorest and most vulnerable economies, especially if there are knock-on effects on the willingness of developed countries to live up to their promises of providing more assistance to strengthen trade capacity in these countries.

Under all three options, an even worse proliferation of preferential trade agreements will occur. This would have two consequences. First, the existing multilateral trading system would be weakened by the preferences and trade diversion generated by these agreements. Second, the preferences would make it even harder to reform the system in the future.

Despite its obvious shortcomings, I find the second option the least odious. Transparency in conceding failure in achieving an ambitious outcome now rather than later is probably best for the system altogether. But time for this option is rapidly running out. In conclusion, the relevant question that has confronted WTO members, how can the WTO save the Doha Round? soon may change to how can the WTO be saved from the Doha Round?

Does this imply that the analyses included in the book are no longer relevant? To the contrary, they are as important as ever. Understanding the impacts of changes in world prices on the incomes of households in poor countries, and—which is more important—what can and should be done to increase the benefits of trade reforms and expand trade opportunities, is as critical in a world without a Doha Round as it is in one where a round is eventually negotiated.

References

UN (United Nations) Millennium Project. 2005. *Trade for Development.* London and Sterling, Va.: Earthscan for the UN Task Force on Trade (www.unmillenniumproject.org/reports/tf_trade.htm [February 2007]).

WTO (World Trade Organization). 2001. "The Doha Ministerial: Culmination of a Two-Year Process." Doha WTO Ministerial Briefing Notes. Geneva, October (www.wto.org/english/thewto_e/minist_e/min01_e/mindecl_e.htm [February 2007]).

Zoellick, Robert B. 2006. "The WTO and New Global Trade Negotiations: What's at Stake." Speech delivered at the Council on Foreign Relations, Washington, October 30.

PART ONE

The Doha Agenda

1

The Challenges to Reducing Poverty through Trade Reform: Overview

BERNARD HOEKMAN AND MARCELO OLARREAGA

In 2001 in Doha, Qatar, members of the World Trade Organization (WTO) agreed to launch the Doha Development Agenda, a round of multilateral negotiations to reduce the use of trade-distorting policies and to bolster the development relevance of the WTO.[1] The Doha agenda spans numerous issues, including reducing agricultural support policies, liberalizing market access for goods and services, and strengthening WTO rules and dispute settlement procedures. As has been stressed in virtually all of the research on the potential impacts of broadly based global trade reform, the potential benefits for the world economy are significant. Global trade reforms can also do much to attain the Millennium Development Goal (MDG) of halving poverty by 2015. But not all groups and individuals will gain, which helps to explain why progress has been slow.

Progress on removing distortionary trade policies has been especially slow in the key area of agriculture. Sometimes the reason for limited progress on market access is seen to be the lack of "enough on the table" to interest exporters. But this ignores the fact that large emerging market countries maintain much higher tariffs and other barriers to trade than do Organization for Economic Cooperation and Development (OECD) countries. By reducing their barriers, these countries will benefit OECD exporters and bolster South-South trade. This prospect should help to mobilize the political support needed in the

1. The ministerial declaration launching the Doha Round uses the word "development" more than fifty times in its ten pages.

OECD to implement reforms. For these emerging market countries, then, the problem is not the agenda. It is that freeing trade is costly for those groups that currently benefit from trade protection.

For many smaller and poorer countries, potential adjustment costs are of concern. But a more critical problem is that they lack the international competitiveness and supply capacity with which to benefit from a freer global trade regime. Some developing countries stand to lose from trade reforms that will enhance global welfare—in particular, from deep nondiscriminatory trade liberalization that will erode the value of the trade preferences they receive or increase the import prices they pay for some staples. For poor countries that have not diversified their economies and depend on preferential access to major markets, there may be little immediate gain from multilateral trade reforms, especially if they do not reform their own trade and domestic economic policy to improve their competitiveness.

Adjustment costs in developing countries would be an inevitable outcome of ambitious global trade reform. The more ambitious these countries' own reforms, the greater the medium-term benefits for incomes are likely to be, but the greater, too, are the likely short-term adjustment costs. Addressing such costs, and putting in place a policy environment that assures households that the reforms will result in new job opportunities, is therefore an important political imperative.[2] This need spans both industrial high-income countries and developing countries.

A more open international trade regime is desirable for a number of reasons: it will lead to a better allocation of world resources, expand consumption opportunities, raise production efficiency, and help to move economies to a higher growth path. But changes in trade policy also have important distributive consequences within and across countries. Some countries and many individuals will lose as a result of trade liberalization. In principle, aggregate gains will exceed aggregate losses,[3] and, as noted in international economics textbooks, this implies that after a reform it is possible to redistribute incomes to compensate the losers while still generating net benefits for the gainers from the reform. In practice, however, political and technical constraints preclude full compensation. Political constraints include equity considerations—for example, should those who introduced past trade-distorting policies at the cost of society as a whole be compensated? Technical constraints include limitations on the ability to tax and redistribute and, more important, on the ability to identify losers and design compensation programs in a way that does not distort the incentives to adjust. These factors make compensation within countries very difficult to implement.

2. Bhagwati (2004); Zedillo and others (2005).
3. Losses are the sum of adjustment costs and the present discounted value of the difference between the prereform and postreform incomes of those individuals unable to find employment that pays wages at or above their prereform levels.

A major conclusion of most of the studies in this volume is that, even if such short-term adjustment concerns are addressed and market access liberalization can be agreed, the results will not be sufficient to harness trade for development and poverty reduction. Significant gains in poor countries from global trade reforms will depend on actions to create new jobs, raise wages, and move producers out of subsistence agriculture. Global trade reform by itself will not ensure these outcomes. Domestic supply constraints are the main reason for the lack of trade growth and diversification in many of the poorest developing countries. Without action to improve supply capacity, reduce transport costs from remote areas, increase farm productivity through extension services, and improve the investment climate, trade opportunities cannot be fully exploited and the potential gains from trade will not be maximized. The needed reforms span numerous areas, many of them "behind the border." The specific interventions that will generate the largest payoffs must be determined case by case. The associated analysis and subsequent actions to address identified priorities will generally require resources that are likely to be in short supply in most poor countries, giving rise to a strong case for additional "aid for trade" as a complement to global trade reform.[4]

The need for aid for trade has both a within- and an across-country dimension. Some countries may be net winners, and some may be net losers from global trade reform. Three questions are of particular interest: Could poorer countries be hurt by a move toward a more open trade regime? *Within* poor countries, will poorer households be negatively affected? And, if so, what can be done ex ante to reduce the incidence of any losses? These questions are at the heart of this book.

This book was motivated by the Doha Development Agenda, the multilateral trade round that was launched by WTO members in 2001. At the time of writing (end 2006), it remains unclear whether the trade round can be brought to a conclusion. As Ernesto Zedillo notes in the introduction to this volume, the prospects are dim. Although the potential policy shock that drives the country studies constituting the bulk of this book is a global liberalization negotiated as part of a Doha Round outcome, the failure of Doha—should this occur—is not particularly relevant for the conclusions of the various authors. The basic questions addressed are of general interest from a development perspective.

Trade Policy Changes and the Poor

Changes in trade policy have direct and indirect effects on the poor. Direct effects on the poor arise through two main channels. First, reforms may affect

4. Prowse (2006).

the demand for their labor and other assets they own and therefore have an impact on their income. Second, trade reforms will change the price of the consumption bundle. Indirect effects will operate through changes in the incentives to invest and to innovate, which generate the potential for higher economic growth. Indirect effects can be quite important, but they are not considered in the country studies in this volume, in part because they have been the subject of much research.[5] In this book the focus is on the direct effects of global trade liberalization.

Both theory and practice suggest that the poverty impacts of a common trade policy shock will vary widely across countries. Whether the poor will benefit or not from global trade reforms depends on the country and the individual. For example, the poor in Cambodia consume and produce different products than the poor in Ethiopia, and the trade policies of these countries are also quite different. The same is true of other policies, market structures, infrastructure, regulatory regimes, and so forth. Such differences will lead to different transmission mechanisms and thus different impacts at the level of the individual and household. One cannot expect the impact of a common shock to be similar across poor households in different (poor) countries.

The goal of this book is to assess the likely impact of multilateral trade liberalization on the poor of some of the poorest countries in the world. The country studies focus on seven small poor countries spanning three regions: three countries in Africa (Ethiopia, Madagascar, and Zambia), two in Asia (Cambodia and Vietnam), and two in Latin America (Bolivia and Nicaragua). An important consideration in the selection of countries was the availability of good data on household incomes and expenditure. Such data are critical to capture the impact of global trade policy reforms at a disaggregated level within each country.

By focusing on a spectrum of poor countries across different regions, we hope to provide general guidelines regarding the likely impacts of implementing multilaterally agreed liberalization commitments and what could be done to enhance the development impacts of such reforms. The analysis in this book complements other recent research on trade and poverty linkages, such as the work by Harrison and by Hertel and Winters.[6] First, it focuses exclusively on very low-income countries for which no previous attempt has been made to measure the impacts of global trade liberalization on the poorest segments of the population. Second, it uses high levels of disaggregation at both the household and trade levels.

5. See, for example, Harrison (2005).
6. Harrison (2005); Hertel and Winters (2006). The contributions to Harrison (2005) do not analyze a common set of policy changes, and they go beyond trade to include migration and foreign direct investment. Hertel and Winters (2006) do focus on the impact on poverty of a common shock—a Doha Round liberalization—but the authors of the papers in that volume use a variety of methodological approaches.

Several methods can be used to study the impact of trade on poverty: statistical methods that rely on microeconometrics using household surveys, simulation techniques using computable general equilibrium models, and cross-country regressions. The studies here all use a similar methodology, based on statistical approaches that combine information on trade policy at the product level with income and consumption data at the household level; they also use microeconometrics to measure the responses of individuals or households to trade shocks. The use of similar empirical methods that employ the same set of global policy shocks to evaluate the impact of trade reforms allows for a deeper and more robust comparison of results across countries.

The analysis proceeds in two steps. First is the estimation of the global impact of two potential outcomes of the Doha Round on the prices of traded goods: a limited-ambition, "business-as-usual" result and a more ambitious outcome. These two scenarios are described in more detail below. The second step involves applying the estimated changes in prices and quantities at the country level, mapping the vectors of changes in global price and trade quantity that were generated in the first step onto the household survey data for each country, so as to assess the direct impact on the incomes and consumption of the poor. These impacts are partly estimated and partly calculated. Each of the country studies starts by using household survey data sets to "locate" or characterize the poor in terms of the goods and services they produce and consume. The object is to identify what assets the poor own or control, such as their type of labor, skill, land, and capital, as well as what goods they consume (their consumption bundle). Once the poor have been "located," the question analyzed is how the specific trade policy shocks affect the returns on their assets and the prices of the goods they consume as well as how easy it is for them to adjust to the new relative prices.

The first step of the project is the subject of chapter 2 by Kee, Nicita, and Olarreaga, who develop a simple multiproduct, multicountry trade model to estimate the impact of the alternative Doha outcomes on world prices, exports, and imports at the six-digit level of the Harmonized System of Goods Classification. Both country and product disaggregation are a distinct feature of the analysis, as the goal is to identify individual small, poor countries as well as the differences among countries in patterns of trade and revealed comparative advantage. This is not something that global general equilibrium models can do, as most poor countries are not identified separately in the available databases, and the level of product disaggregation is limited. The approach has the additional advantage of using estimated elasticities at the six-digit product level, which allows the associated standard errors to be used to calculate confidence intervals. Moreover, the impacts on wages, employment, and domestic prices of the simulated global price-quantity changes are estimated wherever possible. Thus a distinguishing feature of the analysis is a heavy reliance on the econometric estimation of key variables rather than on assumptions about how markets and households would react to the trade shocks.

Two potential outcomes of the Doha Development Agenda are considered. The first, termed *business as usual,* involves a 40 percent reduction in the bound tariffs of WTO members, with applied tariffs that vary depending on the difference between current applied and bound levels; a reduction of all tariff peaks to a maximum of 50 percent; a 40 percent reduction in commitments for domestic agricultural support (the aggregate measure of support); elimination of agricultural export subsidies; and an improvement in trade facilitation corresponding to a 2 percent increase in imports.

The second Doha scenario is a more ambitious one of the type advocated by the United Nations Millennium Project Task Force on Trade.[7] Termed the *ambitious* scenario, it involves the full elimination of tariffs and subsidies and the same improvement in trade facilitation as under the business-as-usual scenario, plus a 50 percent reduction in the restrictiveness of nontariff measures (tariff quotas, antidumping, and health and safety standards). As documented by the World Bank and International Monetary Fund (IMF), nontariff measures account for a large proportion of the total trade restrictiveness of the national policies applied by OECD countries (see figure 1-1).[8]

Worldwide, a business-as-usual outcome from the Doha Round would lead to a $59 billion gain in real incomes (with a 95 percent confidence interval of $46 billion to $72 billion), of which $23 billion would be captured by developing countries. While these aggregate gains may seem small, especially in light of estimates of the global gains from multilateral trade reforms that have been generated by various global general equilibrium models, they are within the range of estimates in more recent studies.[9] Under the more unlikely ambitious scenario, global welfare gains would be around $269 billion (with a 95 percent confidence interval of $253 billion to $285 billion), of which developing countries would capture $112 billion.[10]

7. UN Millennium Project (2005).
8. World Bank and IMF (2005).
9. Anderson, Martin, and van der Mensbrugghe (2006); Hertel and Winters (2006); Polaski (2006). There are several reasons why more recent global model estimates of the potential gains from multilateral liberalization are lower than previous ones. One important reason is that earlier analysis used data for the early to mid-1990s in the calibration of models (that is, pre–Uruguay Round protection levels, including the Multifiber Arrangement), did not incorporate China's accession to the WTO (and the significant liberalization undertaken by China in this process), and tended to assume that Doha would lead to full liberalization. More recent analysis generates lower estimates of the potential global gains because to some extent the earlier potential has now been realized: there has been significant liberalization since the early 1990s.
10. Both the business-as-usual and the ambitious estimates ignore the potential gains from service trade liberalization and foreign direct investment flows. This is also true in almost all of the literature analyzing global liberalization, including Anderson, Martin, and van der Mensbrugghe (2006) and Polasky (2006).

Figure 1-1. *Agricultural Protection in OECD Countries*
Percent

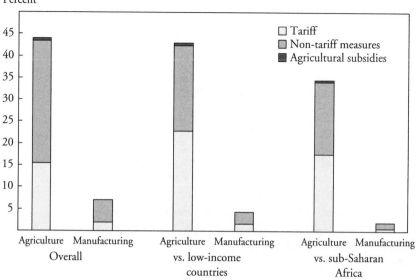

Source: World Bank and IMF (2005).

Although these are estimates, and eventual outcomes would differ substantially depending on the specifics that are eventually negotiated in the Doha Round or a subsequent round, what matters is the difference in overall magnitude across the two scenarios. Clearly, ambition matters. Moreover, in both scenarios, reducing the barriers to market access matters most for the world market prices of the products that are traded by developing countries. This is not surprising, given the finding that subsidies account for only a small share of the total trade restrictiveness of OECD countries.[11]

While the size of the global gains is affected by the type of scenario assumed, in both scenarios the gains are much greater for high-income OECD countries than for other countries. More important, under the business-as-usual scenario some forty countries are predicted to experience either no gains or a *fall* in real income (welfare). Their probable losses are mostly quite small in absolute terms, but from a poverty perspective it is noteworthy that the losers include many of the least developed countries and poor Central Asian economies. Under the ambitious Doha scenario, the number of losers falls to around twenty countries,

11. See Hoekman, Ng, and Olarreaga (2004, fig. 1); World Bank and IMF (2005). While subsidies have much less of an impact overall, at the commodity level this is not always the case, cotton being a prominent example. Indeed, for a number of African countries subsidies matter much more than market access.

and many of the least developed countries that would lose under the business-as-usual outcome register gains, sometimes substantial ones. Income inequality is estimated to remain almost unchanged under both Doha scenarios, increasing slightly under business as usual.

The simulation results imply that efforts to open up market access are vitally important, in contrast to focusing primarily on reducing subsidies and thus achieving only limited progress on market access liberalization, including non-tariff measures.

Even an ambitious outcome, however, would not be enough to make the Doha Round truly a "development round," given that the gains are likely to be skewed toward high-income OECD countries. This asymmetry could be offset by redistributing some of the gains. Such transfers to the South, if used to reduce trade costs within poor countries and to increase farm productivity (through extension services, for example), could have significant impacts, improving the outcomes for the poorest segments of the population in the poorest countries and allowing them to benefit from the new opportunities offered by multilateral trade liberalization.

The Country Studies

The analysis in chapter 2 concludes that most of the countries for which case studies were undertaken would be affected only marginally by a business-as-usual Doha scenario and that several would stand to lose slightly. By contrast, the more ambitious Doha outcome would yield gains for all the countries studied. The country studies explore the implications for poverty within each country and identify the extent to which impacts would be pro-poor—that is, benefit poorer households disproportionately—within each country. Their findings also allow an exploration of what countries could do to maximize the benefits (or reduce the potential losses for poor households) from Doha-related global liberalization.

As noted, all the country studies assume the same global reforms. Table 1-1 summarizes the broad impacts across the seven countries of the different reforms considered: implementation of an ambitious Doha deal, a business-as-usual Doha deal, poor countries' own trade liberalization, and complementary (non-trade policy) domestic reforms. While there is a lot of heterogeneity, the ambitious scenario would bring important increases in income for the poor in all seven countries studied. Implementation of business as usual would only bring significant income gains for the poor in Madagascar, Nicaragua, and Vietnam.

None of the case studies finds that the poor (on average) would be seriously hurt by the changes in trade policy proposed in the Doha Round. Thus the finding that some *poor countries* may lose in the aggregate from a round of liberalization does not necessarily imply that *poor households within these countries* would lose. This is an important distinction. A more likely outcome is that the

Table 1-1. *Summary of Country Study Findings*

Impact	Ambitious Doha	Business as usual	Own trade liberalization	Complementary reforms
Income changes				
Poor gain[a]	All	Madagascar, Nicaragua, Vietnam	Madagascar, Zambia	All
Poor unaffected[b]	None	Bolivia, Cambodia, Ethiopia, Zambia	Cambodia	None
Poor lose[c]	None	None	Ethiopia	None
Inequality				
Falls[d]	Bolivia, Madagascar, Vietnam	Bolivia, Vietnam		All
Unchanged[e]	Cambodia, Nicaragua, Zambia	Zambia		None
Increases[f]	Ethiopia	Ethiopia, Madagascar, Nicaragua		None

a. The poor gain if their average real income rises more than 1 percent.

b. The poor are unaffected if their average real income changes between −1 and +1 percent.

c. The poor lose if their average real income falls more than 1 percent.

d. Income inequality falls when the percentage increase in real income of the poorer 50 percent of individuals is at least 0.5 percentage point larger than the increase in real income of the richer 50 percent.

e. Income inequality remains unchanged when the percentage increase in real income of the poorer 50 percent of individuals is within 0.5 percentage point of the increase in real income of the richer 50 percent.

f. Income inequality increases when the percentage increase in real income of the poorer 50 percent of individuals is at least 0.5 percentage point less than the increase in real income of the richer 50 percent.

poor would remain unaffected. In terms of income inequality (as defined in table 1-1), the picture is ambiguous. Income inequality would fall in only three countries under the ambitious scenario: Bolivia, Madagascar, and Vietnam. Thus an ambitious outcome from the Doha Round is likely to benefit the poor, but not necessarily by proportionately more than it benefits the rich.

In addition to the distributional impacts of the Doha Round, the country studies analyze a wide range of complementary reforms that poor countries might pursue in conjunction with global trade reform. The findings reveal the importance of domestic actions to magnify the impact of a Doha deal. "Own" trade liberalization by individual countries is one possible reform, and in Madagascar and Zambia this would bring important gains to the poor. Indeed, in Madagascar, half of the real income gains for the poor obtained under the ambitious scenario would stem from the country's own trade liberalization. By contrast, if Ethiopia were to liberalize its trade policies, the poor would lose,

Figure 1-2. *Poverty Impact of a 10 Percent Increase in Agricultural Yields, by Region*

Percent poverty reduction

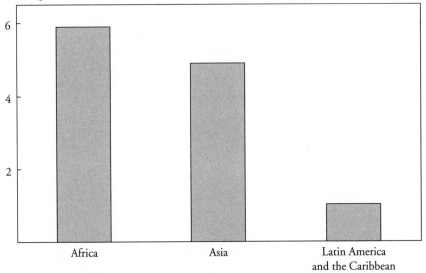

Source: Thirtle, Lin, and Piesse (2003).

because their consumption and production bundles are such that the net overall effect of the associated price and wage changes would be negative. Among other possible complementary reforms, the studies focus on actions in poor countries to move households out of subsistence production and into the market, so that they can benefit from the trade opportunities created by the Doha Round (or indeed from existing opportunities).

The results suggest that, without complementary reforms in low-income countries and without additional development assistance to pursue such reforms, multilateral reform would do much less than it could to deliver on the development promise. This finding will not be very surprising to development economists, but it has not been highlighted in most of the trade-oriented research. Given that poverty is concentrated in rural areas that depend heavily on agriculture, trade opportunities can raise incomes, but only if products are produced for the market. This may require active intervention to help households to make the switch—through extension services, access to credit, and investments in infrastructure. Moreover, such actions may also be needed to improve agricultural yields and raise productivity—a key requirement for reducing poverty in Africa (see figure 1-2). The following paragraphs summarize key findings from each country study.

In chapter 3 Alessandro Nicita concludes that in Ethiopia poor households would benefit substantially less than nonpoor households from multilateral trade liberalization. The regions that are expected to benefit the most are the urban areas of Addis Ababa and Dire-Dawa; rural and remote regions would be barely affected. Overall, multilateral trade liberalization would have only a small impact on Ethiopian households. This is partly because the likely policy changes would have only small impacts on the world prices of products exported by Ethiopia and partly because exports represent only a small part of Ethiopia's GDP, so that even hypothetically doubling the country's export values would not have much impact on overall poverty. Moreover, within Ethiopia, markets are poorly interconnected, and households largely engage in subsistence activities, with the consequence that the price and quantity effects of trade polices will not reach remote regions where most of the poor live. Finally, low agricultural productivity hinders the capacity of Ethiopian households to increase their supply to external markets.

In chapter 4, on Madagascar, Nicita concludes that a business-as-usual outcome from the Doha Round would have only a small impact on households, amounting to an increase in real income of about 0.6 percent. More ambitious multilateral trade liberalization would raise average real incomes by some 1.8 percent. The households that would benefit most are those in poverty, which would gain between 2 and 3 percent. The richest households would benefit the least in percentage terms (0.5 percent). Poor households would benefit most from price effects (due to the expected increase in agricultural prices) and from export effects (due to the expected rise in international demand for Malagasy products). Richer households would tend to benefit from the new employment opportunities in export production rather than from changes in consumer or producer prices.

In Madagascar as in Ethiopia, multilateral trade liberalization would have only small effects on the prices and international demand of export products for which Madagascar has a comparative advantage. The expected increases in the prices of cereals would not have a large net positive effect, but rather would redistribute real income from consumers to producers (from urban to rural areas). Again as in Ethiopia, Madagascar's low supply response and the insulation of poor households from market shocks—due to lack of infrastructure, missing markets, and pervasive subsistence production—make international trade policies of little direct relevance to most of the poor.

In chapter 5 Jorge Balat, Irene Brambilla, and Guido Porto find that in Zambia, too, only small impacts can be expected from a business-as-usual outcome from Doha, again because this would generate only small changes in prices for Zambian exports and imports and again because home-produced goods account for very large shares of both income and expenditure for households. An ambitious outcome would yield more significant welfare gains. To reduce poverty, Zambia would need to complement international trading opportunities with domestic reforms. This conclusion is illustrated by analyses of agricultural extension services, cotton marketing reforms, and programs supporting job opportunities for heads of households.

In chapter 6 Isidro Soloaga finds that in Cambodia trade liberalization is likely to have important effects on the rice market. A business-as-usual Doha outcome would produce a small average loss of 0.2 percent in household purchasing power, whereas an ambitious outcome would generate a substantial increase of about 7.5 percent—losses to producers from lower global rice prices would be more than offset by gains to consumers. Cambodia itself imposes high tariffs on semiprocessed and consumer goods at present, and simulations show that if Cambodia would change its tariff structure to a 7 percent flat rate, this would raise average household real income by about 3.7 percent, almost half as much as the estimated gain from ambitious global liberalization; most of the benefit would come from lower tariffs on foods. An expansion of textile exports would raise demand for labor, with potentially highly beneficial effects on the real incomes of households with at least one member switching into the new jobs; most of these households would be in the poorer 40 percent of the income distribution. For the population at large, there would be a small gain of 0.2 percent of real income. If Cambodia takes measures to improve the paddy-to-rice yield and to reduce post-harvest losses, as well as to lower transaction costs in general, the real income of the poorer half of the population could rise by more than 10 percent under the ambitious Doha scenario.

In chapter 7 Aylin Işık-Dikmelik concludes that in Vietnam neither Doha scenario would have a big effect on the overall poverty rate, but that both scenarios would cause an important redistribution of purchasing power in favor of the poor. For Vietnam, most of the changes that would follow from multilateral liberalization would result from changes in the demand for and price of rice, which is a key component of household income and expenditure as well as of exports. In the short run, real average household income would decline by 0.2 percent under business-as-usual and by 0.6 percent under the ambitious scenario. The long-run effects, which include changes in export demand and employment, would be somewhat more significant, with real income gains of 0.9 and 1.1 percent, respectively. Although actual gains and losses would depend on the level of trade liberalization implemented, urban households would almost always lose, while rural households—which include 90 percent of the country's poor—would gain much more than the average. With ambitious multilateral liberalization, over the long run Vietnam's rice sellers would gain by 10 percent of their purchasing power, and buyers would lose by 4.5 percent. Although 70 percent of all households produce rice, most of the urban poor are net buyers, but only 60 percent of the rural poor are net buyers; as a result, liberalization would have a positive effect on the rural poor.

In chapter 8 Gabriel Lara and Isidro Soloaga assess the impacts in Bolivia. The business-as-usual Doha scenario would generate an average loss equivalent

to 0.7 percent of household spending, while an ambitious outcome would produce an average gain of 1.3 percent. In this latter scenario, all would benefit
except the poorest 10 percent of households. Over the longer run, considering
the implied changes in exports, the estimated impacts would increase, with
households in deciles two through seven obtaining gains in real income of
more than 4 percent. The authors also assess the impact of potential domestic
policies to raise the demand for labor. Agricultural expansion could raise average household income by 7 percent—more than the gain that would result
from an ambitious Doha outcome. Generating such increases is therefore
important, and the growth that has taken place in the share of nontraditional
products such as soybeans and Brazil nuts in Bolivia's exports suggests that it
should be feasible. Success in the Doha Round would permit further increases
in exports of nontraditional products, raising the demand for labor with correspondingly positive effects on household incomes. The authors also estimate
that 50,000 people moving into manufacturing jobs, in response to growth in
demand for manufactured exports, would produce an average increase of about
2 percent in real incomes, with the richest 30 percent of households benefiting
the least. Thus the effects on welfare of increased labor demand induced by
changes in export demand would be greater than the effects of changes in
prices and quantities and would be more pro-poor.

In chapter 9 Ania Gomez and Isidro Soloaga find that in Nicaragua a limited outcome from the Doha Round would induce an average loss equivalent
to 0.6 percent of household purchasing power, with poorer households losing
more. By contrast, an ambitious global reform would produce an average gain
of 4.6 percent, with poorer households gaining more. The expected expansion
in labor demand coming from an increase in exports of manufactured goods
would generate an average real income gain of about 2 percent. The authors
also consider potential policies to strengthen agricultural extension services and
improve road infrastructure. They estimate that these policies would raise the
incomes of poorer families in Nicaragua, either by increasing the productivity
of coffee producers (of whom about 25 percent are in extreme poverty) or by
increasing market participation. If poor subsistence farmers could switch to
(rural) wage employment, they could expect to raise their real incomes by
about 44 percent.

Global Policy Implications: Aid for Trade and Complementary Policies

The global modeling and the country studies illustrate that, to achieve the
promise of the Doha Development Agenda, trade reforms need to be ambitious
to maximize the potential poverty-reducing impacts. But even ambitious multilateral trade reform would not achieve a major impact on global poverty and, in

particular, on outcomes in the poorest countries. Hoekman thus argues, in chapter 10, that complementary action is needed in two key areas:

—Significantly expanding dedicated grant-based funding to bolster supply capacity and improve productivity, through an "aid-for-trade" integration mechanism that identifies and addresses trade priorities and capacity constraints on a country-by-country basis, and

—Putting greater emphasis on realizing development goals and the impacts of trade policies in developing countries as opposed to focusing on defining exemptions from rules.

Dedicated Funding for Aid for Trade: A Multilateral Trade Integration Program

An ambitious freeing of market access would benefit developing countries as a group. However, as illustrated in this volume, some countries—especially the poorest—may not gain much even from an ambitious round, given their economic structures and the discouraging environments they provide for investment and business. Numerous complementary policies can and should be pursued so that more households can benefit from trade opportunities. Many of these policies will require resources for their implementation.

An important first step toward mobilizing additional resources to bolster trade capacity was the commitment by the G-8 heads of government in 2005 to increase aid to developing countries to build physical, human, and institutional capacity for trade and to grant additional support to build the capacity of developing countries to take advantage of the new opportunities for trade that would result from a positive conclusion of the Doha Round.[12]

In absolute terms, multilateral trade liberalization would yield greater economic benefits to high-income countries than to developing countries. Given that, for many poor countries, the overall gains from trade reform would be relatively limited, there is a case for transferring some of the gains that would accrue to rich countries to those that are less well off. Building capacity for trade is arguably also a good use of some of the additional aid that OECD countries have agreed to provide independent of the outcome of the Doha Round: bolstering the trade capacity of poor countries would help to achieve development goals by increasing economic growth and expanding employment.[13] But providing additional aid for trade in the context of an ambitious outcome from

---

12. See G-8, Gleneagles 2005, Africa text: para. 22(a), available at www.fco.gov.uk/Files/ kfile/PostG8_Gleneagles_Africa,0.pdf [February 2006].
13. The pursuit of development goals through trade-induced growth and employment suffers from not being able to target specific MDGs directly, but it may be more sustainable, because the associated improvements in areas such as primary education will be demand driven rather than exogenously induced by aid aiming to create schools and train teachers.

Doha—in effect redistributing some of the global gains from trade—could also deliver the desired ambitious outcome by increasing political support for deep trade reforms. Aid for trade can never substitute for progress on market access or unilateral domestic reform. But it can greatly increase the benefits of trade opportunities for many poor countries by supporting their own reforms and can help to deliver the global public good of substantially freer trade.

Although the modalities of how additional funding should be administered, allocated, and monitored will need to be resolved, the basic principles that should be satisfied by an aid-for-trade integration mechanism are simple: support should take the form of grants, be credible and predictable, cover more countries than just the least developed, be based on a process of identifying needs for trade capacity that is truly country driven and country owned, and have its processes and outcomes monitored independently.[14]

Particularly important are the credibility and predictability of funding.[15] Previous "best endeavor" promises to provide assistance for trade were only partly realized, and more promises provide little assurance to low-income countries that their concerns will be addressed. Experience shows the need for a mechanism that is dedicated to identifying and addressing the constraints on a nation's trade competitiveness, augmenting the gains from global trade reforms, and helping to offset the adjustment costs of reform.

The elements of such a mechanism have been created in recent years in the form of the Integrated Framework for Trade-Related Technical Assistance. As detailed in chapter 10 of this volume, the integrated framework brings together six multilateral agencies—the International Monetary Fund, the International Trade Center, the United Nations Conference on Trade and Development (UNCTAD), the UN Development Program, the World Trade Organization, and the World Bank. The basic purpose is twofold: to help countries to define a trade agenda by identifying and prioritizing a set of trade-related adjustment and capacity-building needs and associated complementary reforms and to provide support to embed the resulting trade agenda into a country's overall development strategy (usually the poverty reduction strategy), so as to assist the country concerned in seeking financing for needed investments from donors and international institutions.

At the September 2005 IMF and World Bank annual meetings, agreement was reached on expanding the integrated framework by providing it with

14. Prowse (2005).

15. For more in-depth discussion, see Zedillo and others (2005); Prowse (2006). See Basu (2006) for a particularly ambitious proposal to generate funding for such schemes, arguing for the introduction of an equity tax that would be redistributed to workers hurt by globalization. As Basu notes, such a tax would need to be coordinated at the global level, as unilateral adoption of such a tax would lead to capital outflows, lower wages, and higher unemployment.

additional resources to analyze trade needs and to ensure that these needs are considered by governments and donors through existing development assistance mechanisms—poverty reduction strategy papers and roundtables of consultative groups and donors. There was also agreement to consider extending the approach to span additional countries and recognition of the need to consider whether there should be a mechanism to address requirements related to regional integration rather than just country-specific actions. A report by the first WTO Task Force on Aid for Trade, established at the Hong Kong WTO ministerial meeting in December 2005, sketched a number of the key elements of operationalizing a concerted effort to expand aid for trade and make this more effective in strengthening trade capacity and performance. This includes mechanisms to define demand for assistance better and to ensure that a supply of funds and expertise will be made available to address demands. The task force stresses the importance of more regular monitoring of the development assistance provided by members to developing countries in the trade area.[16]

Much remains to be done to define and put in place the modalities for moving forward on aid for trade. This is important whatever the ultimate outcome of the Doha Round, as an effective mechanism for making additional resources available to help developing countries to implement their trade strategies and benefit from trade opportunities will have a high return independent of the WTO process. Indeed, in the event of a Doha failure, WTO members are likely to pursue a very similar agenda in the context of preferential trade and regional integration agreements.

From Exceptions for Developing Countries to Helping Achieve Development Goals

One of the important questions facing policymakers in the Doha Round concerns the circumstances, if any, under which international rules should allow developing countries to use trade policies to pursue development (for example, by using import barriers to protect domestic industries). While the basic trade policy rules of the WTO make good sense for all countries, high-income and developing alike, these rules ignore the fact that governments may be forced to use trade policy because more efficient instruments are not available (for example, a country's weak tax base may preclude the government from using subsidies). Compliance with basic WTO rules is also more costly for low-income than for high-income WTO members, insofar as the negotiated rules reflect the status quo in industrial countries.

Providing exemptions for the use of trade policies by developing countries—the traditional WTO approach and the focus of much of the Doha negotia-

16. WTO (2006).

tions on special and differential treatment—is not the best way to achieve development objectives. For example, in a recent paper, Stern and Deardorff argue that special and differential treatment can actually hurt countries that are supposed to benefit from it, as trade negotiations undertaken by countries participating in the liberalization effort are likely to result in a deterioration in the terms of trade for those staying on the sidelines.[17] Instead of focusing exclusively on exemptions to allow the use of trade policy instruments, the trading system could support development by providing independent monitoring of the development impact of trade and trade-related policies, together with the proposed aid-for-trade integration mechanism. A more proactive approach is needed to help developing countries to attain their trade-related objectives.[18]

This could be achieved by creating a mechanism in the WTO that focuses on a country's trade agenda and priorities and links them to the enhanced aid-for-trade integration program mentioned above. The goals of such a mechanism would be to reduce governments' perceived need to use costly trade policy tools, to place the implementation of WTO disciplines in a national context, and to monitor the effects of trade and related policies.

Different complementary options can be considered to operationalize this idea. The most limited of these is to build on the agreement that was reached in the area of trade facilitation, making the implementation (enforcement) of negotiated disciplines conditional on developing countries' receipt of adequate assistance from industrial countries. A more ambitious option would be to establish a multilateral mechanism to help developing countries to pursue national objectives through instruments that do not distort trade. A specific way to do this would be for WTO members to agree to a set of "core" disciplines that apply to *all* members and to allow developing countries to invoke a "development defense" in disputes alleging the violation of non-core rules.[19] Agreement to consider options that would move in this direction is one way in which the WTO could help to achieve the goal of greater policy coherence for development.

Concluding Remarks

In its report, the UN Millennium Task Force on Trade stresses that an ambitious outcome from the Doha Round could do much to achieve the Millennium Development Goal of halving poverty.[20] Trade can and should play an

---

17. Stern and Deardorff (2006).
18. Zedillo and others (2005).
19. Hoekman (2005).
20. UN Millennium Project (2005).

important role in allowing countries to achieve development objectives. The country studies in this volume support this conclusion: an ambitious outcome from the Doha Round would help to reduce the incidence of poverty. At the same time, as the task force report notes, not all countries will gain in the short run, and all countries will face adjustment costs. From the perspective of the poorest countries, a Doha Round outcome that liberalizes market access on a nondiscriminatory basis would be beneficial, but by no means sufficient, to bolster growth prospects. Indeed, many countries may not benefit much from a Doha Round in the short run, whether ambitious or not, as many of their poorest households are connected only tenuously to markets.

Moreover, some poor countries stand to lose as a result of preference erosion; the deeper are the most favored nation (MFN) reforms that are agreed, the more existing preferential access will be eroded. This issue was not incorporated into the analysis in this volume, given that recent research on this topic suggests that the aggregate impact of preference erosion would be limited for most poor countries.[21] Preference erosion is an important issue for some countries, but they are mostly middle-income economies.[22]

Expanded, dedicated funding for an aid-for-trade mechanism that provides predictable resources to address national competitiveness constraints, addresses regulatory weaknesses, and deals with adjustment costs—including by providing assistance to help countries to deal with preference erosion and replace trade-distorting policies with alternative policy instruments that enhance the benefits of global trade policy reforms—would enhance the benefits of trade for a larger group of countries. The creation of a dedicated aid-for-trade mechanism could also facilitate a more ambitious Doha outcome on market access—or, in the event of failure of the Doha Round, lay the foundations for a subsequent effort to pursue multilateral liberalization—as well as provide tangible evidence that rich WTO members are taking development objectives seriously. As noted, the need for aid for trade is not conditional on trade negotiations or trade agreements: it should be pursued independently.

The studies in this volume illustrate the importance of detailed microeconometric analysis of the impacts of policy reforms—both global and national—on poor households. Much remains to be done to improve the methods used for such analyses and to collect the type of data needed. For example, several of the studies flag the need to incorporate market imperfections explicitly into the analysis. These are an important dimension of reality in many countries and

---

21. Administrative requirements (rules of origin), the exercise of market power by importers (retailers, distributors), product exclusions, and low most favored nation tariffs for most manufactures and natural resource–based products all imply that the effective value of preferential access is limited.

22. Alexandraki and Lankes (2004).

tend to be neglected in most general equilibrium numerical analyses, which assume that markets exist and that they clear. The different contributors to this volume have employed different approaches, and it is not clear which are most appropriate.[23] Thus many open questions remain, and the chapters in this volume constitute just a step toward more realistic modeling of the impacts of (global) trade reforms on poverty in individual countries.

References

Alexandraki, Katerina, and Hans Peter Lankes. 2004. "Estimating the Impact of Preference Erosion on Middle-Income Countries." IMF Working Paper WP/04/169. Washington: International Monetary Fund.

Anderson, Kym, Will Martin, and Dominique van der Mensbrugghe. 2006. "Market and Welfare Implications of Doha Reform Scenarios." In *Agricultural Trade Reform and the Doha Development Agenda,* edited by Kym Anderson and Will Martin. Washington: Palgrave-Macmillan and the World Bank.

Basu, Kaushik. 2006. "Globalization, Poverty, and Inequality: What Is the Relationship? What Can Be Done?" *World Development* 34, no. 8: 1361–73.

Bhagwati, Jagdish. 2004. *In Defense of Globalization.* New York: Oxford University Press.

Harrison, Ann, ed. 2005. *Globalization and Poverty.* University of Chicago Press.

Hertel, Thomas, and L. Alan Winters, eds. 2006. *Poverty and the WTO: Impacts of the Doha Development Agenda.* Washington: Palgrave-Macmillan and the World Bank.

Hoekman, Bernard. 2005. "Operationalizing the Concept of Policy Space in the WTO: Beyond Special and Differential Treatment." *Journal of International Economic Law* 8, no. 2: 405–24.

Hoekman, Bernard, Francis Ng, and Marcelo Olarreaga. 2004. "Agricultural Tariffs or Subsidies: Which Are More Important for Developing Countries?" *World Bank Economic Review* 18, no. 2: 175–204.

Polasky, Sandra. 2006. *Winners and Losers: Impact of the Doha Round on Developing Countries.* Washington: Carnegie Endowment.

Prowse, Susan. 2006. " 'Aid for Trade': A Proposal for Increasing Support for Trade Adjustment and Integration." In *Economic Development and Multilateral Trade Cooperation,* edited by Simon Evenett and Bernard Hoekman. Washington: Palgrave-Macmillan and the World Bank.

Stern, Robert M., and Alan V. Deardorff. 2006. "Globalization Bystanders: Does Trade Liberalization Hurt Countries That Do Not Participate?" *World Development* 34, no. 8: 1419–29.

Thirtle, Colin, Lin Lin, and Jennifer Piesse. 2003. "The Impact of Research-Led Agricultural Productivity Growth on Poverty Reduction in Africa, Asia, and Latin America." *World Development* 31, no. 12: 1959–75.

---

23. The methods developed to assess the incidence of job creation across households are an example: Is it better to use a matching labor approach to model the effects of an increase in employment opportunities or a probabilistic approach whereby all potential workers have the same probability of finding a job? Similarly, how should capital market imperfections and access to finance be modeled?

UN (United Nations) Millennium Project. 2005. *Trade for Development.* London and Sterling, Va.: Earthscan for the UN Task Force on Trade (www.unmillenniumproject.org/
reports/tf_trade.htm [February 2007]).

World Bank and IMF (International Monetary Fund). 2005. *Global Monitoring Report 2005.*
Washington.

WTO (World Trade Organization). 2006. "Recommendations of the Task Force on Aid for
Trade." WT/AFT/1. Geneva, July 27.

Zedillo, Ernesto, and others. 2005. "Strengthening the Global Trade Architecture for Economic Development: An Agenda for Action." Yale University, Yale Center for the Study of
Globalization (www.ycsg.yale.edu [February 2007]).

2

Estimating the Effects of Global Trade Reform

HIAU LOOI KEE, ALESSANDRO NICITA,
AND MARCELO OLARREAGA

The Doha Round has been termed the Doha Development Agenda. Much has been written by researchers and policy advocates on what would constitute a good outcome from a development perspective. Most would agree that deep trade liberalization would be beneficial for the world as a whole—and, in particular, for consumers and taxpayers in Organization for Economic Cooperation and Development (OECD) countries and for exporters in large emerging market countries with a clear comparative advantage in labor-intensive manufactures and agricultural products. There is much less agreement that deep global trade reforms would benefit the poorest countries. Indeed, many would argue that these countries may lose from global reforms as a result of their weak competitiveness and the erosion of preferential access to rich-country markets.

As discussed in chapter 1, to assess how global trade reforms are likely to affect households in poor countries, it is necessary to estimate the impacts of these reforms on prices and quantities. Such estimates are the goal of this chapter, which focuses on the impact of two possible outcomes from the Doha trade negotiations on the welfare of 165 countries. It uses a simple trade model to assess the effects of these policy "shocks" on the world prices, exports, and imports of some 5,000 goods.

The two contrasting scenarios are as follows. The first, termed business as usual, is what the Doha negotiations seem likely to accomplish if one judges by past experience and the state of negotiations at the time of writing. It involves a

40 percent reduction in the bound tariffs of World Trade Organization (WTO) members (with applied tariffs varying, depending on the difference between current applied and bound levels), a reduction in all tariff peaks to a maximum of 50 percent of average nominal tariffs, a 40 percent reduction in commitments of support for domestic agriculture (the aggregate measure of support), the elimination of agricultural export subsidies, and an improvement in trade facilitation corresponding to a 2 percent increase in imports—in line with estimates by François, van Meijl, and van Tongeren.[1]

The second scenario, termed ambitious, is close to what is often associated with "Doha" in simulation exercises, but it would probably require many more concessions than have been observed thus far.[2] It entails the elimination of all applied tariffs, a 50 percent cut in the restrictiveness of nontariff barriers (tariff quotas, antidumping measures, and health and safety standards),[3] the elimination of agricultural domestic support and export subsidies, and an improvement in trade facilitation that will lead to a 2 percent increase in world trade.

This chapter is organized as follows. The first section presents the multicountry and multiproduct trade model, and the second discusses data sources. The third section presents the results, and a final section concludes.

The results suggest that a business-as-usual outcome from the Doha Round would lead to global welfare gains on the order of $59 billion, of which $23 billion would accrue to developing countries. An ambitious outcome would lead to global gains of around $269 billion, with $112 billion going to developing countries.[4] More important, of the fifty-six countries that experience a welfare loss under the business-as-usual scenario (due essentially to the deterioration of their terms of trade), thirty-one would have a welfare gain from the ambitious reforms. In the world's poorest region—sub-Saharan Africa—seventeen of the thirty-seven countries in the sample (excluding South Africa) would experience a welfare loss under the business-as-usual scenario, but only four would do so under the ambitious scenario. The prospective changes in world income inequality are slight: the simulation results suggest a small increase under the business-as-usual scenario (a rise of 0.01 percent in the Gini coefficient), as opposed to a small decline under the ambitious scenario (a decline of 0.05 percent in the Gini coefficient).[5]

1. François, van Meijl, and van Tongeren (2005).
2. For an example of such simulation exercises, see World Bank (2004).
3. Nontariff measures account for a large proportion of the total trade restrictiveness of the national policies applied by OECD countries (World Bank and IMF 2005).
4. The welfare changes are very precisely estimated, being statistically significant at the 5 percent level for all but two countries under the ambitious scenario and for 133 out of 165 countries under business as usual. Thus the aggregate welfare gains for the world have a relatively small confidence interval: the 95 percent confidence interval is between $46 billion and $72 billion in the business-as-usual scenario and between $253 billion and $285 billion in the ambitious scenario.
5. Several other inequality indexes are also computed that confirm this result.

A Multicountry and Multiproduct Trade Model

To simulate the shocks associated with the two scenarios, we use a multimarket, multicountry partial equilibrium model. We prefer this over a computable general equilibrium (CGE) modeling approach because our goal is to provide estimates for multiple products and all countries, including the least developed, such as Burundi. Capturing as much of the real-world heterogeneity as possible is important, as our results from this analysis are used as inputs into the case studies that follow. Given that the case studies analyze effects at the level of households, the estimated changes in world prices and trade flows need to be as detailed as possible.

Existing CGE models and their underlying data sets cover only a subset of developing countries and exclude most of the least developed. Relying on aggregate data at the regional level—the approach taken in general equilibrium assessments—would hide many of the differences among countries. This is important because different countries may be affected very differently by a common shock, such as a change in the international trade regime. Our results suggest that it is indeed important to model countries individually: our estimates of changes in welfare associated with the ambitious Doha scenario vary from a loss of 0.5 percent of GDP in Mauritania and Equatorial Guinea to a gain that exceeds 5 percent of GDP in Morocco and Djibouti. An analysis that simply reports results for sub-Saharan Africa as a whole would miss this heterogeneity.

In addition to country aggregation, a CGE approach necessarily involves significant product aggregation, with a resulting aggregation bias. Most common CGE models cannot handle more than thirty industries or so. The reforms implied by the Doha Development Agenda are likely to have very different impacts on specific products, and since individual countries are likely to be quite specialized in specific types of products, it is important to be able to distinguish between salmon and shellfish and between maize and corn and rice. A partial equilibrium approach allows us to identify clearly which products are important for each country. We estimate changes in world prices at the six-digit level of the Harmonized Commodity Description and Coding System (HS), corresponding to almost 5,000 goods.

Another advantage of our partial equilibrium setup is that for each good it depends only on a few parameters, each of which has been carefully and consistently estimated elsewhere.[6] Using the information on the variance of those estimates allows us to bootstrap standard errors for the welfare changes, providing information on the statistical significance of the estimates.

The partial equilibrium setup is not without problems, as some binding structural constraints may not be satisfied. However, it does allow us to abstain

---

6. See Kee, Nicita, and Olarreaga (2004, 2005b).

from making strong assumptions about the functioning of factor markets, an issue that is better dealt with in microeconometric studies.[7]

Model Structure

Import demand and export supply functions are given by:

$$(2\text{-}1) \qquad m_c\left(p_c, Z_c^m\right) \text{ and } x_c\left(p_*, Z_c^x\right),$$

where m_c is the import demand vector of country c (across all goods g), p_c is the domestic price vector of imported goods in country c, Z_c^m is a matrix of exogenous variables determining imports in country c, x_c is the export supply vector of country c (across all goods g), p_* is the vector of world prices, and Z_c^x is a matrix of exogenous variables determining exports in country c. Thus each good g is homogeneous across all countries, but in each country it is an imperfect substitute for all other traded goods. World markets for each good clear, so that:

$$(2\text{-}2) \qquad \sum_c m_c\left(p_c, Z_c^m\right) - \sum_c x_c\left(p_*, Z_c^x\right) = 0.$$

The solution of equation 2-2 with respect to p_* yields the equilibrium world prices. Assume that all world and domestic markets are perfectly competitive, so that:

$$(2\text{-}3) \qquad p_c = p_* \cdot \tau_c,$$

where $\cdot$ is an inner product, τ is a vector (across all goods g) of $\tau_{c,g} = (1 + \tau_{c,g})$, and $\tau_{c,g}$ is the level of protection in country c on good g. For future reference, note that $\tau_{c,g}$ can include tariffs and ad valorem equivalents of nontariff measures and barriers to trade facilitation.

We assume for the moment that all Z_c^m and Z_c^x are constant—these terms are relaxed later to capture the impact of reforms in agricultural subsidies and trade facilitation. Substituting equation 2-3 into equation 2-2 and totally differentiating with respect to changes in tariffs yields:

$$(2\text{-}4) \qquad \sum_c \frac{dm_c}{dp_c}\left[\frac{\partial p_c}{\partial p_*}dp_* + \frac{\partial p_c}{\partial \tau_c}d\tau_c\right] - \sum_c \frac{dx_c}{dp_*}dp_* = 0.$$

Rearranging equation 2-4 and solving for the vector of percentage changes in world prices, $\hat{p}_*$, yields:

---

7. It is not clear to us that it is better to assume that there are perfectly functioning labor markets in all countries than simply to abstract from modeling labor markets.

(2-5)
$$\hat{p}_* = \left[\sum_c E_c^x - \sum_c E_c^m \right]^{-1} \sum_c E_c^m \tau_c,$$

where E_c^m is a squared matrix whose elements are the elasticity of import demand in country c multiplied by the share in world trade of each country's imports of good g. On the diagonal, the matrix has the own-price elasticities of import demand, and off the diagonal there are cross-price elasticities of import demand in each country. Similarly, E_c^x is a squared matrix whose elements are the elasticity of export supply in country c multiplied by the share in world trade of each country's exports of good g. On the diagonal, E_c^x has the own-price elasticities of export supply, and off the diagonal there are cross-price elasticities of export supply in each country.

Equation 2-5 is the basis for our estimation of changes in world prices associated with tariff cuts resulting from the Doha Round. Note that $\hat{\tau}_c$ is not a vector of percentage changes in applied tariffs, but rather a vector of the product of percentage changes in tariffs and $\tau_{c,g}/(1 + \tau_{c,g})$. Also if WTO members agree to reduce bound tariffs by 40 percent, the reduction is only likely to affect those tariff lines that are already bound. Current proposals suggest that tariffs currently unbound are likely to be bound at twice their current applied levels, which implies that a 40 percent reduction in bound tariffs would not affect them. Moreover, given that there is "water" in current bound tariffs (that is, the tariffs applied are lower than their respective bound rates), especially in developing countries, a 40 percent reduction in bound tariffs will not produce as much as a 40 percent reduction in applied tariffs. All this needs to be taken into account when $\hat{\tau}_c$ is computed.

We now relax the assumption that only tariffs will be reduced in the Doha Round: agricultural domestic support will be subject to cuts, export subsidies will be eliminated, and a trade facilitation agreement is likely to reduce trade costs. Allowing the matrixes Z_c^m and Z_c^x to capture these variables, differentiating as in equation 2-4 and rearranging, and solving as in equation 2-5 yields:

(2-6)
$$\hat{p}_* = \left[\sum_c E_c^x - \sum_c E_c^m \right]^{-1} \left(\sum_c E_c^m \hat{\tau}_c - \sum_c \left[E_c^{ms} - E_c^{xs} \right] \hat{s}_c \right.$$
$$\left. - \sum_c E_c^{xxs} \hat{xs}_c + \sum_c \left[E_c^{mf} - E_c^{xf} \right] \hat{f}_c \right),$$

where E_c^{ms} is a matrix of elasticities of imports with respect to domestic support multiplied by the share of imports of country c in world trade in each product; E_c^{xs} is a matrix of elasticities of exports with respect to domestic support in country c multiplied by the share of exports of country c in world trade in each product;[8]

8. Unfortunately, we do not have estimates for the cross-product effects of subsidies; therefore, these matrixes are diagonals with zeros off the diagonal.

$\hat{s}_c$ is a vector of the percentage change in domestic support; E_c^{xxs} is a matrix of elasticities of exports with respect to export subsidies, and $\hat{xs}_c$ is the vector of the percentage change in export subsidies (all multiplied by their respective share in world trade); E_c^{mf} and E_c^{xf} are the matrixes of elasticities of imports and exports with respect to improvements in trade facilitation multiplied by each country's share in world trade in each product; and $\hat{f}_c$ is the percentage change in the trade facilitation indicators in country c.

All the elements of the elasticity matrixes (E) have been estimated—with more or less precision—and therefore an error is associated with our estimates of $\hat{p}_*$. The standard error of $\hat{p}_*$ is obtained through bootstrapping as follows. For each elasticity, we create a normally distributed random variable whose mean and variance are equal to those of the estimated elasticities. We then take fifty draws (with repetition) from these variables for each elasticity and calculate fifty changes in world prices for each tariff line. The standard deviation of these fifty changes provides us with our estimate of the standard error associated with our estimated world price change. This obviously assumes that the covariance of these estimates is 0, which is statistically correct because they were independently estimated, but it could be problematic from an economic point of view. The same approach is followed to estimate the standard errors of the changes in imports, exports, and welfare that are discussed below.

Changes in Imports and Exports

The percentage changes in imports and exports of each country c are given by:

$$(2\text{-}7) \qquad \hat{m}_c = \left[E_c^m \hat{p}_* + E_c^m \hat{\tau}_c + E_c^{ms} \hat{s}_c + E_c^{mf} \hat{f}_c \right] \cdot \theta_c^m ,$$

and

$$(2\text{-}8) \qquad \hat{x}_c = \left[E_c^x \hat{p}_* + E_c^{xs} \hat{s}_c + E_c^{xxs} \hat{xs}_c + E_c^{xf} \hat{f}_c \right] \cdot \theta_c^x ,$$

where θ_c^m is a vector of the inverse of the share in world trade of country c's imports of each product, and θ_c^x is a vector of the inverse of the share in world trade of country c's exports of each product. The first term in the square brackets in equation 2-7 is the change in imports due to liberalization in the rest of the world (through the impact of liberalization on world prices), and the second term is the change in imports due to liberalization at home.[9]

Welfare Changes

The welfare changes associated with these reforms can be easily calculated if one accepts the partial equilibrium nature of this model, where prices of goods

9. As before, a standard error can be provided for $\hat{m}_c$ and $\hat{x}_c$.

in the nontraded sector are kept exogenous. Let us start with the income-expenditure identity in each country c:

$$(2\text{-}9) \qquad e(1, p_c, u_c) = r(1, p_c, v_c) + \tau_c \, p_* m_c,$$

where e is the minimum expenditure necessary to achieve utility level u_c at domestic prices p_c (1 being the price of the *numeraire* good), and r is the maximum revenue that can be achieved given (fixed) endowments v_c and domestic prices p_c. The last term on the right-hand side is tariff revenue (obtained by taking the inner product of the three vectors).

Totally differentiating equation 2-9, using Shephard and Hotelling's lemma and rearranging, allows us to obtain a first-order approximation of the change in welfare:

$$(2\text{-}10) \qquad \Delta W_c = e_u \, du_c = -n_c dp_c + dt_c \, p_* m_c + t_c \, dp_* m_c + t_c \, p_* dm_c,$$

where e_u is the inverse of the marginal utility of income, and n_c are net imports (that is, $n_c = m_c$ if the good is imported and $n_c = -x_c$ if the good is exported). Changes in imports and exports can be calculated using equations 2-7 and 2-8. The change in domestic prices is obtained by totally differentiating equation 2-3:

$$(2\text{-}11) \qquad dp_c = dp_* \tau_c + p_* d\tau_c,$$

where the changes in world prices can be obtained from equation 2-6; $d\tau_c$ is the change in applied levels of border protection implied by the Doha policy changes and is discussed below.

Data Sources

Import and export data come from the United Nations Comtrade database. We take the average between 2001 and 2003 to smooth any year-specific shock. If data are missing for a particular country, we use data for 2000 to calculate an average. For the few countries for which no data are available between 2000 and 2003, we mirror the data using partner countries' trade data (this method is used for twenty-six out of the 165 countries in the sample, most of them in sub-Saharan Africa and Central Asia).

Data on applied and bound most favored nation (MFN) tariffs come from different sources. The main source is the World Trade Organization's Integrated Data Base (IDB). Where no data are available from that source, we use the United Nations Conference on Trade and Development's (UNCTAD's)

TRAINS.[10] Because none of these sources provides ad valorem equivalents of specific tariffs, we use UNCTAD's estimates of these equivalents for Australia, Canada, the European Union, Japan, Norway, Switzerland, and the United States; for other countries, we take ad valorem equivalents from the OECD's Tariffs and Trade CD-ROM for 2003.[11] The tariff data are for the most recent year for which data are available between 2000 and 2004. For more than half the countries, the base year is 2003 or 2004; for only three countries (Peru, Kazakhstan, and Egypt), it is 2000. MFN tariffs missing from these data sources are obtained from the MAcMap database constructed by the International Trade Center (ITC) and Centre d'Etudes Prospectives et d'Informations Internationales (CEPII).[12]

Estimates of ad valorem equivalents of nontariff measures are obtained from Kee and others.[13] Nontariff measures include quantity and price interventions, monopolistic measures, and technical regulations as classified in UNCTAD's TRAINS.

Import demand elasticities (own and cross), as well as their standard errors, come from Kee, Nicita, and Olarreaga.[14] Export supply elasticities (own and cross), as well as their standard errors, come from another work by Kee, Nicita, and Olarreaga.[15] Where estimates of elasticities for particular countries are not available from those papers, we take the trade-weighted average across all countries for those products. In the case of export supply elasticities—where for some tariff lines it is not possible to estimate export supplies at the six-digit level of the Harmonized System—we take the country-specific average across all tariff lines at the four-digit level of the HS; if those are not available, we use average estimates at the two-digit level of the HS. Elasticities of imports and exports with respect to agricultural domestic support and export subsidies are obtained from Hoekman, Ng, and Olarreaga.[16] Elasticities of imports and exports with respect to indicators of trade facilitation come from François, van Meijl, and van Tongeren.[17]

---

10. UNCTAD's TRAINS not only covers the whole tariff schedule for a particular country, but for some countries, it provides information on a few tariff lines that are missing from the WTO's IDB database. In this case, we replace the missing information with what is available in UNCTAD's TRAINS, even when the tariff data are one or two years older.

11. This provides estimates of ad valorem equivalents for all OECD countries, plus Argentina, Bangladesh, Brazil, Czech Republic, Hungary, India, Indonesia, Korea, Malaysia, Mexico, the Philippines, Poland, Romania, Slovak Republic, Sri Lanka, Thailand, Tunisia, Turkey, and Venezuela.

12. See Bouet and others (2003).

13. Kee, Nicita, and Olarreaga (2005a).

14. Kee, Nicita, and Olarreaga (2004).

15. Kee, Nicita, and Olarreaga (2005b).

16. Hoekman, Ng, and Olarreaga (2004).

17. François, van Meijl, and van Tongeren (2005). Their estimates are a little smaller than those in Wilson, Mann, and Otsuki (2004).

Finally, GDP and GDP per capita data are from the World Bank's World Development Indicators database. Again, we take the average for the years with available data between 2000 and 2003.

Results

We consider the two scenarios of multilateral trade liberalization that were outlined above: business as usual and ambitious. An important difference between the two is that in the business-as-usual scenario, applied tariffs are reduced only when the new bound tariff—after a 40 percent cut in the Uruguay Round bound—is smaller than the current applied tariff. In that case, the change in applied tariffs is equal to the difference between the currently applied tariff and the new bound. Obviously, in countries for which we have no data on bound tariffs—either because tariffs are not bound or because the country is not currently a member of the WTO[18]—tariffs will only be affected by the cut in tariff peaks to 50 percent under this Doha scenario. For WTO members with unbound tariffs, this is a reasonable assumption, to the extent that the current Doha Round proposal of binding unbound tariffs at twice their applied level is adopted (in such a case, a 40 percent cut in bound tariffs will not affect applied tariffs).

The importance of distinguishing between cuts in bound and applied tariffs can be seen from table 2-1, which shows the average applied tariffs that would result from two different policy changes: a 40 percent cut in applied tariffs and a 40 percent cut in bound tariffs. The first exercise is straightforward (column 2 of table 2-1): we simply cut applied MFN tariffs by 40 percent across the board. In the second exercise (column 3 of table 2-1), we cut the bound tariffs in force at the end of the Uruguay Round by 40 percent; and then—if and only if the bound is below the current MFN applied level, as discussed above—we replace the new MFN tariff with the value of the new bound. In this second exercise, we also smooth out tariff peaks, constraining all applied tariffs to be below 50 percent of the average applied tariff.

For some countries, there is a big difference in the resulting applied tariffs. Overall, the simple average MFN tariff across all countries in the sample falls from 11.2 to 6.7 percent if a 40 percent cut on *applied* tariffs is introduced, but it only falls to 9.4 percent if the 40 percent cut is undertaken on *bound* tariffs (and peaks above 50 percent are eliminated). The median world tariff falls from 7.0 to 4.2 percent under the cut on applied tariffs, but it remains at 5.0 percent if the cut is undertaken on bound tariffs.

---

18. A number of countries in the data set are neither WTO members nor in the process of accession. They include some Caribbean islands, Iran, Montserrat, Russia, and Syria.

Table 2-1. *Simple Average MFN Tariffs before and after a 40 Percent Doha Cut*[a]

Country	MFN tariff pre-Doha	Post-Doha 40 percent cut		Country	MFN tariff pre-Doha	Post-Doha 40 percent cut	
		Applied tariff	Bound tariff			Applied tariff	Bound tariff
Albania	7.48	4.49	3.87	Lebanon	5.39	3.23	5.14
Algeria	18.68	11.21	18.68	Libya	17.04	10.23	15.09
Angola	8.81	5.29	8.80	Lithuania	3.41	2.05	2.27
Antigua	9.63	5.78	9.56	Macau	0	0	0
Argentina	14.69	8.82	14.04	Madagascar	5.67	3.40	5.65
Armenia	2.96	1.78	2.53	Malawi	13.39	8.04	13.39
Australia	4.16	2.49	3.74	Malaysia	8.63	5.18	4.91
Azerbaijan	8.66	5.20	8.66	Maldives	20.23	12.14	16.45
Bahamas	30.64	18.39	30.35	Mali	11.13	6.68	9.55
Bahrain	7.77	4.66	7.42	Malta	5.68	3.41	5.68
Bangladesh	21.77	13.06	21.66	Mauritania	10.58	6.35	8.98
Barbados	12.37	7.42	10.97	Mauritius	17.35	10.41	13.77
Belarus	11.02	6.61	10.98	Mexico	17.95	10.77	15.29
Belize	10.53	6.32	10.13	Mongolia	6.94	4.16	6.32
Benin	11.98	7.19	10.33	Montserrat	18.05	10.83	18.05
Bermuda	17.46	10.48	17.41	Morocco	30.48	18.29	18.55
Bhutan	16.61	9.97	16.38	Mozambique	12.02	7.21	12.01
Bolivia	9.44	5.66	9.42	Myanmar	5.50	3.30	5.47
Bosnia	6.04	3.62	6.04	Namibia	5.83	3.50	4.86
Botswana	5.83	3.50	4.86	Nepal	13.99	8.39	13.39
Brazil	13.65	8.19	13.18	Netherlands	5.36	3.22	2.91
Brunei	0.80	0.48	0.08	New Zealand	3.97	2.38	2.83
Bulgaria	9.93	5.96	9.09	Nicaragua	4.72	2.83	4.70
Burkina Faso	11.92	7.15	10.33	Niger	11.96	7.18	10.43
Burundi	30.10	18.06	22.41	Nigeria	29.97	17.98	25.21

Country			
Cambodia	16.40	9.84	16.38
Cameroon	18.04	10.83	18.04
Canada	4.95	2.97	2.65
Central African Rep.	18.04	10.83	17.10
Chad	18.04	10.83	18.04
Chile	5.99	3.59	5.99
China	12.46	7.48	6.24
Colombia	12.20	7.32	12.19
Congo, Dem. Rep. of	8.35	5.01	6.48
Congo, Rep. of	18.04	10.83	17.03
Costa Rica	5.41	3.24	5.26
Côte d'Ivoire	11.95	7.17	9.90
Croatia	5.31	3.18	2.94
Cuba	10.87	6.52	10.30
Cyprus	6.23	3.74	5.45
Czech Rep.	4.84	2.90	2.90
Djibouti	30.40	18.24	22.64
Dominica	8.52	5.11	8.42
Dominican Rep.	9.89	5.94	9.37
Ecuador	11.83	7.10	10.88
Egypt	53.07	31.84	15.16
El Salvador	7.05	4.23	6.86
Equatorial Guinea	18.04	10.83	18.04
Estonia	1.69	1.01	1.03
Ethiopia	18.82	11.29	18.82
European Union	5.44	3.26	2.94
Gabon	17.94	10.77	10.61
Georgia	10.64	6.38	4.32
Ghana	14.64	8.78	14.61
Grenada	10.22	6.13	10.07
Norway	7.36	4.42	2.31
Oman	5.66	3.40	4.59
Pakistan	20.02	12.01	17.45
Panama	8.33	5.00	7.42
Papua New Guinea	18.71	11.23	13.49
Paraguay	12.38	7.43	12.06
Peru	13.38	8.03	13.04
Philippines	4.74	2.84	2.80
Poland	14.11	8.46	7.99
Qatar	4.16	2.50	4.01
Moldova	5.10	3.06	4.97
Romania	16.92	10.15	14.43
Russia	10.81	6.49	10.78
Rwanda	19.16	11.49	18.42
South Africa	14.41	8.64	14.41
Saudi Arabia	6.17	3.70	6.09
Senegal	11.92	7.15	11.14
Seychelles	28.30	16.98	24.35
Singapore	0	0	0
Slovakia	4.99	3.00	2.96
Slovenia	9.50	5.70	8.76
Solomon Islands	22.53	13.52	20.57
Sri Lanka	8.25	4.95	3.82
St. Kitts–Nevis	9.35	5.61	9.24
St. Lucia	8.89	5.33	8.78
St. Vincent and the Grenadines	9.80	5.88	9.80
Sudan	24.43	14.66	24.43
Surinam	17.51	10.50	12.55
Swaziland	5.83	3.50	4.86
Switzerland	6.01	3.61	2.70

(continued)

Table 2-1. *Simple Average MFN Tariffs before and after a 40 Percent Doha Cut*[a] *(continued)*

Country	MFN tariff pre-Doha	Post-Doha 40 percent cut	
		Applied tariff	Bound tariff
Guatemala	7.35	4.41	7.32
Guinea	6.46	3.88	6.06
Guinea–Bissau	11.98	7.19	11.98
Guyana	11.02	6.61	10.38
Honduras	6.94	4.16	6.83
Hong Kong	0	0	0
Hungary	9.36	5.62	5.49
Iceland	3.69	2.21	3.09
India	29.31	17.59	24.00
Indonesia	6.80	4.08	6.43
Iran	27.34	16.40	22.42
Israel	7.38	4.43	6.26
Jamaica	7.21	4.33	7.05
Japan	5.89	3.53	1.89
Jordan	14.58	8.75	8.04
Kazakhstan	9.45	5.67	9.24
Kenya	17.06	10.24	17.03
Korea	12.44	7.47	7.00
Kuwait	3.62	2.17	3.57
Kyrgyzstan	4.92	2.95	2.83
Lao	9.62	5.77	9.62
Latvia	3.48	2.09	2.59
Syria	19.61	11.77	17.37
Taiwan	6.87	4.12	6.30
Tajikistan	8.28	4.97	8.28
Tanzania	13.55	8.13	13.55
Macedonia	12.81	7.69	12.68
Thailand	15.99	9.60	11.39
Togo	11.98	7.19	11.98
Trinidad and Tobago	7.91	4.74	7.67
Tunisia	28.69	17.21	13.45
Turkey	10.32	6.19	6.77
Turkmenistan	5.09	3.05	4.32
Uganda	9.01	5.41	9.01
Ukraine	11.37	6.82	9.00
United States	3.78	2.27	1.92
Uruguay	12.75	7.65	12.38
Uzbekistan	11.00	6.60	10.95
Vanuatu	13.80	8.28	13.43
Venezuela	12.70	7.62	12.44
Vietnam	16.41	9.84	16.15
Yemen	12.81	7.69	12.81
Zambia	14.11	8.47	14.11
Zimbabwe	19.03	11.42	17.66

Source: Authors' calculations, based on UN Comtrade database, WTO's Integrated Data Base, UNCTAD's TRAINS, and OECD Tariffs and Trade CD-ROM.

a. Includes an elimination of all tariff peaks above 50 percent.

Figure 2-1. *Percentage Change in Applied Tariffs and GDP per Capita*

Percentage change in applied tariffs

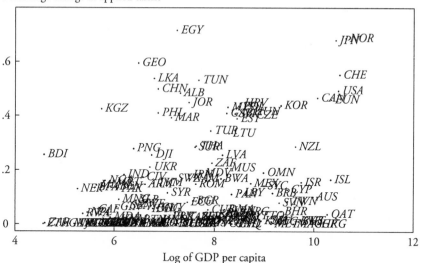

Source: Authors' calculations, based on UN Comtrade database, WTO's Integrated Data Base, UNCTAD's TRAINS, and OECD Tariffs and Trade CD-ROM.

These findings suggest that the extent of tariff reductions implied by the Doha Round may be quite limited in several countries. Indeed, in thirty-five of the 165 countries in our sample (counting European Union members as one), a 40 percent cut in bound tariffs will not affect a single applied tariff. This is the case in Chile, Equatorial Guinea, Ethiopia, Malawi, Uganda, Singapore, and Zambia, for example. Similarly, in almost two-thirds of the countries in the sample, fewer than 10 percent of applied tariffs are affected by a 40 percent cut in bound tariffs accompanied by elimination of peaks above 50 percent.

The average percentage cut in applied tariffs under the business-as-usual scenario seems to increase with GDP per capita (figure 2-1). This mainly reflects the fact that high-income countries tend to apply tariffs that are closer to the bound levels (there is less "water" in these countries' bound tariffs). In this scenario, only thirty-eight countries cut their average applied tariffs by more than 20 percent after a 40 percent cut in bound tariffs. Note that twenty-four countries cut their applied tariffs by more than 40 percent, partly as a result of the elimination of tariff peaks.

Estimated Gains in Welfare

Table 2-2 shows the change in welfare (in millions of U.S. dollars) as well as the standard error associated with the business-as-usual and ambitious scenarios.

Table 2-2. *Welfare Change under Business-as-Usual and Ambitious Scenarios*
Millions of U.S. dollars

Country	MFN tariff pre-Doha	Post-Doha 40 percent cut		Country	MFN tariff pre-Doha	Post-Doha 40 percent cut	
		Applied tariff	Bound tariff			Applied tariff	Bound tariff
Albania	7.48	4.49	3.87	Lebanon	5.39	3.23	5.14
Algeria	18.68	11.21	18.68	Libya	17.04	10.23	15.09
Angola	8.81	5.29	8.80	Lithuania	3.41	2.05	2.27
Antigua	9.63	5.78	9.56	Macau	0	0	0
Argentina	14.69	8.82	14.04	Madagascar	5.67	3.40	5.65
Armenia	2.96	1.78	2.53	Malawi	13.39	8.04	13.39
Australia	4.16	2.49	3.74	Malaysia	8.63	5.18	4.91
Azerbaijan	8.66	5.20	8.66	Maldives	20.23	12.14	16.45
Bahamas	30.64	18.39	30.35	Mali	11.13	6.68	9.55
Bahrain	7.77	4.66	7.42	Malta	5.68	3.41	5.68
Bangladesh	21.77	13.06	21.66	Mauritania	10.58	6.35	8.98
Barbados	12.37	7.42	10.97	Mauritius	17.35	10.41	13.77
Belarus	11.02	6.61	10.98	Mexico	17.95	10.77	15.29
Belize	10.53	6.32	10.13	Mongolia	6.94	4.16	6.32
Benin	11.98	7.19	10.33	Montserrat	18.05	10.83	18.05
Bermuda	17.46	10.48	17.41	Morocco	30.48	18.29	18.55
Bhutan	16.61	9.97	16.38	Mozambique	12.02	7.21	12.01
Bolivia	9.44	5.66	9.42	Myanmar	5.50	3.30	5.47
Bosnia	6.04	3.62	6.04	Namibia	5.83	3.50	4.86
Botswana	5.83	3.50	4.86	Nepal	13.99	8.39	13.39
Brazil	13.65	8.19	13.18	Netherlands	5.36	3.22	2.91
Brunei	0.80	0.48	0.08	New Zealand	3.97	2.38	2.83
Bulgaria	9.93	5.96	9.09	Nicaragua	4.72	2.83	2.83
Burkina Faso	11.92	7.15	10.33	Niger	11.96	7.18	10.43

Country			
Burundi	30.10	18.06	22.41
Cambodia	16.40	9.84	16.38
Cameroon	18.04	10.83	18.04
Canada	4.95	2.97	2.65
Central African Rep.	18.04	10.83	17.10
Chad	18.04	10.83	18.04
Chile	5.99	3.59	5.99
China	12.46	7.48	6.24
Colombia	12.2	7.32	12.19
Congo, Dem. Rep. of	8.35	5.01	6.48
Congo, Rep. of	18.04	10.83	17.03
Costa Rica	5.41	3.24	5.26
Côte d'Ivoire	11.95	7.17	9.90
Croatia	5.31	3.18	2.94
Cuba	10.87	6.52	10.30
Cyprus	6.23	3.74	5.45
Czech Rep.	4.84	2.90	2.90
Djibouti	30.40	18.24	22.64
Dominica	8.52	5.11	8.42
Dominican Rep.	9.89	5.94	9.37
Ecuador	11.83	7.10	10.88
Egypt	53.07	31.84	15.16
El Salvador	7.05	4.23	6.86
Equatorial Guinea	18.04	10.83	18.04
Estonia	1.69	1.01	1.03
Ethiopia	18.82	11.29	18.82
European Union	5.44	3.26	2.94
Gabon	17.94	10.77	10.61
Georgia	10.64	6.38	4.32
Ghana	14.64	8.78	14.61
Grenada	10.22	6.13	10.07

Country			
Nigeria	29.97	17.98	25.21
Norway	7.36	4.42	2.31
Oman	5.66	3.40	4.59
Pakistan	20.02	12.01	17.45
Panama	8.33	5.00	7.42
Papua New Guinea	18.71	11.23	13.49
Paraguay	12.38	7.43	12.06
Peru	13.38	8.03	13.04
Philippines	4.74	2.84	2.80
Poland	14.11	8.46	7.99
Qatar	4.16	2.50	4.01
Moldova	5.10	3.06	4.97
Romania	16.92	10.15	14.43
Russia	10.81	6.49	10.78
Rwanda	19.16	11.49	18.42
South Africa	14.41	8.64	14.41
Saudi Arabia	6.17	3.70	6.09
Senegal	11.92	7.15	11.14
Seychelles	28.30	16.98	24.35
Singapore	0	0	0
Slovakia	4.99	3.00	2.96
Slovenia	9.50	5.70	8.76
Solomon Islands	22.53	13.52	20.57
Sri Lanka	8.25	4.95	3.82
St. Kitts–Nevis	9.35	5.61	9.24
St. Lucia	8.89	5.33	8.78
St. Vincent and the Grenadines	9.80	5.88	9.80
Sudan	24.43	14.66	24.43
Surinam	17.51	10.50	12.55
Swaziland	5.83	3.50	4.86
Switzerland	6.01	3.61	2.70

(continued)

Table 2-2. *Welfare Change under Business-as-Usual and Ambitious Scenarios (continued)*

| Country | MFN tariff pre-Doha | Post-Doha 40 percent cut | | MFN tariff pre-Doha | Post-Doha 40 percent cut | | Country |
		Applied tariff	Bound tariff		Applied tariff	Bound tariff	
Guatemala	7.35	4.41	7.32	19.61	11.77	17.37	Syria
Guinea	6.46	3.88	6.06	6.87	4.12	6.30	Taiwan
Guinea–Bissau	11.98	7.19	11.98	8.28	4.97	8.28	Tajikistan
Guyana	11.02	6.61	10.38	13.55	8.13	13.55	Tanzania
Honduras	6.94	4.16	6.83	12.81	7.69	12.68	Macedonia
Hong Kong	0	0	0	15.99	9.60	11.39	Thailand
Hungary	9.36	5.62	5.49	11.98	7.19	11.98	Togo
Iceland	3.69	2.21	3.09	7.91	4.74	7.67	Trinidad and Tobago
India	29.31	17.59	24.00	28.69	17.21	13.45	Tunisia
Indonesia	6.80	4.08	6.43	10.32	6.19	6.77	Turkey
Iran	27.34	16.40	22.42	5.09	3.05	4.32	Turkmenistan
Israel	7.38	4.43	6.26	9.01	5.41	9.01	Uganda
Jamaica	7.21	4.33	7.05	11.37	6.82	9.00	Ukraine
Japan	5.89	3.53	1.89	3.78	2.27	1.92	United States
Jordan	14.58	8.75	8.04	12.75	7.65	12.38	Uruguay
Kazakhstan	9.45	5.67	9.24	11.00	6.60	10.95	Uzbekistan
Kenya	17.06	10.24	17.03	13.80	8.28	13.43	Vanuatu
Korea	12.44	7.47	7.00	12.70	7.62	12.44	Venezuela
Kuwait	3.62	2.17	3.57	16.41	9.84	16.15	Vietnam
Kyrgyzstan	4.92	2.95	2.83	12.81	7.69	12.81	Yemen
Lao	9.62	5.77	9.62	14.11	8.47	14.11	Zambia
Latvia	3.48	2.09	2.59	19.03	11.42	17.66	Zimbabwe

Source: Authors' calculations, based on UN Comtrade database, WTO's Integrated Data Base, UNCTAD's TRAINS, and OECD Tariffs and Trade CD-ROM.

The differences in the overall welfare change associated with the two scenarios are striking. For the world as a whole, the business-as-usual scenario yields estimated welfare gains of $59 billion, but the ambitious scenario yields gains four to five times as large, at $269 billion. In the business-as-usual scenario, more than two-thirds of the gains, or $41 billion, stem from liberalization in agriculture. In the ambitious scenario, around two-thirds of the gains come from the 50 percent reduction in nontariff measures, and $125 billion in gains come from liberalization in agriculture.

The standard error for the point estimates of the welfare changes is estimated using standard errors for all the estimated parameters of the trade model.[19] Using bootstrapping, we take fifty random draws with repetition from the distribution of parameters. We then compute for each of these draws changes in world prices and welfare using the model described above. The standard error is computed by taking the standard deviation across different draws. The estimates of welfare changes are generally very precise. They are statistically significant at the 5 percent level for 133 countries out of 165 under the business-as-usual scenario and for all but two countries (Costa Rica and Sri Lanka) under the ambitious scenario. Aggregating across countries, the 95 percent confidence interval for the change in world welfare is between $46 billion and $72 billion under the business-as-usual scenario and between $253 billion and $285 billion under the ambitious scenario.

Distribution of Welfare Gains

Looking at the distribution of the estimated welfare gains, we find that high-income countries benefit much more than other countries. In the business-as-usual scenario, developing countries gain $23 billion, of which $3 billion accrues to low-income countries. While the average gain for a developing country is $0.2 billion, the average gain for a high-income OECD country is ten times as large, at $2.1 billion. Once we control for the size of the country (using GDP) the average difference in gains between a high-income OECD country and a developing country is $1 billion. Among the twenty-one high-income OECD countries in our sample, only two (Denmark and Iceland) experience welfare losses. Among the 146 countries that are not high-income OECD members, forty-two (or 29 percent) experience a welfare loss, although the loss is greater than $100 million for only six countries.

In the ambitious scenario, high-income OECD countries capture $158 billion, and the other countries gain $111 billion; $16 billion goes to low-income countries. The average gain for a developing country is $0.8 billion, whereas the average gain for a high-income OECD country is again nearly ten times as large, at $7.5 billion. Once we control for country size using GDP, the average

---

19. We ignore what is likely to be a more important source of uncertainty: model specification.

difference in gains between a high-income OECD country and a developing country is about $2.6 billion. None of the high-income OECD countries in our sample experiences a welfare loss. Among developing countries, twenty-nine (or one in five) see their welfare decline, but only two experience welfare losses greater than $100 million.

If the average high-income OECD country stands to gain ten times as much as the average developing country, one may argue that high-income OECD countries experience larger gains simply because their economies are larger. This is partly true; welfare changes add 1.9 percentage points to the GDP of developing countries, but only 0.7 percentage point to the GDP of high-income OECD countries.

However, there are significant differences among individual countries, especially within the developing world. Among high-income OECD countries, the gains in welfare vary from 0.3 to 2.9 percent of GDP, and among developing countries, the range is from −1.7 to 9.4 percent of GDP.

To illustrate this heterogeneity and suggest the impact that reforms stemming from the Doha Round may have on cross-country income inequality, figure 2-2 shows the densities of the welfare change as a share of GDP for

Figure 2-2. *Distribution of Welfare Changes in Rich and Poor Countries*
Density

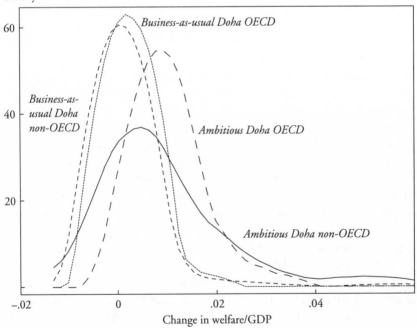

Source: Authors' calculations, based on UN Comtrade database, WTO's Integrated Data Base, UNCTAD's TRAINS, and OECD Tariffs and Trade CD-ROM.

high-income and developing countries under both scenarios. We see that, while the ambitious scenario yields larger gains than business as usual, for both high-income and developing countries, the distribution of high-income countries stochastically dominates the distribution of developing countries (it lies to the right of the developing-country distribution). So, even under the ambitious scenario, a developing country is less likely than a high-income country to increase its welfare by more than a certain fraction of GDP.

Thus it seems that cross-country income inequality may increase after the Doha-related policy changes, regardless of whether we adopt a business-as-usual or an ambitious scenario. To explore this further, we calculate a series of income inequality indexes before and after the implementation of each Doha scenario. We find that the changes in cross-country income inequality associated with these trade policy changes are small, but they all suggest an increase in income inequality in the business-as-usual scenario and a decline in the ambitious scenario. For example, the Gini coefficient rises 0.01 percent under the business-as-usual scenario, and it declines 0.05 percent after the ambitious shock. The coefficient of variation increases 0.03 percent in the business-as-usual scenario and declines 0.11 percent in the ambitious scenario. However, even if the changes in income inequality across countries are quite small, the changes in income inequality within countries can be very large. The latter changes are examined in the country case studies.

Concluding Remarks

This chapter has assessed the potential for the Doha trade negotiations to deliver on their development promise. We have considered two scenarios—a business-as-usual outcome from the negotiations and an ambitious round of trade liberalization—that have very different implications for welfare. Business as usual would produce an estimated increase in world welfare of $46 billion to $72 billion, with a point estimate of $59 billion. The potential gains under the ambitious scenario are estimated to be four to five times as large, at $253 billion to $285 billion, with a point estimate of $268 billion.

While the actual welfare impacts of the Doha negotiations will obviously depend both on what is agreed and on domestic factors that affect the pass-through of international price shocks, both scenarios have an important feature in common: the gains are much greater for high-income OECD countries. Moreover, after both shocks cross-country income inequality is almost unchanged, although under the business-as-usual scenario, it actually increases slightly.

We conclude that for a Doha Round to be a development round, agreeing on freer market access will not be enough. Gains to poor countries can be enhanced through the redistribution to the South of some of the benefits accruing to high-income OECD countries. Several of the case studies that follow illustrate how complementary reforms that reduce trade costs within countries and increase farm productivity (through agricultural extension services, for example) are necessary if the poorest parts of the population in the poorest countries are to benefit from the new opportunities offered by multilateral trade liberalization.

References

Bouet, Antoine, Ivan Decreux, Lionel Fontaigné, Sébastien Jean, and Didier Laborde. 2003. "Computing an Exhaustive and Consistent, Ad Valorem Equivalent Measure of Applied Protection: A Detailed Description of MAcMap-HS6 Methodology." Paris: Centre d'Etudes Prospectives et d'Informations Internationales (CEPII).

François, Joseph, Hans van Meijl, and Frank van Tongeren. 2005. "Trade Liberalization and Developing Countries under the Doha Round." *Economic Policy* 20, no. 42 (April): 349–91.

Hoekman, Bernard, Francis Ng, and Marcelo Olarreaga. 2004. "Agricultural Tariffs versus Subsidies: What's More Important for Developing Countries?" *World Bank Economic Review* 18, no. 2: 405–26.

Kee, Hiau Looi, Alessandro Nicita, and Marcelo Olarreaga. 2004. "Import Demand Elasticities and Trade Distortions." Policy Research Working Paper 3452. Washington: World Bank.

———. 2005a. "Estimating Ad Valorem Equivalents of Non-Tariff Measures." Washington: World Bank.

———. 2005b. "Estimating Export Supply Elasticities." Washington: World Bank.

Wilson, John S., Catherine Mann, and Tsuneshiro Otsuki. 2004. "Assessing the Potential Benefit of Trade Facilitation: A Global Perspective." Policy Research Working Paper 3224. Washington: World Bank.

World Bank. 2004. *Global Economic Prospects.* Washington (www.worldbank.org/prospects/gep2004/ [February 2007]).

World Bank and IMF (International Monetary Fund). 2005. *Global Monitoring Report 2005.* Washington.

PART TWO

Country Studies

3

Ethiopia

ALESSANDRO NICITA

This chapter analyzes how the changes in international prices consequent on the implementation of the Doha Development Agenda would affect household expenditures and incomes in Ethiopia. To explore the variance in the distribution of the effects and to identify potential winners and losers, the effect of multilateral trade liberalization is estimated by broad household groups and by geographic region. Two scenarios are considered: limited multilateral trade liberalization, termed the business-as-usual scenario, and more extensive multilateral trade liberalization, termed the ambitious scenario.[1] The chapter also explores complementary policies that Ethiopia might adopt to help its households take advantage of the opportunities offered by a Doha deal.

The empirical methodology used is based on the trade and poverty framework of Winters and consists of tracking the movement in the prices (and quantities) of goods and factors associated with trade policy reforms and measuring their effect on household welfare.[2] The price and quantity effects of the two Doha scenarios are those estimated by Kee, Nicita, and Olarreaga in chapter 2 of this volume. The present chapter translates price and quantity effects at the border into changes at the regional level, maps them onto household welfare, and ultimately estimates the overall effect on poverty.

1. See chapter 2 for a detailed description of the two scenarios.
2. Winters (2002).

The chapter is organized as follows. It begins by describing the extent and distribution of poverty in Ethiopia and then analyzes Ethiopia's exposure to international trade shocks, tracing the implications for the likely effects of trade reforms on Ethiopian households. This is followed by a section describing the empirical framework used for the simulations and a section explaining the different policy scenarios that are analyzed; these look at the probable effects of multilateral trade liberalization, on its own and when complemented by potential changes in Ethiopia's own policies. A section then presents the results, and a final section concludes.

The analysis suggests that multilateral trade liberalization would have only a small effect on poverty in Ethiopia. Even under the most optimistic scenario, when ambitious multilateral liberalization is paired with improved domestic policies, the effects are estimated to be less than a 1 percent increase in real income for most households. The size of the gain differs across household groups: poor households and households in rural areas are expected to gain substantially less than the average. The reasons for the limited impact are to be found in the rudimentary state of Ethiopia's domestic markets. In particular, poor price transmission, the pervasive subsistence economy, weak infrastructure, and the overall weak supply response from producers severely thwart the country's ability to benefit from implementation of the Doha agenda.

Poverty in Ethiopia

Poverty is a major concern and a chronic problem in Ethiopia. Regional political instability, recurring droughts, and inappropriate policies have exacerbated the problem, making Ethiopia one of the poorest countries in the world. Ethiopia's GDP per capita is estimated at about $110, compared to about $450 for sub-Saharan Africa on average. Other indicators also place Ethiopia at the bottom of the list: life expectancy is forty-two years, and literacy rates are around 40 percent. Recent estimates put the number of poor—defined as people who cannot afford the minimum expenditure needed to guarantee an intake of 2,200 calories per day—at about 25 million, or about 44 percent of the total population.[3] More realistically, using a $2 a day poverty line, the percentage of poor is about 80 percent, or about 45 million people. Poverty has remained fairly stable, declining by about 1 percent between 1995 and 2000.

At least half the poor (23 million) are in rural areas,[4] but Ethiopia is a very diverse country, and poverty varies greatly across regions (table 3-1). Tigray, Afar, Benshangul, SNNPR, and Gambella are the poorest, with more than half

---

3. World Bank, World Development Indicators database.
4. This is because rural areas are poorer than urban areas and because the overwhelming majority of the population lives in rural areas (85 percent).

Table 3-1. *Geographic Incidence of Poverty (Headcount Index) in Ethiopia*[a]

Region	Poverty, HC (percent)	Rural poverty, HC (percent)	Urban poverty, HC (percent)	Rural poor (thousands)	Urban poor (thousands)
Addis Ababa	36	27	36	11	716
Afar	56	68	27	121	20
Amhara	42	43	31	5,773	429
Benishangul	54	56	29	343	13
Dire Dawa/ Harari	33	33	33	36	88
Gambella	51	55	38	60	14
Oromiya	40	40	36	7,655	786
SNNPR	51	52	40	5,877	341
Somali	38	44	26	185	58
Tigray	61	62	61	1,895	327
Total	44	45	37	21,957	2,791

Source: Author's calculations.

a. HC is the headcount index—that is, the share of the population whose total consumption falls below the poverty line.

of their people in poverty. Regions that fare better are Addis Ababa, Harari, and Dire Dawa, all of which are urban enclaves.

Ethiopia's Exposure to International Price Shocks

The extent to which multilateral trade liberalization will reduce poverty in Ethiopia depends on the exposure to trade shocks of the Ethiopian economy in general and on that of poor households in particular. Much of Ethiopia's production is for subsistence, largely because markets are poorly developed[5] and because poor infrastructure makes the flow of goods and information difficult. For a large proportion of households, income and expenditures are barely affected by changes in trade policies. The following discussion briefly illustrates Ethiopia's trade structure and the composition of household income and expenditure baskets.

Exports and Imports

Ethiopia's trade flows are not large. The ratio of exports to GDP is about 15 percent, one of the lowest in sub-Saharan Africa. Imports are concentrated in manufacturing ($1.5 billion), while agricultural imports are very small, at $100 million, or less than $0.20 per individual per year, and mostly cereals.[6]

5. For example, households cannot sell their output for lack of local buyers or traders.

6. Additionally, Ethiopia receives large quantities of food and non-food aid. The UN World Food Program has estimated that food aid to Ethiopia was about $150 million for 2004.

Because of the low level of agricultural imports and the segmentation of the domestic market, any movement in the international prices of agricultural products is unlikely to affect greatly the cost of the consumption basket of Ethiopian households.

On the supply side, agriculture and livestock rearing are the main economic activities in Ethiopia. Agriculture is based largely on subsistence production, and cash crops are very few, essentially coffee and *chat*.[7] Even though most of the country's agricultural production is destined for domestic markets,[8] agriculture supplies about 80 percent of Ethiopia's total exports. Agricultural exports totaled about $400 million in 2002.[9] Major exports are coffee (which accounts for about a third of total exports), *chat,* oilseeds, leather products, and livestock.

Because exports make up such a small share of GDP, even large percentage increases in exports alone could not substantially alleviate poverty in Ethiopia. It seems likely that the more important constraints on the country's development are the small share of production that is marketed and the consequent low agricultural productivity, rather than lack of access to international markets. These constraints are explored later in the chapter.

Households' Exposure to International Trade Shocks

The poverty effect of trade policies operating through changes in international prices and quantities is determined, within the structure of domestic markets, by the composition of household consumption baskets and by the sources of household income. The easiest way to think about how poor households are affected by trade policies is in terms of the "farm household," which produces goods and services, sells its labor, and consumes. In this setup, an increase in the price of a good for which a household is a net seller increases the household's real income, while a decrease reduces it.

To show which products Ethiopian households are most exposed to, figure 3-1 summarizes income sources and figure 3-2 shows the composition of the

7. *Chat (qat)* is a mild stimulant exported mostly to neighboring countries and to Great Britain for the use of Somali immigrants. The plant is illegal in the United States and most European countries. In Ethiopia *chat* is widely cultivated and represents an increasingly important source of cash for Ethiopian farmers. The plant has the advantages of growing well in dry climates, requiring little tending, and producing a harvest in only one season. This makes it substantially easier and more remunerative to cultivate than coffee. Another important advantage is that it generates immediate revenues. Although the cultivation of *chat* is not encouraged, the government benefits from it by licensing its export and theoretically setting the price.

8. A large part of the cereal produced in the country is consumed locally. Even in the case of coffee, less than half of total production is exported.

9. However, official exports are underreported, especially for those products exported mainly to neighboring countries (chat, livestock, and, to a minor degree, coffee).

Figure 3-1. *Sources of Household Income in Ethiopia, by Household per Capita Income Group*
Percent

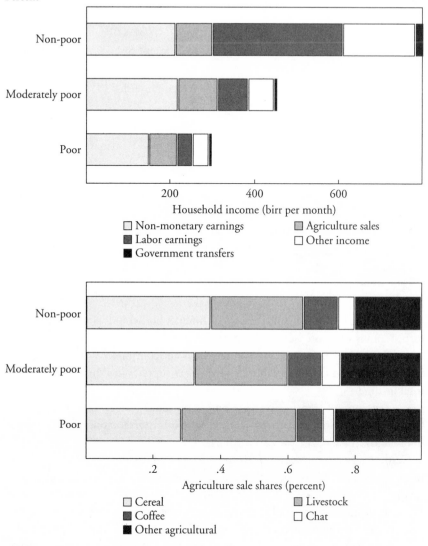

Source: Author's calculations.

consumption baskets. Households are classified as poor (below the 2,200 calorie poverty line), moderately poor (below the $2 a day poverty line but above 2,200 calories), and non-poor.

Figure 3-1 reveals four important facts:

—The average cash flow of poor households is less than Br200, equivalent to about $25, per month.

Figure 3-2. *Composition of Household Expenditure in Ethiopia, by Household per Capita Income Group*

Percent

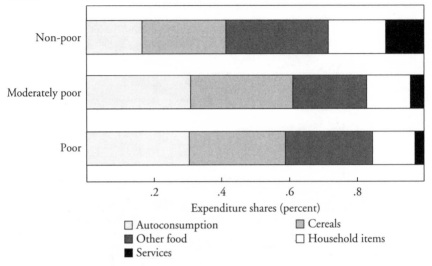

Expenditure shares (percent)

□ Autoconsumption   ▨ Cereals
■ Other food   □ Household items
■ Services

Source: Author's calculations.

—About half of the income of poor Ethiopian households is in nonmonetary form[10] and is therefore isolated from price effects.

—The main source of monetary income is agricultural sales (mostly of cereals, livestock, and coffee), while work for wages supplies less than 15 percent of total income.

—Government transfers provide only a minimal part of the income of the households, and other sources of income are important only for non-poor households.

Within agricultural sales, cereals (mostly *teff* and maize) and livestock supply more than 60 percent of the cash receipts of households. This large percentage is related to the pervasive subsistence economy. Almost all rural households in Ethiopia produce cereals and livestock, and households sell their excess production while keeping what they need for subsistence. Cash crops such as coffee and *chat* represent about 10 percent of the agricultural sales of poor households and 15 percent of those of moderately poor and non-poor households. Other agricultural products represent slightly less than 25 percent of the sales of poor households. Compared with moderately poor households, the poorest households rely more heavily on livestock and less on cereal production.

On the consumption side, figure 3-2 shows the allocation of the household expenditure basket among five product groups. On average, households' own

10. This is represented mostly by products produced and consumed within the household.

Figure 3-3. *Share of Income from Subsistence Activities in Ethiopia, by Decile of Household per Capita Income*[a]

Percent

Income decile

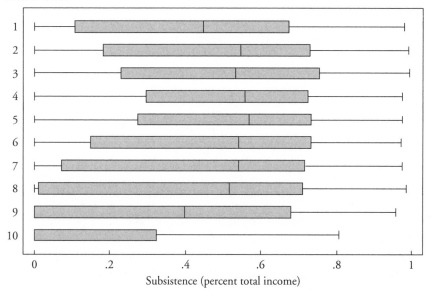

Subsistence (percent total income)

Source: Author's calculations.
a. Excludes outside values.

produce supplies about one-third of their total consumption. For poor households, about 30 percent of total spending goes for cereals, and other food takes another 25 percent;[11] 10 percent goes for household items; and less than 5 percent goes for services. Non-poor households have a slightly different spending pattern: subsistence production represents a smaller share of their consumption, and they spend proportionately more on household items and on services.

For a household that does not participate in markets, changes in the prices of the goods it produces or consumes have no direct effect on income. Figure 3-3 illustrates the amounts of income originating from subsistence activities, in households ranked by income decile. The bars in the figure contain observations between the twenty-fifth and seventy-fifth percentiles. The line in the middle represents the median.[12] The figure indicates that subsistence production is present in all income deciles, and its importance fades only for the richer households.

11. Pulses, meat, and dairy products represent more than 50 percent of the category of other food.
12. For the tenth decile the median is 0.

Table 3-2. *Changes in Prices and Exports in Ethiopia:*
Business-as-Usual and Ambitious Scenarios

	Business as usual		Ambitious Doha	
Item	Change in prices (percent)	Change in exports (millions of U.S. dollars)	Change in prices (percent)	Change in exports (millions of U.S. dollars)
Cereal	5	0.7	8	1.5
Coffee	1	3.1	3	3.5
Chat	0	0.0	0	0.0
Livestock	2	0.1	3	1.1
Other agriculture	−1	−0.3	−7	−6.5
Other goods	0	3.1	1	8.9
Employment (number of workers)		70,000		160,000

Source: Author's calculations.

For poor households, median levels of reliance on subsistence production are around 50 percent.

In summary, Ethiopian households rely heavily on subsistence activities, and as a result a large part of their income is isolated from international trade shocks. Cereals are the most important item in both their income and consumption baskets, so any change in the price of cereals is likely to create substantial income redistribution between producers and consumers. Among other agricultural products, those that substantially affect household income are livestock, coffee, and *chat.*

Implications of the Doha Development Agenda for Ethiopia

Within the analytical framework of this chapter, the implications for Ethiopian households of implementing the Doha Development Agenda depend on three factors:

—Impact on prices of goods produced and consumed by Ethiopian households,

—Impact on world demand for Ethiopian products, and

—Impact on employment in Ethiopia.

The estimates by Kee, Nicita, and Olarreaga in chapter 2 indicate that successful implementation of the Doha Development Agenda would change the prices and quantities of products of importance to the Ethiopian economy (table 3-2).

Under the business-as-usual scenario, the price changes for products of importance to Ethiopian households vary from 5 percent (cereals) to −1 percent (other agriculture). The price of coffee rises, but only by 1 percent. Slightly larger changes in prices are estimated for the ambitious Doha scenario: prices rise by about 8 percent for cereal and 3 percent for coffee and fall by 7 percent for other agricultural products.[13]

Table 3-2 also reports supply responses for the two scenarios. In the business-as-usual scenario, the supply responses of the Ethiopian economy total about $7 million. Most of the increases are estimated to be in coffee and "other goods." In the ambitious scenario, the increase in exports is estimated at about $10 million, also coming mainly from coffee and other goods.

Estimated changes in exports, combined with input-output tables and employment statistics from the Global Trade Analysis Project (GTAP) database are used to calculate the expected change in employment in Ethiopia. The export increases are estimated to create about 70,000 new jobs in the business-as-usual scenario and about 160,000 in the ambitious scenario (table 3-2).[14]

Using the changes identified in international prices and demand for Ethiopian exports, as well as the expected changes in employment, the following section describes the method used to measure how these effects translate into household welfare.

Empirical Framework

To estimate the impact of implementing the Doha Development Agenda on households in Ethiopia, first, changes in the prices and demand for internationally traded products important for Ethiopian households are translated into changes in domestic prices and export supply; second, the increase in supply is distributed across households; third, the impact on employment is mapped onto households;[15] and finally, all these changes are fed into the household welfare function to measure changes in real income and poverty.[16]

The analysis relies mostly on data originating from two household surveys: the 1999/2000 Welfare Monitoring Survey (WMS) and the 1999/2000 Household Income, Consumption, and Expenditure Survey (HICES). Both surveys use a stratified two-stage sample design (three-stage for some areas) and are nationally representative of Ethiopia's non-nomadic population at the regional level. Data on prices at the regional and zonal levels were obtained from two reports published by the Ethiopian Central Statistical Authority.[17] Trade data

13. Given the peculiarity of *chat* (*qat*), the effect of the multilateral trade liberalization on the price of this crop is assumed to be negligible.

14. These increases in labor demand are estimated using labor-output ratios by sector from the GTAP database for the "rest-of-sub-Saharan Africa" (Ethiopia is not represented individually in the current version of GTAP). Assuming that labor-output coefficients remain unchanged, the change in total employment is calculated by summing over sectors the product of the change in net exports multiplied by the labor-output ratio obtained from GTAP.

15. Given the vast reserve of labor in Ethiopia, wages are assumed to be constant in real terms. Similarly, public and private transfers are also fixed in real terms.

16. This framework follows Winters (2002).

17. CSA (various years).

were obtained from the UN Comtrade database. Remaining data were obtained from the *Statistical Abstract* published annually by the CSA, from other national accounts statistics, and from the World Bank World Development Indicators database.

International and Domestic Prices

To measure the effect on poverty that would result from movement in international prices, it is necessary first to estimate the extent to which retail prices (those faced by households) reflect changes in international prices (those affected by multinational agreements).

As is widely recognized, the international prices of products and their retail prices are linked only loosely; even without import barriers such as tariffs, many factors such as transport costs and local supply of substitute products act as filters between the two.[18] This is particularly true in developing countries where local markets are poorly developed or missing.[19] It is also found that, in most cases, the correlation between international and domestic local prices diminishes as distance from major urban centers increases. This implies that most remote areas are likely to be little affected by economic policies that operate through changes in prices.[20]

To capture empirically the pass-through from international prices to domestic prices in Ethiopia, it is assumed that prices in Addis Ababa or Dire Dawa reflect the full extent of the change in prices in international markets. Then the domestic price transmission between Addis Ababa or Dire Dawa and eight regions is estimated econometrically, so as to capture the pass-through coefficient between the border and each of the regions.[21]

To estimate the extent of domestic price transmission, this chapter uses a simple model that captures the changes in the price of a basket of products in eight regions relative to the price of the same basket in Addis Ababa and Dire Dawa.[22] A simple ordinary least squares estimation is used to obtain the (short-run) pass-through price elasticities for each region. The estimation takes the form:

$$(3\text{-}1) \qquad \Delta P_{jit} = \beta_1 D_i + \beta_2 D_i A_{jt} + \beta_3 J_j + \varepsilon_{jit},$$

18. Frankel, Parsley, and Wei (2005); Winters, McCulloch, and McKay (2004).

19. When there is a good or service that individuals would like to purchase (at a price at which that good could be produced profitably) but that is not available in the market, the market for that good or service is said to be missing. More generally, when there is no market in which a good or service can be bought or sold, the market is said to be missing.

20. Nicita (2004).

21. This is not necessarily an unrealistic setup, since most of Ethiopia's imports and exports are marketed and pass through either Addis Ababa or Dire Dawa.

22. The product basket includes an equal proportion of maize, wheat, *teff*, barley, sorghum, coffee, oils, and beans.

Table 3-3. *Domestic Price Transmission in Ethiopia, by Region*
Short-run pass-through elasticities

Region	Price transmission
Addis Ababa	1.000
Afar	0.323
Amhara	0.430
Benishangul	0.399
Dire Dawa	1.000
Gambella	0.228
Oromiya	0.371
SNNPR	0.383
Somali	0.192
Tigray	0.376

Source: Author's calculations.

where ΔP_{jit} is the change in the price of good j in region i between time t and $t-1$, D_i is a regional dummy, A_{jt} is the change in the price of good j in Addis Ababa, and J is a product dummy.

The results for domestic price transmission are shown in table 3-3 (for more detailed econometric results, see table 3A-1 in the appendix to this chapter).

Excluding the capital and Dire Dawa, domestic price transmission is well below 50 percent and varies from about 43 percent (Amhara) to about 19 percent (Somali). In their simplicity, these coefficients seem to reflect the remoteness of each region: Amhara is a fairly well-connected region south of the capital, while the Somali area is largely a desert and, by most standards, one of the most remote regions of Ethiopia.

These results suggest that regions such as Somali or Gambella will likely experience little effect from any Doha scenarios concerning prices, simply because prices in those regions do not respond much to changes in international prices.

Export Supply

Implementation of the Doha Development Agenda is estimated to evoke an increase in demand for Ethiopian exports of about $7 million a year in the business-as-usual scenario. However, an increase in demand for Ethiopian exports will not necessarily have much effect on poverty.

The reasons are threefold. First, poor households may not be producing the goods for which there is increased demand; as noted, these households tend to produce largely for their own consumption, not for the market. Second, poor households have a large part of their income tied to subsistence agriculture and have less ability to switch to the more remunerative export crops.[23]

23. Poor households tend to engage in less risky activities and are usually more resistant to innovation.

Third, there is a cost associated with increasing the supply for the export market. Changes in exports can be decomposed into a quantity effect (the change in volume supplied to the export market) and a price effect (the change in the value of exports that takes place because of the change in price). To mimic the costs associated with the increase in quantity, it is assumed that the gains originate only from the increased prices, which now apply to the larger volume of production.[24] The increase in export quantities is assumed to be proportional to the marketed production of each household and to follow the price pass-through mechanism. (This implies that households that are producing only for their own consumption will not increase their production and that households in regions where there are no changed price signals will not adjust their production.)

Impact on Employment

As noted, multilateral trade liberalization would create about 70,000 jobs in Ethiopia in the business-as-usual scenario and about 160,000 in the ambitious scenario. To allocate those jobs to households, the labor market is assumed to comprise two sectors, formal and informal. The increase in employment is assumed to occur in the formal sector and, consequently, to affect poverty depending on two factors: the extent to which the new jobs are filled by poor workers and the wage premium paid for the formal jobs relative to informal ones.

To estimate who will fill the new jobs, workers in the informal sector are ranked according to their probability of finding a job in the formal sector. For this purpose, a matching methodology is used to estimate propensity scores for individual workers.[25] Propensity scores represent the predicted probability that each individual has of working in the formal sector based on his or her observed characteristics. They are estimated with a logit model:

(3-2) $$L_i = \beta_0 + \beta_1 X_i + \beta_2 H_i + \varepsilon_i,$$

where L_i is the logit of a dichotomous variable that takes the value 1 if the ith individual is employed in the formal sector and 0 otherwise, X_i is a vector of individual characteristics, and H_i is a vector of household characteristics.

In this setup, the probability that each worker has of moving into the formal sector is a function of his or her demographic characteristics. These include gender, age, level of education, urban or rural location, and detailed regional

---

24. Input costs are not reported in the data. In practice this assumption represents the lower bound. A more accurate estimate would add the profits (value of output minus input costs) multiplied by the increase in quantity.

25. Heckman, Ichimura, and Todd (1998).

location.[26] The workers are then ranked according to their estimated probabilities, and, for those with the highest rank, the sector of employment is switched from informal to formal.

Having estimated which workers are more likely to fill the jobs created by the expanding economy, the next step is to estimate the impact that the new employment would have on the income of each worker. To do so requires an estimate of the wage differential between the informal and formal sectors. The latter is estimated using household data and following the wage premium literature.[27] The estimation regresses the log of worker i's wages ($\ln W_{ij}$) on a vector of worker i's characteristics (X_{ij}) and a set of industry indicators (I_{ij}) and takes the Mincerian form:[28]

$$(3\text{-}3) \qquad \ln W_{ij} = \beta_0 + \beta_1 X_{ij} + \beta_2 I_{ij} + \varepsilon_{ij}.$$

Again, workers' characteristics are taken to include gender, age, educational level, urban, or rural location, and detailed regional dummies so as to reflect the segmentation of markets. The coefficient on the formal sector dummy captures the wage premium paid in the formal sector as compared to the informal sector.[29] The results, controlling for individual characteristics, show that the average wage is just 6 percent higher in the formal than in the informal sector.

Changes in Household Welfare

With these results, it is now possible to calculate the changes that would take place in household welfare. In developing countries, most households both produce and consume goods, and in analyzing how any policy affects household welfare, this dual role must be acknowledged. The farm household model of Singh, Squire, and Strauss fits this purpose.[30] In this model, a change in real income (dy_h) can be expressed as follows:

$$(3\text{-}4) \quad dy_h = \underbrace{\sum_g \theta_h^g dP_h^g\, y_h}_{ag.income\,(price\,effect)} + \underbrace{\sum_g dQ_h^g dP_h^g}_{ag.income\,(export\,effect)} + \underbrace{\theta_h^l dw_h\, y_h}_{labor\,income} - \underbrace{\sum_g \phi_h^g dP_h^g\, y_h}_{consumption},$$

26. For this purpose, Ethiopia is divided into 108 geographic areas.
27. Krueger and Summers (1988).
28. The Mincerian wage equation is a popular model showing how an individual's characteristics affect his or her wage.
29. In other words, the coefficient of the sector dummy represents the part of the variation in wages that cannot be explained by the worker's own characteristics, but can be explained by the worker's sector affiliation.
30. Singh, Squire, and Strauss (1986).

where, dP_h^g is the percentage change in prices of good g faced by households $h;$[31] θ_h^g is the share of income obtained from the sale of good g by household h, θ_h^l is the share of income obtained in the labor market, ϕ_h^g is the share of the consumption basket devoted to good g, and y_h is the income of the household.[32] The change in quantity is given by:

$$(3\text{-}5) \qquad\qquad dQ_h^g = \Delta Exp^g \frac{y_h^g}{\sum\limits_h y_h^g},$$

where ΔExp^g is the total change in export of good g, and y_h^g is the income originating from the sale of good g by household h; and

$$(3\text{-}6) \qquad\qquad dw_h = \sum_i w_i \left(zw_i \right) R_i,$$

where dw_h is the percentage change in wages across the labor income of individuals in household h, w_i is the share of individual i in the total labor income in household h, and zw_{iA} is the percentage wage differential for individual i estimated by equation 3-3. R_i takes the value of 1 for those individuals who best match the characteristics of those employed in the formal sector (estimated according to equation 3-2), and 0 otherwise.

In this setup, equation 3-4 suggests that a change in the price of good g favors or harms the household to the extent given by the net exposure of the household's budget to that particular good. Moreover, an increase in exports of a particular good favors the household in proportion to its marketed production of the good, and new employment favors those households whose workers have the best matching characteristics. Finally, the change in welfare is distributed across household members, expenditures are equated to the new level of income, and new welfare indicators are calculated at the new level of consumption.

Simulation Results

Two sets of simulations are used to analyze the impact of the business-as-usual and ambitious multilateral trade liberalization scenarios on Ethiopian households. The first simulation mimics the status quo in Ethiopia: domestic price transmission is kept at the estimated level, households' supply responses are fixed at their observed level, and subsistence households remain outside the market economy.

31. Changes in prices are equal for households in the same region.
32. Income is equated to expenditures.

The second set of simulations measures the effect of multilateral trade liberalization when matched by a number of complementary policies that Ethiopia could potentially introduce to improve the effect of the Doha liberalization on Ethiopian households. The first of these four policies would increase the participation of subsistence producers in the market. The second would increase the supply response of agricultural producers. The third would improve the transmission of price signals to remote areas, and the last would remove all of Ethiopia's tariff barriers. The assumptions made about these complementary policies are detailed below.

Increased Market Participation by Subsistence Producers

Because of the costs associated with an increase in supply, the net gains from an increase in demand for Ethiopian exports are likely to be small under current conditions. Ethiopia may be able to support the increase in international demand with complementary policies aimed at increasing the volume of output that is marketed. Households would respond to these policies by channeling part of their subsistence production to the market. Clearly, they would gain not the full income from their additional sales, but rather this income minus the value of the subsistence production that they have to give up. More precisely, the increase in their real income is determined by the premium from switching from subsistence to the more remunerative cash crop. Given the paucity of data for Ethiopia, the premium is simply approximated by the difference in percentage terms of the average yield (in value) from the cultivation of *teff* (the most common staple crop in Ethiopia) and the average yield of cash crops.[33]

The determinants of poor price transmission and subsistence are often similar and are usually linked to trade costs, market competitiveness, and local supply. Policies aimed at lowering transaction costs often make markets work better and consequently increase the market participation of households. In addition, subsistence production is usually correlated with distance from services (remoteness), credit constraints, lack of skills and knowledge, and ultimately the inability to hedge the risks of a volatile or remote environment.

The following equation is used to identify possible complementary policies that might increase the proportion of output that is marketed:

$$(3\text{-}7) \qquad AC_i = \beta_0 + \beta_1 X_i + \beta_2 K_i + f_r + \varepsilon_i,$$

where AC_i is the share of income originating from subsistence activities (agriculture and gathering) for household i, X_i is a vector of the household's specific characteristics (which include household assets, household size, and household

---

33. The premium is estimated to be about 50 percent. Data on yield were obtained from the Food and Agriculture Organization but do not include the cost of production (inputs).

Table 3-4. *Determinants of Subsistence Production in Ethiopia*

Policy variable	Impact on subsistence income
Access to credit	−3.20%
Distance from markets	0.30% per km
Distance from roads	0.04% per km
Distance from public transportation	0.10% per km

Source: Author's calculations.

head's gender, age, and education), and K_i is a vector of policy characteristics (which include access to credit and distance to markets, roads, and public transport).

The estimation is performed across all households. Geographic differences are controlled using fixed effects (f_r) by administrative zone, further subdivided into urban and rural areas.[34] In this setup, the coefficients on some of the variables may indicate which determinants are more important in reducing a household's dependence on subsistence production. Table 3-4 summarizes the findings; details are reported in the appendix to this chapter.

Table 3-4 shows that access to a limited supply of credit reduces the share of subsistence income by about 3.2 percentage points. Another determinant of the importance of subsistence production is a household's distance from basic services. The percentage of income originating from subsistence income increases by about 3 percent for every 10 kilometers of distance from markets. The comparable rate is about 0.4 percent for distance from roads and about 1 percent for distance from public transportation.

The results from equation 3-7 are paired with the Doha scenarios of table 3-2 to calculate the effects on welfare of this combination of policies. In the simulation exercise, the assumption is that all households are provided with limited access to credit and that distance to services (roads, telephone, and public transport) is reduced equally for all households, until the value of the additional marketed production reaches the value of the increase in international demand directly attributable to the Doha agenda.[35]

Productivity

Perhaps the increase in international demand originating from the Doha Round could be met by an increase in the productivity of Ethiopian farmers. For this purpose, complementary policies to train farmers to use inputs better and to improve their cultivation techniques would need to be implemented effectively.

34. The estimation accounts for 108 geographic areas.
35. Distance from roads, telephone, and public transport is reduced in percentage terms. To create an increase in marketed supply to match the increase in international demand would require that the distance to these services be cut in about half.

Indeed, one of the most serious constraints preventing Ethiopia from escaping poverty is its very low agricultural productivity. The policy-improved scenario assumes an increase in the productivity of the Ethiopian economy so that the increase in exports could be supplied at zero monetary costs for farmers. In this scenario, the full amount of the increase in exports is allocated to the income of households.

Price Transmission

One of the characteristics of the Ethiopian economy is the segmentation of its domestic markets. As noted, this is reflected in the limited transmission of price signals, which softens the effect of trade policies on the poor. To explore the effect of better domestic price transmission, the simulation exercise assumes that price transmission is now twice as efficient as the pattern that was shown in table 3-3.[36]

The results show that better domestic price transmission would have two basic effects. The first of these is a greater impact on products consumed and produced by households. The second is redistributive: better price transmission is associated with a higher supply response, and therefore the supply for export markets is now allocated more uniformly.

Ethiopian Trade Liberalization

Ethiopia's economy is relatively open. The import-weighted average tariff is about 13 percent, and the tariff on agricultural products averages about 12 percent. However, tariffs on basic food crops are much lower than this: *teff* and wheat, the most important cereals in Ethiopia, face a tariff of 5 percent. Livestock products are more protected, with a tariff of about 20 percent. Coffee is the exception, with a tariff of 40 percent.[37] Tariffs on manufactured products average about 13 percent, and among them, textiles and apparel face the highest levels of protection, with average tariffs of about 30 percent. Motor vehicles are also heavily protected, with a tariff of about 20 percent.

To calculate the effect of a complete removal of Ethiopia's tariffs, it is assumed that the removal of tariffs will decrease the price of the affected goods (including their domestic varieties), subject to the price transmission mechanism.[38] For example, the removal of the tariff on wheat would affect the price of wheat by the amount of the tariff multiplied by the price transmission coefficient estimated in regression 3-6.

---

36. Although the elasticity is not allowed to be larger than 1.

37. Whatever the tariff on coffee, the large internal production, paired with consumer preferences for local varieties, is likely to keep imports of coffee virtually at zero.

38. Given the importance of coffee in Ethiopian society and the consumers' preferences for domestically produced varieties, the tariff on coffee is assumed not to have any impact on the domestic price.

Trade liberalization is politically difficult for a developing country to implement, because it tends to reduce government revenues. Ethiopia is no exception. National statistics indicate that the Ethiopian government budget relies substantially on tariff revenues: about 25 percent of total revenue is collected from taxes on foreign goods. If that revenue is not replaced, the reduction in tariff revenue would indirectly depress household welfare. To take this into account, the loss of revenue is reflected uniformly (in percentage terms) across households, causing a reduction of about 0.3 percent in real income.

Results: Effects of the Doha Development Agenda on Poverty

This section first presents the effects of multilateral trade liberalization (both in the business-as-usual and ambitious scenarios) and then describes the effects of multilateral trade liberalization paired with complementary domestic policies. The effects on household welfare are reported as percentage changes in household real per capita income, which are more suitable for this purpose than standard indicators of poverty.

Multilateral Trade Liberalization: Business-as-Usual and Ambitious Scenarios

The results suggest that implementing the Doha agenda, whether in the business-as-usual case or the ambitious scenario, would not substantially affect poverty in Ethiopia (table 3-5).

This outcome is not unexpected, for several reasons. First the impact on prices and quantities of products exported by Ethiopia would not be very large. Second, because Ethiopia's exports are only a minimal part of its GDP, even a doubling of current export values would not have much impact on poverty. Third, Ethiopia's domestic markets are poorly interconnected, and the price and quantity effects of trade policy would not easily reach the rural areas where most of the poor live. Finally, Ethiopian households, especially the poorest, depend heavily on subsistence production and so are isolated from market shocks and trade policies.

In the business-as-usual case, losses in real income are estimated at about 0.4 percent for the poorest households. Among regions, Addis Ababa is the only one where the overall average effect is positive (a small real income increase of 0.2 percent). In the ambitious scenario, the overall effect improves, but it still involves a fall in real income for all but the non-poor households.

The reason why these outcomes are not more propitious is to be found in the increase in the cost of living consequent on the increase in the price of consumption goods, particularly cereals. This translates into a more expensive consumption basket for Ethiopian households and hence a loss of purchasing power. The probable increases in the value of production, quantity produced,

Table 3-5. *Effects on Household Welfare in Ethiopia:*
Business-as-Usual and Ambitious Scenarios
Percent

Effects A	Changes in real income	
	Business as usual	Ambitious
Overall effects		
Poor	−0.4	−0.3
Moderately poor	−0.3	−0.1
Non-poor	−0.1	0.3
Overall	−0.3	−0.1
Regional effects		
Addis Ababa	0.2	1.6
Afar	−0.3	−0.2
Amhara	−0.5	−0.6
Benishangul	−0.3	−0.3
Dire Dawa	−0.8	0.5
Gambella	−0.7	−0.4
Oromiya	−0.3	−0.3
SNNPR	−0.1	0.3
Somali	−0.1	0.1
Tigray	−0.5	−0.5

B	Change in real income due to					
	Consumption effect		Income effect		Employment effect	
	Business as usual	Ambitious	Business as usual	Ambitious	Business as usual	Ambitious
Effects decomposition						
Poor	−0.5	−0.5	0.1	0.1	0.0	0.1
Moderately poor	−0.5	−0.4	0.1	0.2	0.1	0.2
Non-poor	−0.5	−0.4	0.1	0.1	0.3	0.5

Source: Author's calculations.

and employment opportunities are too small to counteract the increase in the cost of living.

Multilateral Trade Liberalization Accompanied by Complementary Policies

The additional gains when multilateral trade liberalization is associated with the four complementary policies are illustrated in table 3-6.

The results show that the complementary policies would in general lead to larger gains. The increase in productivity for export production would have the

Table 3-6. *Effects on Household Welfare in Ethiopia, by Household per Capita Income Group and Region: Business-as-Usual and Ambitious Scenarios*

Percent

Complementary policy effects decomposition	Reduction of subsistence farming		Increase in productivity		Own trade liberalization		Doubling the price pass-through	
	Business as usual	Ambitious	Business as usual	Ambitious	Business as usual	Ambitious	Business as usual	Ambitious
Household group								
Poor	0.2	0.3	0.4	0.5	-0.2	-0.2	0.2	0.4
Moderately poor	0.2	0.3	0.4	0.6	-0.1	-0.1	0.2	0.3
Non-poor	0.1	0.2	0.2	0.3	0.2	0.2	0.1	0.2
Region								
Addis Ababa	0.0	0.0	0.0	0.0	1.7	1.7	-0.4	-0.8
Afar	0.1	0.2	0.1	0.2	-0.1	-0.1	0.2	0.5
Amhara	0.1	0.1	0.2	0.4	-0.3	-0.3	0.1	0.2
Benishangul	0.1	0.2	0.3	0.5	-0.3	-0.3	0.1	0.2
Dire Dawa/Harari	0.0	0.1	0.1	0.1	1.6	1.6	0.0	0.0
Gambella	0.2	0.3	0.6	1.0	0.5	0.5	0.1	0.2
Oromiya	0.2	0.3	0.4	0.6	-0.2	-0.2	0.2	0.4
SNNPR	0.3	0.5	0.5	0.8	-0.2	-0.2	0.4	0.9
Somali	0.1	0.2	0.1	0.2	-0.2	-0.2	0.4	0.8
Tigray	0.2	0.3	0.3	0.5	-0.2	-0.2	0.1	0.1

Source: Author's calculations.

largest effect, and its benefits would add half a percentage point to the real income of the poor. Improving the price pass-through to remote areas also would have a substantial positive effect on the poor, especially in the ambitious scenario. Complementing the multilateral trade liberalization with an increase in the marketed proportion of farm output would have a slightly smaller impact. Trade liberalization by Ethiopia would have a marginal effect in aggregate, but it would tend to increase income inequality, as the rich would benefit more than the poor.[39]

If the Doha agenda were implemented and accompanied by all four complementary Ethiopian reforms, then Ethiopia's poor would see an increase in real income of around 0.2 percent under the business-as-usual scenario and 0.7 percent under the ambitious scenario. The non-poor would gain by at least twice as much as the poor.

Table 3-6 also reports the effects of the complementary policies by region. Those complementary policies aimed at an increase in marketed agricultural output or an increase in productivity would benefit mostly the agricultural regions. Liberalizing Ethiopia's trade and the associated reduction in the cost of imports would benefit mostly the urban areas (Addis Ababa and Dire Dawa), while decreasing real income in agricultural regions. Improvement of domestic price pass-through would have a positive effect in the remote areas and a negative effect in Addis Ababa.[40]

Conclusions

This chapter has investigated the effects on Ethiopian households to be expected from the multilateral trade liberalization proposed by the Doha Development Agenda. The results suggest that, without complementary policies, multilateral trade liberalization would have a negative, though very small, impact on the Ethiopian poor. The reason lies in the price effect. The trade reforms would raise prices and hence would push up the cost of the consumption baskets of households, ultimately reducing real income. This negative price effect would be softened, but—for most households—not counterbalanced, by increases in the value of production, employment, and exports. The poor would lose real income in both the business-as-usual and ambitious scenarios. In the ambitious scenario, Doha would have a positive effect on non-poor households.

Multilateral trade liberalization such as proposed by the Doha agenda would have a more beneficial effect if complemented by domestic reforms. Particularly

39. It is assumed that Ethiopia's own trade liberalization does not interact with the changes in world prices under the business-as-usual and ambitious scenarios. Hence the marginal (or additional) impact of own trade liberalization is the same under both scenarios.

40. The negative impact in Addis Ababa is due to the fact that a larger price transmission implies that the supply for export markets originates more uniformly across regions.

important in the Ethiopian context is a policy reform to raise productivity for agricultural export products.

Whether positive or negative, however, the effects would be small. Even in the most optimistic case (the ambitious scenario complemented with an increase in farm productivity and better pass-through of price signals to domestic producers), multilateral trade liberalization would produce at most a 1 percent increase in real income for most households. And the distribution of the effects across income groups indicates that poor households would benefit substantially less than the non-poor. The regions that are expected to benefit the most are the urban areas of Addis Ababa and Dire Dawa; rural and remote regions would be barely affected.

To conclude, a Doha deal may offer an opportunity, albeit small, for the Ethiopian economy to integrate into the world economy. However, to benefit from this integration, Ethiopia would need to improve the workings of its domestic economy.

References

CSA (Central Statistical Authority). Various years. "Report on Quarterly Average Retail Prices of Goods and Services in Rural Areas by *Killil* and Zone" and "Report on Average Retail Prices of Goods and Services by Urban Center." Addis Ababa.

Frankel, Jeffrey, David Parsley, and Shang-Jin Wei. 2005. "Slow Pass-Through around the World: A New Import for Developing Countries?" NBER Working Paper 11199. Cambridge, Mass.: National Bureau of Economic Research, March.

Heckman, James, Hidehiko Ichimura, and Petra Todd. 1998. "Matching as an Econometric Evaluation Estimator." *Review of Economic Studies* 65, no. 2 (April): 261–94.

Krueger, Alan B., and Lawrence H. Summers. 1988. "Efficiency Wages and the Inter-Industry Wage Structure." *Econometrica* 56, no. 2: 259–93.

Nicita, Alessandro. 2004. "Who Benefited from Trade Liberalization in Mexico? Measuring the Effects on Household Welfare." World Bank Working Paper 3265. Washington: World Bank.

Singh, Inderjit, Lyn Squire, and John Strauss, eds. 1986. *Agricultural Household Models, Extensions, Applications, and Policy.* Washington and Baltimore, Md.: World Bank and Johns Hopkins University Press.

Winters, L. Alan. 2002. "Trade Liberalization and Poverty: What Are the Links?" *World Economy* 25, no. 9: 1339–67.

Winters, L. Alan, Neil McCulloch, and Andrew McKay. 2004. "Trade Liberalization and Poverty: The Evidence So Far." *Journal of Economic Literature* 42, no. 1: 72–115.

Regression Results

Table 3A-1. *Price Pass-Through: Regression Results from Estimating Equation 3-1*[a]

Dependent variable: change in price (by region, product, time)

Variable	Coefficient	Standard error
Regional dummy (Tigray)	6.961***	(1.3725)
Regional dummy (Afar)	6.589***	(1.4001)
Regional dummy (Amhara)	8.051***	(1.3626)
Regional dummy (Benishangul)	7.976***	(1.3796)
Regional dummy (Somali)	1.140	(1.4319)
Regional dummy (Oromiya)	4.988***	(1.3669)
Regional dummy (SNNPR)	8.975***	(1.3793)
Regional dummy (Gambella)	6.734***	(1.3997)
Regional dummy (Addis-Dire Dawa)	6.029***	(1.3980)
Regional dummy * Price change (Tigray)	0.376***	(0.0090)
Regional dummy * Price change (Afar)	0.323***	(0.0082)
Regional dummy * Price change (Amhara)	0.430***	(0.0078)
Regional dummy * Price change (Benishangul)	0.399***	(0.0081)
Regional dummy * Price change (Somali)	0.192***	(0.0135)
Regional dummy * Price change (Oromiya)	0.371***	(0.0089)
Regional dummy * Price change (SNNPR)	0.383***	(0.0085)
Regional dummy * Price change (Gambella)	0.228***	(0.0090)
Regional dummy * Price change (Addis-Dire Dawa)	(dropped)	
Number of observations	2,307	
R-squared	0.5967	

a. Fixed effect by product (thirteen products).
***Significant at .01 percent; **significant at .05 percent; *significant at .10 percent.

Table 3A-2. *Propensity Scores: Regression Results from Estimating Equation 3-2*[a]

Dependent variable: logit (1 = individual employed in formal sector)

Variable	Coefficient	Standard error
Education (years)	0.016**	(0.0074)
Education squared	0.006***	(0.0006)
Age (years)	0.035***	(0.0044)
Age squared	0.000***	(0.0001)
Gender (1 = male)	−0.042**	(0.0180)
Married (1 = yes)	−0.010	(0.0120)
Constant	−0.887**	(0.5046)
Number of observations	39,258	
R-squared	0.2197	

a. Fixed effect by geographic areas (109 areas).
***Significant at .01 percent; **significant at .05 percent; *significant at .10 percent.

Table 3A-3. *Wage Equation: Regression Results from Estimating Equation 3-3*[a]

Dependent variable: logarithm wage

Variable	Coefficient	Standard error
Wage differential	0.056**	(0.0270)
Education (years)	0.056***	(0.0079)
Education squared	0.001**	(0.0006)
Age (years)	0.034***	(0.0042)
Age squared	0.000***	(0.0000)
Gender (1 = male)	0.094***	(0.0238)
Constant	6.876***	(0.0964)
Number of observations	4,712	
R-squared	0.5506	

a. Fixed effect by geographic area (109 areas).

***Significant at .01 percent; **significant at .05 percent; *significant at .10 percent.

Table 3A-4. *Subsistence: Regression Results from Estimating Equation 3-7*[a]

Dependent variable: percentage of household income from subsistence production

Variable	Coefficient	Standard error
Gender (1 = male)	0.033***	(0.0039)
Age (years)	0.000***	(0.0001)
Household size	0.006***	(0.0008)
Agricultural assets (1 = yes)	−0.023***	(0.0007)
Accest to credit (1 = yes)	−0.033***	(0.0051)
Education (years)	−0.006***	(0.0006)
Distance markets (km)	0.006***	(0.0005)
Distance markets squared	0.000***	(0.0000)
Distance road (km)	0.004***	(0.0003)
Distance road squared	0.000	(0.0000)
Distance public transport (km)	0.001***	(0.0003)
Distance public transport squared	0.000***	(0.0000)
Constant	1.347***	(0.0323)
Number of observations	16,177	
R-squared	0.6251	

a. Fixed effect by geographic area (109 areas).

***Significant at .01 percent; **significant at .05 percent; *significant at .10 percent.

4

Madagascar

ALESSANDRO NICITA

As shown in chapter 2 of this volume, the overall impact of multilateral trade liberalization is expected to be minor in Madagascar, as in most other least developed countries. However, a small overall effect might still mean a large impact for some parts of the population. This chapter analyzes the effects that multilateral trade liberalization would have across income groups and between urban and rural areas, identifying possible winners and losers. The analysis explores the effects on households' real income of the two scenarios introduced in chapter 2: a business-as-usual scenario, which involves a 40 percent reduction in bound tariffs, and a more ambitious multilateral trade liberalization.

The empirical approach is based on the trade and poverty framework developed by Winters.[1] First, changes in prices and quantities of goods and factors consequent on changes in trade policy are estimated using the partial equilibrium model described by Kee, Nicita, and Olarreaga in chapter 2. Then these changes are mapped onto the consumption and production bundles of individual Malagasy households.

This chapter is organized as follows. A brief section describes the extent and distribution of poverty in Madagascar, followed by a section analyzing Mada-

The author wishes to thank Jorge Balat, Marcelo Olarreaga, Guido Porto, and Isidro Soloaga for helpful comments and discussions.

1. Winters (2002).

gascar's exposure to international shocks by looking at household production and consumption patterns to gauge the likely effects of changes in trade policy on household welfare. A third section sets out the empirical framework used for the simulations, a fourth section presents the results, and a final section concludes.

The findings suggest that the implementation of a business-as-usual multilateral trade liberalization would have little impact on household real income and even less impact on overall poverty in Madagascar (on average, it would produce an increase of about 0.6 percent in real income). The implementation of more ambitious trade liberalization would have a larger impact on household real income (an average increase of 1.8 percent), with rural areas benefiting slightly more than urban. In the ambitious scenario, poor households would benefit the most; their real income would rise by between 2 and 3 percent.

There are several reasons why multilateral trade liberalization (and in particular in the business-as-usual scenario) would have only a limited effect on poverty in Madagascar. First is the small supply response of the Malagasy economy to movements in international prices. Second is the limited effect of the proposed liberalization measures on the products that are exported by Madagascar and for which Madagascar has a comparative advantage. Third is the weak infrastructure and pervasive subsistence economy in the country's rural areas, which largely isolate households from the effects of international price changes.

Poverty in Madagascar

Madagascar is one of the poorest countries in the world. Macroeconomic indicators suggest that the nation became steadily poorer over the forty years prior to 2001.[2] In that year, about 70 percent of the population lived in poverty. The 2002 political crisis produced a rapid rise in the poverty rate so that 73.6 percent of the population was estimated to be poor in 2003.

Poverty rates are quite different across geographic regions and between urban and rural areas. Table 4-1 reports the percentage of people living in poverty as observed from household surveys.

Among the different regions, poverty rates have been worsening the most in Taomasina, Fianarantsoa, and rural Toliara. By contrast, poverty rates have fallen dramatically in the Antananarivo region, especially in urban Antananarivo, where poverty has declined from about 52 percent in 1997 to 29 percent in 2001.

Over the past decade, poverty has receded somewhat in urban areas but increased in rural areas. Urban areas benefited from growth in the export sectors during the late 1990s, which created employment and pushed up labor earnings.[3] But rural areas have lagged behind, and three-quarters of

---

2. Per capita GDP declined from about $430 to $230 between 1960 and 2001.
3. Nicita and Razzaz (2003).

Table 4-1. *Percentage of Population in Poverty (Headcount Index) in Madagascar, 1993–2001*[a]

Location	1993			1997			1999			2001		
	Total	*Urban*	*Rural*	*Total*	*Urban*	*Rural*	*Total*	*Urban*	*Rural*	*Total*	*Urban*	*Rural*
National	70	50.1	74.5	73.3	63.2	76	71.3	52.1	76.7	70.1	48.1	76.5
Province												
Antananarivo	68	42.4	76.2	66.4	52	72.1	61.7	43.3	69.3	49.3	29.2	57.5
Fianarantsoa	74.2	64.9	75.3	75.1	83.1	73.6	81.1	55.8	85.9	83.3	59.4	87.8
Taomasina	77.9	55.8	81.1	79.8	76.3	80.8	71.3	52.6	76.4	83.1	61.1	89.1
Mahajanga	53.2	37.3	56.7	73.8	68.2	75.1	76	65.2	78.8	72.6	50.2	78.5
Toliara	81.1	66.9	84.2	82	69.1	84.9	71.6	66.5	73.1	75.9	50.2	83.4
Antsiranana	60.2	49.5	63.7	62.3	27	69.5	72.6	31.3	80.6	69.7	27.9	79.3

Source: Author's calculations, based on data in the *Enquête Prioritaire Auprès des Ménages* for 2001.

a. Headcount index is the share of the population whose total consumption falls below the poverty line.

Table 4-2. *Percentage of Population in Poverty (Headcount Index) in Madagascar, by Economic Sector, 1993–2001*

Sector	1993	1997	1999	2001
Agriculture	76.1	76.5	77.4	77.5
Manufacturing	57.7	57.4	52.6	41.8
Services	53.2	48.2	44.0	37.1

Source: Author's calculations, based on data in the *Enquête Prioritaire Auprès des Ménages* for 2001.

their people are poor. This trend is reflected in the poverty rates by economic sector (table 4-2).

Throughout the 1990s, living standards fell for households employed in agriculture, while they rose significantly for households employed in services and, especially, manufacturing. In particular, during the few years of high economic growth from 1999 to 2001, the poverty rate for people in manufacturing dropped by more than 10 percentage points, while in the service sector poverty was reduced by about 7 percentage points.

In summary, poverty in Madagascar is primarily a rural and agricultural phenomenon. Urban poverty rates are admittedly high, but they are much lower than rural poverty rates, and while urban poverty rates responded to macroeconomic shocks, rural poverty rose persistently throughout the 1990s. The lack of response in rural areas to economic reforms that have established a more open and competitive market since 1996 suggests that liberalizing the market, while necessary, will not be sufficient to address the issue of rural poverty. Development of institutions and rural infrastructure in order to integrate rural areas into domestic and world markets is a prerequisite for alleviating poverty.

Madagascar's Exposure to International Shocks

Successful implementation of the Doha Development Agenda will change the international prices of Madagascar's exports and imports and alter the demand for Malagasy products. In this context, it is important to analyze the trade structure of Madagascar in general, and the composition of the income and expenditure baskets of poor households in particular, so as to gauge the exposure of the Malagasy poor to the effects of the implementation of Doha.

Exports and Imports

Madagascar's economy is relatively open in comparison to those of other low-income countries in sub-Saharan Africa. Madagascar widely liberalized its economy in the early 1990s, and the average tariff is now about 5 percent. Most agricultural goods face a tariff of 5 percent or less.

The share of exports in GDP is about 30 percent. Exports total about $750 million, and three-quarters of them are in only four product groups: textiles and apparel ($270 million), vanilla ($150 million), cloves ($90 million), and crustaceans ($100 million).

Imports totaled about $1.1 billion in 2003 and are mainly of manufactured products ($1 billion), particularly fuel, machinery, and semiprocessed textile fibers used by the apparel industry. Agricultural imports are much smaller and are dominated by rice ($50 million) and oils and fats ($30 million). Madagascar's low reliance on agricultural imports suggests that the poor will not be greatly affected by movements in international prices. Notably, in the case of rice, imports supplied just 7 percent of total consumption in 2003.

Household Exposure

The poverty effect of economic policies that, like multilateral trade liberalization, operate through changing prices depends on the composition of the household consumption basket and the sources of household income. The easiest way to think about how poor households are directly affected by trade policies is in terms of the "farm household," which produces goods and services, sells its labor, and consumes. In this setup, an increase in the price of a good for which a household is a net seller increases the household's real income, while a decrease reduces it.

To show which products Malagasy households are most exposed to, figure 4-1 summarizes the income sources of Malagasy households. Households are classified

Figure 4-1. *Sources of Household Income in Madagascar, by Decile of per Capita Expenditure*

Income shares (percent)

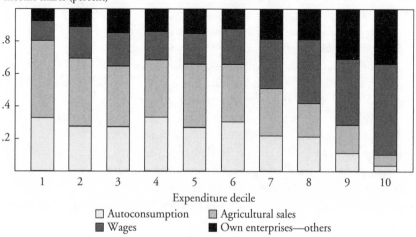

Source: Author's calculations.

by deciles of adult-equivalent per capita expenditure, with the poorest households categorized into decile one.

Figure 4-1 shows the following:

—Subsistence production, or "auto consumption" (the imputed income
of goods produced and consumed within the household), contributes about
30 percent to the income of poor households, and its share declines rapidly as
households become richer.

—Sales of agricultural products represent about 40 percent of the income of
the poor. This percentage, too, declines rapidly as households become richer.

—The richer the household is, the more important is labor income from
wages and households' own enterprises.

To better identify where the poor obtain their incomes, figure 4-2 disaggre-
gates agricultural income by crop and earned income by broad economic sector.
The composition of agricultural sales, illustrated by the left-hand panel of the
figure, shows the following:

—Regardless of their income level, households obtain more than three-
quarters of their monetary income from sales of basic crops (rice and other
cereals; fruit and vegetables).

—Vanilla is an important source of cash, but only for richer households.

—Poor households produce a wider selection of agricultural products than
do richer households and obtain a larger part of their cash income from the sale
of "other crops."[4]

The right-hand panel of figure 4-2, which differentiates labor by broad
economic sector, shows the following:

—Most of the labor income of poor households comes from agriculture.

—The service sector (which includes petty and informal activities) is second
in importance for the poorest households, but rapidly becomes the main source
of cash for higher-income households.

—The manufacturing sector, and in particular the textile and apparel sector,
is only a minor source of employment for the poor.

On the consumption side, figure 4-3 shows the composition of the average
expenditure basket of households categorized by expenditure deciles. Food
expenditures (whether the imputed value of subsistence production or actual
purchases) take up about 70 percent of the total expenditures of the poor.
Manufactured goods (household items) take about 10 percent, services take less
than 20 percent, and the remainder is taken by other items such as imputed rent.

The right-hand panel of figure 4-3 explores the composition of household
food expenditure. Subsistence production supplies a large part of the food
consumed by the poorer households and about half of that consumed by the

4. This is also related to the prevalence of subsistence agriculture among poor households.
Subsistence households tend to produce a wider variety of food crops.

Figure 4-2. *Sources of Household Income in Madagascar, by Decile of per Capita Expenditure*

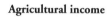

Agricultural income

Agricultural income shares (percent)

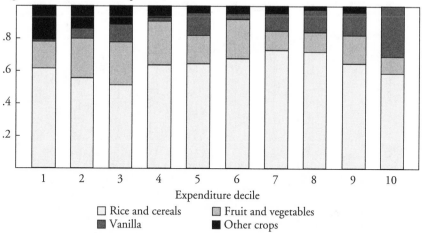

Expenditure decile

☐ Rice and cereals   ▨ Fruit and vegetables
■ Vanilla   ■ Other crops

Labor income

Earned income shares (percent)

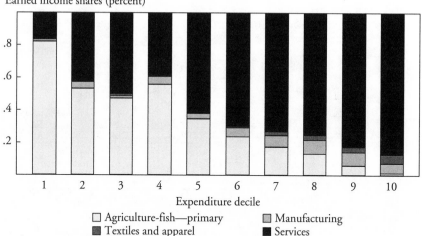

Expenditure decile

☐ Agriculture-fish—primary   ▨ Manufacturing
■ Textiles and apparel   ■ Services

Source: Author's calculations.

poorest decile. Except among the richest 10 percent of households, cereals (mainly rice) dominate the consumption basket. Meat, dairy, vegetables, and other food products become a larger part of the expenditure basket as a household's income increases.

In summary, the most important source of cash for poor households is the sale of agricultural products. Among these, rice alone supplies about 20 percent of the

Figure 4-3. *Composition of Household Expenditure in Madagascar, by Decile of per Capita Expenditure*

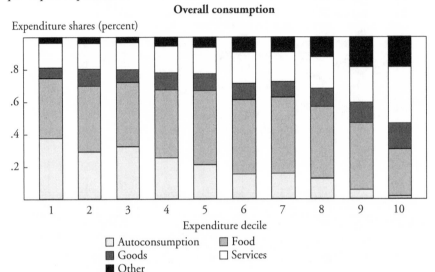

Overall consumption

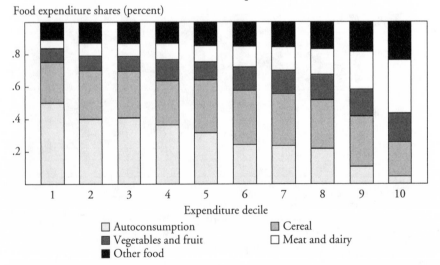

Food consumption

Source: Author's calculations.

income of the average household. Income from labor is also important for the poor, who obtain about 15 percent of their total income from wages and profits from enterprises they own. On the consumption side, most of the purchases of poor households are of food, and, among these, rice and other cereals account for about 15–20 percent. Finally, a substantial part of household income and expenditure arises from the production of subsistence crops (mostly rice, maize, and cassava) that are consumed within the household. This large share reflects decisions by poor households on how best to cope with risk, and it has the effect of isolating a large part of the household budget from market shocks.

Implications of the Doha Development Agenda for Madagascar

For Madagascar's economy in general, and the Malagasy poor in particular, the implications of the multilateral trade liberalization discussed in the Doha Round depend on three factors:

—Impact on prices of goods produced and consumed by the poor,

—Impact on world demand for Malagasy products produced and sold by the poor, and

—Impact on employment and the extent to which this affects the poor.

The changes in prices and world demand associated with the two Doha scenarios are estimated by Kee, Nicita, and Olarreaga in chapter 2. Implementation of the Doha agenda is expected to change the prices and quantities of several products of importance to the Malagasy economy, as reported in table 4-3.

Madagascar's most important product is rice. The removal of protection is expected to raise the price of rice by about 6 percent in the business-as-usual scenario and by about 19 percent in the ambitious scenario. A Doha deal would also have a large impact on the prices of other cereals, which are expected to increase by about 7.5 and 11.4 percent in the two scenarios, respectively.

Table 4-3. *Doha Effects on Prices and Quantities in Madagascar: Business-as-Usual and Ambitious Scenarios*

Product group	International price change (percent)		Export changes (thousands of U.S. dollars)	
	Business as usual	Ambitious Doha	Business as usual	Ambitious Doha
Rice	6.1	18.9	0	0
Other cereals	7.5	11.4	44	83
Cloves	0.0	1.0	1,826	10,790
Vanilla	0.0	0.2	2,912	6,343
Other agriculture	0.5	2.2	5,228	7,966
Livestock	0.3	6.3	1,074	2,570
Minerals	0.3	0.9	894	3,401
Textiles and apparel	0.2	0.5	12,356	33,960
Food industry	0.8	2.5	604	1,494
Other manufacturing	−0.5	0.1	2,306	7,183
Employment (number)			22,000	65,000

Source: Author's calculations, based on data in the *Enquête Prioritaire Auprès des Ménages* for 2001.

Although business as usual is not expected to affect greatly the prices of other products important in Madagascar, the ambitious scenario is expected to produce larger price increases, given that it involves larger cuts in protection. In the ambitious scenario, prices of livestock products are expected to rise by about 6.3 percent; those of cloves, an important export crop, by about 1 percent; and those of other agricultural products by about 2.2 percent. The price of vanilla, Madagascar's major export crop, would not be affected appreciably.

The rise in overall demand for Malagasy products is expected to be about $27 million under business as usual and about $75 million in the ambitious scenario. Most of the increases would be in textiles and apparel. Among agricultural products, international demand for Malagasy cloves is expected to increase by about $2 million in the business-as-usual scenario and by about $11 million in the ambitious scenario. Demand for vanilla from Madagascar is expected to increase by about $3 million and $6.5 million, respectively, in the two scenarios.

Given the expected changes in price and quantity, the impact on employment can be calculated using input-output tables and employment statistics from the Global Trade Analysis Project; it is assumed that the percentage change in sectoral employment is equal to the percentage change in production. Driven largely by an expansion of the textile and apparel industry, employment would grow by an estimated 22,000 jobs in the business-as-usual scenario and by about 65,000 jobs in the ambitious scenario.

Empirical Framework

The analysis relies mainly on data from the 2001 *Enquête Prioritaire Auprès des Ménages* (EPM). The household-level data used for the analysis were collected by the Direction des Statistiques des Ménages (DSM) of the Institut National de la Statistique (INSTAT) in Madagascar. The surveys are stratified, multi-staged, and clustered. The 2001 survey was collected from September to November 2001 and is representative of the entire population. The surveys are designed to be representative at the regional level (*faritany*) as well as the urban-rural level within each region. They include data on income, consumption, household characteristics, and individual characteristics. Trade data were obtained from the UN Comtrade database. Remaining data were obtained from the *Statistical Abstract* published annually by the CSA, from other national accounts statistics, and from the World Bank World Development Indicators database.

To explore the effects of trade liberalization on the poor in Madagascar, changes in the prices of and demand for internationally traded products are translated into domestic prices and then mapped onto household welfare using a farm household model. The analysis proceeds in four stages: first, international prices are translated into domestic prices; second, the increase in exports of agricultural products is distributed to households; third, the impact on employment is mapped onto the household; and, finally, these changes are fed into the household welfare function to measure the overall changes in real income.[5]

Supply of Exports

To allocate the increase in exports to individual households, the increase in international demand for Malagasy products is assumed to be met by an increase in marketed production by households. Here it is assumed that those households that are already more exposed to markets will be more responsive as suppliers. Therefore, supply responses are correlated with marketed quantities and not with overall production.[6] As a further assumption, the full value of the increase in exports is allocated to the households. This implies that households currently have unused resources (particularly labor) and that the increase in export supply is produced at zero costs, fueled by a better allocation and use of productive assets. This is not an unreasonable assumption in the case of Madagascar, where productivity is very low.

Doha and Employment

To measure the extent to which the poor benefit from the growth in employment associated with more liberal world trade, the labor market is assumed to consist of two sectors, formal and informal. The growth in employment is assumed to occur in the formal sector and to affect the poor depending on two factors: the extent to which the new jobs are filled by the poor and the wage premium paid for work in the formal relative to the informal sector.

To estimate who will fill the new jobs, workers are ranked according to their probability of finding employment in the formal sector, using a matching methodology to estimate their propensity scores.[7] Propensity scores represent the predicted probability that each individual has of working in the informal sector, based on his or her observed characteristics—gender, age, level of education, and urban-rural and regional location—and are estimated with a logit model:

$$(4\text{-}1) \qquad L_i = \beta_0 + \beta_1 X_i + \beta_2 H_i + \varepsilon_i,$$

where L_i is the logit of a dichotomous variable that takes the value 1 if the ith individual is employed in the formal sector and 0 otherwise, X_i is a vector of individual characteristics, and H_i is a vector of household characteristics. The workers are then ranked according to their individual propensities, and, for those with the highest rank, the sector of employment is changed from informal to formal.

---

5. This framework follows Winters (2002).

6. Therefore, the increase in exports is not allocated to households that produce only for subsistence.

7. Heckman, Ichimura, and Todd (1998).

Having estimated which individuals are more likely to fill the jobs created by the expanding economy, the next step is to estimate the impact that the new employment will have on the income of each worker. To do so requires an estimate of the wage difference between the informal and formal sectors. The latter is estimated using the household data and following the wage premium literature.[8] The estimation regresses the log of worker i's wages ($\ln W_{ij}$) on a vector of worker i's characteristics (X_{ij}) and a set of industry indicators (I_{ij}) and takes the Mincerian form:[9]

(4-2) $$\ln W_{ij} = \beta_0 + \beta_1 X_{ij} + \beta_2 I_{ij} + \varepsilon_{ij}.$$

Workers' characteristics include gender, age, education, urban-rural, and regional dummies. The coefficient on the formal sector dummy captures the wage premium paid in the formal sector as compared to the informal sector.[10]

The results show an average wage premium of about 27 percent for work in the formal sector; details of the estimation are presented in the appendix to this chapter.[11]

Regarding labor earnings, the link between implementation of the Doha agenda and the returns to labor is identified by economic theory that links movements in prices (caused by trade liberalization) to the wages faced by households. For the sake of simplicity, and for lack of data, the movements in wages are here assumed to reflect the movements in prices, so that real wages are kept fixed.[12] In this context, the estimated increase in Madagascar's manufactured exports is assumed to originate exclusively from an increase in employment rather than an increase in productivity. This is not an unreasonable assumption in a country where wages, especially those of the poor, are likely to be kept stable by a large pool of reserve labor.

Changes in Household Welfare

With these results, it is now possible to calculate changes in household welfare. In developing countries, most households are simultaneously consumers and produc-

---

8. Krueger and Summers (1988).

9. The Mincerian wage equation is a popular model showing how an individual's characteristics affect his or her wage.

10. In other words, the coefficient of the sector dummy represents the part of the variation in wages that cannot be explained by the worker's own characteristics, but can be explained by the worker's sector affiliation.

11. The monetary income of households is increased by the old (observed or imputed) wage multiplied by 1.27.

12. A more sophisticated approach would require the estimation of price-wage elasticities for different products and different types of labor. For example, see Nicita (2004) or Porto (2003). However, this would require appropriate data and would make the analysis more cumbersome, while adding very little to the overall outcome.

ers of the same goods, and in analyzing how a policy affects household welfare, this dual role must be acknowledged. The farm household model fits this purpose.[13] In this model, a change in real income (dy_h) can be expressed as follows:

$$(4\text{-}3) \quad dy_h = \underbrace{\sum_g \theta_h^g dP_h^g y_h}_{ag.income\ (price\ effect)} + \underbrace{\sum_g dQ_h^g dP_h^g}_{ag.income\ (export\ effect)} + \underbrace{\theta_h^\ell dw_h y_h}_{labor\ income} + \underbrace{\sum_g \phi_h^g dP_h^g y_h}_{consumption},$$

where dP_h^g is the change in prices of good g faced by households h,[14] θ_h^g is the share of income obtained from the sale of good g by household h, θ_h^ℓ is the share of income obtained in the labor market, ϕ_h^g is the share of the consumption basket devoted to good g, and y_h is the income of the household.[15] The change in quantity supplied is given by:

$$(4\text{-}4) \qquad\qquad dQ_h^g = \Delta Exp^g \frac{y_h^g}{\sum_h y_h^g},$$

where ΔExp^g is the total change in export of good g, and y_h^g is the income originating from the sale of good g by household h; and

$$(4\text{-}5) \qquad\qquad dw_h = \sum_i w_i (zw_i) R_i,$$

where dw_h is the percentage change in wages averaged across the labor income of individuals in household h, w_i is the share of individual i in total labor income in household h, zw_i is the percentage wage differential for individual i estimated by equation 4-3, and R_i takes the value 1 for the individuals who best match the characteristics of those employed in the formal sector (estimated according to equation 4-2) and 0 otherwise.

In this setup, equation 4-3 suggests that a change in the price of good g favors or harms the household to an extent given by the net exposure of its budget to that particular good. Moreover, an increase in the export of a particular good favors households in proportion to their marketed production of the good, and new employment favors households with the best matching characteristics. Finally, the change in welfare is distributed across household members, expenditures are equated to the new level of income, and new welfare indicators are calculated at the new level of consumption.

13. Singh, Squire, and Strauss (1986).
14. Changes in prices are equal for households in the same region.
15. Income is equated with expenditures.

Simulation Results

This section illustrates the results of simulations using the empirical framework discussed above. First we explore the business-as-usual and the ambitious Doha scenarios, and then we analyze what the effect would be if the ambitious implementation of Doha were complemented by trade liberalization on the part of Madagascar itself. The effects on household welfare are calculated as percentages of current household expenditure per capita. Households are arrayed by decile of per capita expenditure. A policy change is pro-poor if it provides extra spending power for households in the first five deciles.

Business-as-Usual Scenario

Under the business-as-usual scenario, multilateral trade liberalization would have little impact on poverty in Madagascar. This is not unexpected, given that the proposed liberalization measures are not likely to have much effect on products of importance for the Malagasy economy.

The changes in real income in this scenario are estimated to be small. Overall, real household income would rise by about 0.6 percent. The gains would be larger for urban households than for rural and be distributed unequally along the income scale. Except for households in the two richest deciles, in percentage terms the gains would increase along with the income of households (figure 4-4).

The histograms in figure 4-4 differentiate the effects of changes in prices (the difference between the cost of the expenditure baskets and the value of agricul-

Figure 4-4. *Effects on Household Welfare in Madagascar, by Decile of per Capita Expenditure: Business-as-Usual Scenario*

Change in real income (percent)

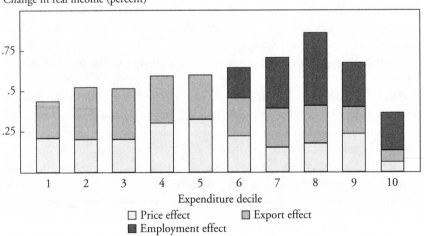

Source: Author's calculations.

tural production), exports (the increase in export quantities), and employment (the income from employment created as a consequence of Doha implementation). This decomposition indicates that poor households would gain mostly from the price and export effects and urban households would capture all the gains from the creation of employment.

Ambitious Scenario

The ambitious multilateral trade liberalization would produce an overall increase of about 1.8 percent in real income. Rural areas would gain mostly from the increases in the value of agricultural production and the quantity exported, while urban areas again would reap all the benefits from the increase in employment. Price effects are negative in urban areas—where consumers would lose as a consequence of higher prices—and positive in rural areas—where producers would gain from higher agricultural prices. Increases in exports, due to the increase in international demand for Malagasy agricultural products, would cause a rise of about 0.6 percent in real income for rural households and about 0.3 percent for urban households.

Poor households would gain the most, with increases in their real income ranging from 2 to almost 3 percent (figure 4-5). Most of their gains would come from price effects (the poor tend to be net producers of agricultural products), while employment effects would dominate the gains of households in higher income brackets. For the richest households, price effects would be negative.

Figure 4-5. *Effects on Household Welfare in Madagascar, by Decile of per Capita Expenditure: Ambitious Scenario*

Change in real income (percent)

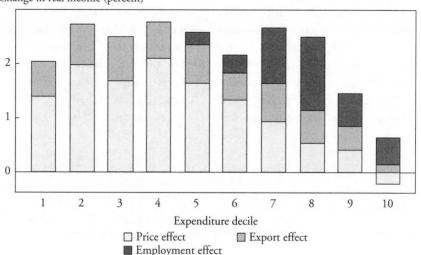

Source: Author's calculations.

In summary, the simulations show that a business-as-usual implementation of the Doha proposals would have only a small effect on households' real income in Madagascar, but that a more ambitious multilateral trade liberalization would yield an increase of about 1.8 percent. Relative to the business-as-usual scenario, poorer households would benefit by at least an additional 1.5 percent of purchasing power.

In either case, however, the likely benefits for Madagascar are not large. The main reason is that most of Madagascar's exports are of products little affected by the Doha agenda (vanilla, cloves, textiles, and apparel). Products for which multilateral trade liberalization is expected to have a larger impact (cereals, especially rice) are produced in Madagascar but barely traded. The reduction of tariffs in developed countries that is proposed by the Doha Development Agenda, and the associated increase in the price of cereals, would redistribute income from Madagascar's consumers to producers (from urban to rural areas) rather than produce a large net gain.

A second reason for the small impact of multilateral trade liberalization on Malagasy households is the low supply response of the Malagasy economy. Given the lack of infrastructure, the rudimentary state of markets, and the pervasive subsistence economy in rural areas, even large increases in prices may not induce rural producers to increase their supply to urban or international markets. Similarly, low productivity and the poor supply response limit the capacity of Madagascar's economy to increase supply to world markets when international demand increases.

Ambitious Doha Plus Own Trade Liberalization

The results suggest that, on its own, the reduction of trade barriers in developed countries cannot solve Madagascar's poverty problems. A final simulation combines the effects of the ambitious multilateral trade liberalization with those of a complete potential removal of tariffs by Madagascar itself.[16] In this simulation, the effects of Madagascar's own trade liberalization are restricted to the first-order effect on prices, without considering effects on exports or employment.

Madagascar's current tariff schedule is relatively low and simple, as mentioned, with the notable exception of rice, for which the tariff is 15 percent.[17]

---

16. Complete trade liberalization is politically difficult to implement in developing countries, as it affects not only domestic prices but also government revenues. National statistics indicate that Madagascar's government budget relies heavily on tariff revenues. The removal of tariffs on imports would reduce government revenues by about $2 per household per month. Hence, assuming no replacement revenue and assuming that households uniformly benefit from public goods and services financed by tariff revenues, the removal of Madagascar's tariffs would further reduce the welfare of poor households.

17. The tariff on rice is one of the most politically controversial issues for Madagascar and has been adjusted with almost every change in political power.

Figure 4-6. *Effects on Household Welfare in Madagascar, by Decile of per Capita Expenditure: Ambitious Scenario Paired with Malagasy Trade Liberalization (Price Effects)*

Change in real income (percent)

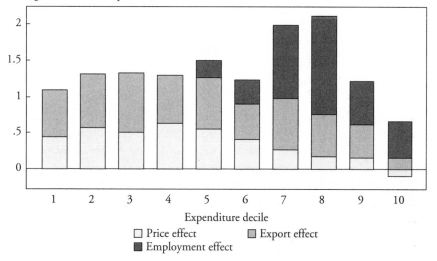

Source: Author's calculations.

Madagascar's removal of tariff barriers would substantially reduce the prices paid by consumers for imported goods. For the products of most importance for Madagascar, the decrease in the prices of imports contrasts with the outcome from multilateral trade liberalization alone, which, in most cases, would result in an increase in prices.

The ambitious implementation of Doha, paired with Madagascar's own trade liberalization, would produce average gains of about 1.4 percent in real household income. The results of this simulation are summarized in figure 4-6. The gains for poor households would range between 1 and 1.5 percent of real income. Households that would benefit the most are those near the poverty line (the seventh and eighth deciles), and for them the gains would be driven largely by an increase in employment. Real income is expected to rise by about 1.6 percent in urban areas and by about 1.3 percent in rural areas.

The removal of existing tariffs, and the consequent decrease in import prices, would benefit consumers at the expense of agricultural producers. This change in the terms of trade could pose a problem especially for the local economies of rural areas, for which the tariffs offer an essential advantage relative to imports. If Madagascar would remove its own tariffs, rural households would lose about 0.5 percent of their real income with respect to the ambitious scenario without Malagasy trade liberalization.

Clearly, this simulation provides only a rough approximation; trade liberalization may have many positive effects, such as an increase in the overall competitiveness of the economy, availability of a wider selection of goods, and so on. To estimate those effects is beyond the scope of this work, but in any case, because poor households are occupied largely in import-competing agriculture—particularly rice production—it seems clear that undertaking its own trade liberalization would not be a cure-all for Madagascar.

Conclusions

This chapter has investigated the effects on Malagasy households of the multilateral trade liberalization proposed in Doha. The empirical work suggests that a business-as-usual implementation of these proposals would have only a small impact on Malagasy households, amounting to an increase in real income of about 0.6 percent. Deeper multilateral trade liberalization (the ambitious scenario) would produce a somewhat larger gain, of about 1.8 percent. In this case, the benefits would go disproportionately to the poor. Households living in poverty would see their real incomes rise by between 2 and 3 percent. The richest households would benefit the least, with a 0.5 percent increase in their real income. The gains for poor households would arise mostly from price effects (due to the increase in agricultural prices) and export effects (due to the increase in the international demand for Malagasy products). Richer households would tend to benefit more from new employment opportunities. The distribution of gains in the business-as-usual scenario would be similar.

In any case, but especially in the business-as-usual scenario, the effects of the proposed multilateral trade liberalization would not be large for Madagascar. There are three main reasons why. First is the limited relevance of the Doha agenda to the export products in which Madagascar has a comparative advantage (vanilla, cloves, textiles, and apparel). The Doha proposals would have a larger impact on cereals, particularly rice, which Madagascar now produces but barely trades. Hence the implementation of the Doha proposals would redistribute purchasing power from consumers to producers (and from urban to rural areas). A second reason for the small impact of Doha on Malagasy households is the low supply response of the economy; exports respond only modestly to changes in international prices. A third reason is that poor households are isolated from market shocks; the lack of infrastructure, rudimentary state of markets, and the pervasive subsistence economy make it very difficult for international trade policies to reach the majority of the poor. For Madagascar the development of institutions and rural infrastructure, in order to integrate rural areas into domestic and world markets, is a prerequisite for alleviating poverty.

References

Heckman, James, Hidehiko Ichimura, and Petra Todd. 1998. "Matching as an Econometric Evaluation Estimator." *Review of Economic Studies* 65, no. 2 (April): 261–94.

Krueger, Alan B., and Lawrence H. Summers. 1988. "Efficiency Wages and the Inter-Industry Wage Structure." *Econometrica* 56, no. 2: 259–93.

Nicita, Alessandro. 2004. "Who Benefited from Trade Liberalization in Mexico? Measuring the Effects on Household Welfare." World Bank Working Paper 3265. Washington: World Bank.

Nicita, Alessandro, and Susan Razzaz. 2003. "Who Benefits and How Much? How Gender Affects Welfare Impacts of a Booming Textile Industry." World Bank Working Paper 3029. Washington: World Bank.

Porto, Guido. 2003. "Trade Reforms, Market Access, and Poverty in Argentina." World Bank Working Paper 3135. Washington: World Bank.

Singh, Inderjit, Lyn Squire, and John Strauss. 1986. *Agricultural Household Models, Extensions, Applications, and Policy.* Washington and Baltimore, Md.: World Bank and Johns Hopkins University Press.

Winters, L. Alan. 2002. "Trade Liberalization and Poverty: What Are the Links?" *World Economy* 25, no. 9: 1339–67.

Winters, L. Alan, Neil McCulloch, and Andrew McKay. 2004. "Trade Liberalization and Poverty: The Evidence So Far." *Journal of Economic Literature* 42, no. 1: 72–115.

APPENDIX

Regression Results

Table 4A-1. *Propensity Scores: Regression Results from Estimating Equation 4-1*

Dependent variable: logit (1 = individual employed in formal sector)

Variable	Coefficient	Standard error
Age (years)	0.012***	0.0015
Education (years)	0.104***	0.0048
Techical skill (1 = yes)	0.220***	0.0396
Region dummy 1	0.343***	0.0667
Region dummy 2	−0.376***	0.0741
Region dummy 3	−0.353***	0.0757
Region dummy 4	−0.527***	0.0793
Region dummy 5	−0.168**	0.0782
Urban dummy (urban = 1)	0.140***	0.0422
Gender dummy (male = 1)	0.489***	0.0381
Constant	−1.379***	0.0845
Number of observations	12,809	
Pseudo R-squared	0.0955	

Table 4A-2. *Wage Equation: Regression Results from Estimating Equation 4-2*

Dependent variable: Logarithm wage

Variable	Coefficient	Standard error
Age (years)	0.620***	0.055
Age squared	−0.008***	0.001
Education (years)	0.801***	0.026
Education squared	−0.039***	0.002
Formal sector premium	0.270***	0.033
Region dummy 1	2.155***	0.061
Region dummy 2	1.622***	0.065
Region dummy 3	1.724***	0.067
Region dummy 4	1.731***	0.078
Region dummy 5	1.970***	0.079
Marital status (1 = single)	−1.113***	0.038
Urban dummy (1 = urban)	0.269***	0.038
Number of observations	10,247	
R-squared	0.6912	

5

Zambia

JORGE F. BALAT, IRENE BRAMBILLA,
AND GUIDO G. PORTO

The trade reforms that are on the so-called Doha Development Agenda would introduce new opportunities and new challenges for poor households in developing countries. These opportunities and challenges are multidimensional: as consumers, households will face changes in the prices of goods they buy, and as income earners, they will face changes in wages, employment, the profitability of different crops, and agricultural income.

Our analysis of these impacts on poverty in Zambia builds on two links, one connecting trade reforms with prices and quantities and another connecting household income and consumption patterns with those price and quantity changes. The estimated changes in price and quantity are drawn from chapter 2, in which Kee, Nicita, and Olarreaga lay out a global model of world supply and demand. To link the price changes to household consumption in Zambia, we describe patterns of household expenditure. On the income side, we examine income sources in rural and urban Zambia separately. Since rural households derive income mostly from agricultural activities, such as growing cash crops, we estimate agricultural income gains using predictions of growth in agricultural exports. Since in urban areas the major sources of income are wages and

The authors thank Bernard Hoekman, Alessandro Nicita, and Isidro Soloaga for comments and suggestions. Special thanks to Marcelo Olarreaga for comments and endless encouragement. The discussion at the Latin American and Caribbean Economic Association (LACEA) meeting in San José, Costa Rica, was useful and improved the interpretation of our results.

employment, we look at the income gains originating in increases in wages and employment due to trade. We trace the implications of the two scenarios that were introduced in chapter 2: the base case, referred to as business as usual, involves a 40 percent reduction in bound tariffs in developed countries. The second, the ambitious scenario, entails much deeper trade liberalization: tariffs and subsidies in agriculture are eliminated, and nontariff barriers are cut in half. We also explore the welfare impacts of complementary domestic policies to improve agricultural productivity and augment urban employment.

This chapter is organized as follows. The first section provides an overview of trade and poverty in Zambia. The next two sections analyze the gains or losses in household income and expenditure, respectively, from multilateral trade liberalization in the business-as-usual scenario and from complementary domestic policies. A fourth section estimates the overall impacts at the household level. A fifth section summarizes the impacts of the ambitious Doha scenario, alone and with complementary domestic policies. A final section concludes.

We find that the business-as-usual scenario would have only a negligible impact on welfare in Zambia. The explanation lies in the small estimated changes in the international prices of goods important to Zambia's economy and severe limitations in household supply responses. The ambitious Doha scenario would yield more significant gains, spanning the entire income distribution. Jobs would be lost in this scenario, which includes the removal of Zambia's own tariffs and the protection they accord domestic producers. But the effects of lower prices for key consumption goods would outweigh these losses, so the Zambian population on average would reap small gains in real income. Greater gains can be expected if Zambia pursues complementary policies in agriculture that improve the supply response to new opportunities for trade.

Poverty and the Economy

Zambia, one of the world's poorest countries, is a landlocked country in southern central Africa. In 2000 its 10.7 million inhabitants had a per capita GDP of only $302.

Poverty

Zambia suffered from rising poverty during the 1990s (table 5-1),[1] although poverty rates differ widely across regions (table 5-2). Zambia is a large country, and its provinces differ in the quality of land, weather, access to water, and

---

1. This section is based on Balat and Porto (2005). Poverty analysis can be done using the 1991 Priority Survey and the 1996 and 1998 Living Conditions Monitoring Surveys (LCMS). The 2002 LCMS was not available at the time this chapter was written. For more details on these sources of data, see Balat and Porto (2005).

Table 5-1. *Poverty Headcount in Zambia, by Rural and Urban Area, 1991–98*[a]
Percent

Area	1991	1996	1998
National	69.6	80.0	71.5
Rural	88.3	90.5	82.1
Urban	47.2	62.1	53.4

Source: Authors' calculations, based on Zambian Priority Survey for 1991, Living Conditions Monitoring Survey for 1996, and Living Conditions Monitoring Survey for 1998. Poverty lines are taken from official figures from the Zambia Central Statistical Office.

a. The poverty headcount is the percentage of the population with an income below the poverty line. This poverty line is the monetary value of a bundle of goods that would allow the consumer to reach a minimum caloric intake and cover minimal non-food expenses.

access to infrastructure. The capital, Lusaka, and the Copperbelt are the most economically advanced, the Central and Eastern provinces produce cotton, the Southern province boasts the Victoria Falls and benefits from tourism, and the remaining provinces are less developed. In 1998 (the most recent year for which comprehensive data are available), all provinces had aggregate poverty counts higher than 60 percent, except for Lusaka, which contains the capital city (48 percent). Poverty was much more prevalent in rural than in urban areas. Urban poverty nowhere exceeded 70 percent of the population. In Lusaka, a mostly urban province, more than 75 percent of the rural population was poor, but in the Western province, more than 90 percent of the rural population was poor.

Table 5-2. *Poverty Headcount in Zambia, by Province, 1998*[a]
Percent

Province	Total	Rural	Urban
National	71.5	82.1	53.4
Central	74.9	82.3	60.5
Copperbelt	63.2	82.1	57.5
Eastern	79.1	80.6	64.4
Luapula	80.1	84.6	52.4
Lusaka	48.4	75.7	42.4
Northern	80.6	83.3	66.4
North-Western	74.3	77.4	54.1
Southern	68.2	73.0	51.8
Western	88.1	90.3	69.5

Source: Authors' calculations, based on the Living Conditions Monitoring Survey for 1998.

a. The poverty headcount is the percentage of the population with an income below the poverty line.

Trade Trends

Zambia's major trading partners are the Common Market for Eastern and Southern Africa (COMESA), the European Union, and Japan.[2]

Zambia's exports have been dominated by copper, and diversification into nontraditional exports has become important only recently. In 1990 metals accounted for 93 percent of the country's commodity exports, but by 1999, their share had fallen to 61 percent; nontraditional exports—mainly primary products, horticultural products, textiles, processed foods, and animal products—made up the remaining 39 percent.[3]

Zambia's main imports are metals (iron, steel), with 17 percent of total imports in 1999; petroleum (13 percent); and fertilizers (13 percent). Other important import lines include chemicals, machinery, and manufactures.

Tariffs are Zambia's main trade policy instrument. Although quantitative restrictions have been largely eliminated, the country also maintains some import controls based on environmental, sanitary, or security issues. Agriculture is the most protected sector, with an average tariff of 18.7 percent, followed by manufacturing, with an average tariff of 13.2 percent. As of 2002, the tariff structure had four bands (0, 5, 15, and 25 percent), with an average rate of around 13 percent. Most tariff lines are ad valorem, and items are rarely subject to seasonal, specific, compound, variable, or interim tariffs. The most common tariff rate is 15 percent, which is applied to around 33 percent of the tariff lines. Almost two-thirds of the tariff lines are subject to either a 15 percent or a 25 percent tariff, while 21 percent of the tariff lines (1,265 lines) enter duty free. The latter include books, pharmaceutical products, and productive machinery for agriculture. Raw materials and industrial or productive machinery face tariffs in the 0–5 percent range. Intermediate goods are generally taxed at 15 percent, and a 25 percent tariff is applied to final consumer goods and agriculture-related tariff lines. The average applied most favored nation tariff in mining and quarrying is 8.2 percent.

Exports have largely been liberalized; there are no official export taxes, charges, or levies, and export controls and regulations are minimal. Maize exports, however, are sometimes subject to bans for national food security reasons, as happened in 2002.

Income

By affecting wages and cash income from agriculture, trade opportunities are likely to have large impacts on household resources and on poverty. As argued by Deaton and others, the short-run effects of price changes on household welfare can be assessed by looking at the sources from which households derive their

---

2. This section is based on Balat and Porto (2005).
3. For more details, see WTO (1996).

income and the goods and services on which they spend it.[4] The description of income shares is also useful because it highlights the main channels through which trade opportunities can affect household income.

As shown in table 5-3, the main sources of income for the average Zambian household are the household's own production (28 percent), non-farm businesses (22 percent), and wages (21 percent). The sale of food crops accounts for 6 percent of total income—more than twice the share of cash crops (2.5 percent). Livestock and poultry and remittances account for 5.5 and 5 percent of household income, respectively.

Income sources differ significantly between poor and non-poor households. While subsistence production—the production of food for the family's own consumption—supplies a third of income in the average poor household, it provides less than a fifth in non-poor families. And while wages account for only 14 percent of the income of the poor, they provide a third of the income of the non-poor. The shares of income generated in non-farm businesses are 21 and 25 percent in poor and non-poor households, respectively. The poor earn a larger share of income from the sale of both food and cash crops and from livestock and poultry than do the non-poor.

As expected, income sources also differ between rural and urban areas. In rural areas, 43 percent of total income derives from the family's own production; the comparable share in urban areas is only 3 percent. Non-farm income in rural areas is 17 percent, compared with 32 percent in urban areas. In urban areas, wages supply 45 percent of household income, and the contribution of agricultural activities is much smaller.

In rural areas, households derive most of their income from subsistence agriculture and from nontradable services (non-farm income), while cash crop activities and agricultural wage labor supply a smaller fraction. In urban areas, the important determinants of income are labor markets, employment, and wages. Thus, in what follows, we study income gains in rural and urban areas separately.

Multilateral Trade Reform and Welfare Gains in Rural Areas

Trade reforms have an effect on prices and on quantities produced and exported. To see how these changes affect the household, consider cotton, one of Zambia's major cash crops. The elimination of U.S. subsidies on cotton would lead to a reduction in world supply and thus to an increase in world prices. Since U.S. supply would be lower and producer prices would be higher, the quantity of cotton produced in Zambia and exported would increase. We can interpret these effects as generating two sources of gain for Zambian farmers. First, since prices are higher, farmers would receive a higher net price for their cotton. This is a first-order gain whose effect on household welfare can be estimated using data on

4. Deaton (1989, 1997).

Table 5-3. *Sources of Household Income in Zambia, by National, Rural, and Urban Area and Income Group*
Percent

Source of income	National			Rural			Urban		
	Total	Poor	Non-poor	Total	Poor	Non-poor	Total	Poor	Non-poor
Own production	28.3	33.3	19.1	42.5	42.9	42.0	3.3	4.4	2.4
Sale of food crops	6.3	7.6	3.8	9.1	9.5	7.6	1.4	1.7	1.1
Sale of non-food crops	2.5	3.0	1.3	3.8	4.0	2.9	0.1	0.1	0.1
Livestock and poultry	5.5	6.8	2.9	8.1	8.7	5.9	0.8	1.0	0.7
Wages	20.8	14.4	32.9	16.8	5.9	10.3	45.3	40.3	49.4
Non-farm income	22.3	20.9	24.9	6.9	16.3	18.3	32.0	34.7	29.7
Remittances	4.9	5.0	4.8	5.3	5.0	6.1	4.3	4.9	3.9
Other sources	9.5	9.0	10.3	7.5	7.7	6.9	12.8	13.0	12.7
Total	100.0	100.0	100.0	100.0	100.0	100.0	100.0	100.0	100.0

Source: Authors' calculations, based on Living Conditions Monitoring Survey for 1998.

Table 5-4. *Changes in Price and Quantity in Zambia: Business-as-Usual Scenario*
Percent

Product	Price changes	Quantity changes
Cotton	3.51	5.51
Vegetables	−0.05	−0.19
Tobacco	1.30	17.95
Hybrid maize	3.99	9.63
Groundnuts	−0.12	0.83

Source: Authors' calculations, based on Living Conditions Monitoring Survey for 1998.

the composition of household income as in table 5-3. Second, farmers can now increase their output of cotton and sell it in international markets. This supply response is generally a second-order effect and will be relatively small unless the household has idle resources (land, labor) or enjoys increases in productivity.

To gauge the impacts of Doha-related multilateral trade reforms on agricultural household welfare and poverty, we start by looking at the international price and quantity changes that are likely to be induced by the business-as-usual scenario. Zambia's main crops are cotton, tobacco, maize, vegetables, and groundnuts. In column 1 of table 5-4, we reproduce the price changes for these commodities, which were estimated by Kee, Nicita, and Olarreaga in chapter 2 for this scenario.

A key observation here is that the price changes for these crops are quite small. This means that income earners in Zambia would not benefit much from these price changes alone and hence that the supply responses of producers to changes in export demand would be critical for poverty reduction.[5] Column 2 reports the estimated changes in the quantity of supply for the major cash crops in Zambia. Tobacco exports would increase by 17.95 percent, those of maize by 9.63 percent, and those of cotton by 5.5 percent; exports of vegetables and groundnuts would not be much affected.[6]

Given the price and quantity changes reported in table 5-4, our task now is to estimate the resulting changes in household welfare and to assess the poverty impacts. We assume that all households face the same price changes. This may not be true if some households are better connected to the market than others, but we do not have good data to assess this.[7]

5. For some analyses of supply responses, trade, and poverty, see Heltberg and Tarp (2001); Lopez, Nash, and Stanton (1995); Porto (2004); and Balat and Porto (2005).
6. Both the Doha scenarios include an exogenous increase in exports of 2 percent, attributed to improvements in trade facilitation. This explains why price declines in groundnuts can be accompanied by quantity increases.
7. Nicita (2005) studies the role of price transmission in the event of trade liberalization in Mexico.

Another concern is how to allocate the quantity changes among producers. We adopt a procedure that allocates the quantities exported in proportion to an individual household's propensity to produce each exportable commodity. A household's propensity score $p(x)$ is its estimated probability of producing a specific agricultural commodity, as a function of household characteristic x. That is,

$$(5\text{-}1) \qquad p(x_i) = P(D = 1|x_i),$$

where D is an indicator of whether the household is a producer of the commodity in question.[8]

In short, we begin by estimating a probability model for being a cotton producer, a tobacco producer, a hybrid maize producer, a vegetable producer, or a groundnut producer. Next, we rescale these probabilities by the sum of the individual propensity scores as follows:

$$(5\text{-}2) \qquad \tilde{p}(x_i) = \frac{p(x_i)}{\sum_i p(x_i)},$$

This rescaling transforms the estimated propensity score into weights that we can use to allocate the increased exports to producer households. That is, we allocate the estimated growth in exported quantities according to the relative propensity score given by equation 5-2.

It is important to note that we allow for supply responses from subsistence households, not only from households that are already producing for the market; that is, we allow for a movement of farmers out of subsistence agriculture and into cash crop agriculture. Of course, households that are already involved in cash cropping probably have a higher propensity to produce cash crops, and so they are more likely to have a higher propensity score. This feature of the model is plausible, since it is likely that a farmer producing for the market will continue doing so once market opportunities expand.

Our main findings are shown in table 5-5. Here, we report the first- and second-order effects on household welfare of the price and quantity changes based on our procedure to allocate these changes among households. The first-order effect is the product of the estimated price changes of the different goods and the income shares of the different Zambian households; the second-order effect can be captured by multiplying the quantity change in the household's output by the price change times 0.5. The effects are expressed as percentages of

---

8. For more details on estimating the propensity score, see Dehejia and Wahba (2002); Heckman and others (1996); Heckman, Ichimura, and Todd (1997, 1998); Rosenbaum and Rubin (1983); and Rubin (1977).

Table 5-5. *Welfare Gains from Key Export Crops in Zambia, by Decile of per Capita Expenditure: Business-as-Usual Scenario*
Percent

Decile	Cotton	Vegetables	Tobacco	Hybrid maize	Groundnuts	Total
1	0.11	−0.002	0.007	0.07	−0.001	0.19
2	0.09	−0.001	0.006	0.05	−0.002	0.15
3	0.05	−0.001	0.002	0.05	−0.001	0.10
4	0.07	−0.001	0.003	0.05	−0.001	0.12
5	0.05	−0.001	0.002	0.04	−0.001	0.09
6	0.04	−0.001	0.001	0.04	−0.001	0.08
7	0.03	−0.001	0.003	0.05	−0.001	0.08
8	0.03	−0.001	0.001	0.03	−0.001	0.06
9	0.02	−0.001	0.002	0.04	−0.001	0.06
10	0.02	−0.001	0.001	0.04	−0.001	0.07
Total	0.05	−0.001	0.003	0.05	−0.001	0.10

Source: Authors' calculations, based on Living Conditions Monitoring Survey for 1998.

current household expenditure per capita, for rural households arrayed by decile of per capita expenditure.

As shown by table 5-5, the business-as-usual scenario does not significantly affect the purchasing power of a typical rural household in Zambia. Its overall effect is positive but very small: a gain of only 0.10 percent. There are somewhat larger gains for the poorest households (see the results for the first decile), but the magnitudes are too small to deserve further attention.

There are two key elements behind these results: the small changes in price generated by multilateral liberalization in this scenario and the small shares of household income derived from marketed output. It is worth asking whether there are circumstances in which a Doha deal would have a bigger impact on poverty.

One way in which developing countries may benefit from new trading opportunities is by increasing their producers' supply responses to international price changes. We believe that this requires improvements in productivity: important benefits can be achieved only if households can keep their costs down while increasing their output. For example, households may be able to produce more output with the same inputs, or they may have underemployed land or family labor that could be put to use.

Let us assume that households can increase their marketed output of crops, as reported in column 2 of table 5-4, at no additional costs. Table 5-6 reports the welfare gains that result from this relaxation of supply constraints. It shows that even these gains remain quite small, adding only 0.62 percent to initial per capita expenditure for the average rural household. The gains are higher among the poorest rural households: for households in the poorest three deciles they are

Table 5-6. *Additional Welfare Gains in Zambia, by Decile of per Capita Expenditure: Complementary Reforms*[a]
Percent

Decile	Cotton	Vegetables	Tobacco	Hybrid maize	Groundnuts	Total
1	0.27	−0.012	0.62	1.20	0.023	2.11
2	0.16	−0.005	0.16	0.73	0.013	1.06
3	0.12	−0.003	0.28	0.49	0.010	0.89
4	0.09	−0.002	0.06	0.31	0.008	0.47
5	0.06	−0.002	0.04	0.38	0.004	0.49
6	0.05	−0.001	0.03	0.22	0.003	0.29
7	0.02	−0.001	0.10	0.21	0.003	0.33
8	0.02	−0.001	0.01	0.14	0.002	0.17
9	0.02	−0.001	0.03	0.20	0.002	0.25
10	0.01	−0.001	0.01	0.11	0.002	0.13
Total	0.08	−0.003	0.13	0.40	0.007	0.62

Source: Authors' calculations, based on Living Conditions Monitoring Survey for 1998.

a. The results are based on the simulated effects of the elimination of supply constraints in agriculture. See text for details.

2.11, 1.06, and 0.89 percent, respectively, but they are less than half of a percentage point at the middle and upper tail of the income distribution.

To calculate the total welfare gains to rural households from the business-as-usual scenario, we add the figures in table 5-6 to the first- and second-order effects reported in table 5-5.

The magnitude of the estimated changes in income conveys an important message: by itself, a business-as-usual outcome from the Doha Round will not do much to reduce poverty in Zambia. What is needed is a combination of multilateral trade liberalization and a set of complementary domestic policies that would allow rural households to capture the full benefits of the new trading opportunities. In fact, in this case there is evidence to suggest that multilateral trade reforms, accompanied by complementary policies, would benefit the poor proportionately more than the rich.

Domestic actions are needed to facilitate both production and trade of agricultural commodities. As shown in table 5-3, almost all rural households engage in subsistence agriculture, and many derive most of their consumption from this source. To benefit from new opportunities for international trade, subsistence farmers will need to produce for the market. Some households will respond by switching to cash crops, but many others, faced with myriad constraints, will be unable to do so. Several key policies would ease the transition from subsistence to market, including better access to credit, infrastructure, education, markets, and information about markets.

More educated households will be better prepared to face international markets and to adopt new crops and production techniques. Farmers who have access to credit will be better able to afford the initial investments (in seeds, fertilizer, tools) needed to begin growing more lucrative crops. If better infrastructure is provided, transaction and production costs will be lower, facilitating trade in cash crops. And if better marketing opportunities arise, farmers will be "closer" to the market. All these arguments highlight the need for complementary policies if producers are to take full advantage of the new trading opportunities from a Doha deal.

Two recent empirical studies corroborate the idea that education, information, and marketing services are key factors for Zambia in securing gains from an expansion of international trade. Building on an empirical model of cotton yields in Zambia, Balat and Porto find that receiving agricultural extension services[9] raises a household's cotton production per hectare by 8.4 percent. Brambilla and Porto discuss the effects of the elimination of Zambia's cotton marketing board and associated liberalization of cotton production and trade during the 1990s.[10] They find that, after an initial period of failure in these reforms, Zambian farmers increasingly adopted cotton as a major cash crop and that cotton yields significantly increased. This was due to a combination of improved access to inputs, increased know-how, improved marketing information, and increased efficiency in input use. Altogether, these reforms allowed farmers to take advantage of the gains associated with export opportunities for agricultural commodities such as cotton.

Multilateral Trade Reform and Welfare Gains in Urban Areas

Whereas agriculture is key in rural areas, wages and employment are more important in urban areas. For urban households, the benefits from a Doha deal would take effect mostly through an increase in job opportunities.

To estimate the effects on poverty of an increase in jobs, created by growth in demand for exports under the business-as-usual scenario, we estimate a model of employment probability jointly with an earnings regression model. In fact, we implement a Heckman model of wages and employment. Our main assumption is that Zambia has a large pool of unemployed individuals (a reasonable assumption, since the unemployment rate in urban Zambia is more than 15 percent) and hence that the new jobs would be taken by unemployed individuals and that the wage rate would remain roughly constant.

---

9. Balat and Porto (2005). These are services provided by the government (and some agricultural intermediaries) that give farmers information and support on a variety of issues, such as markets, prices, buyers, sellers, technology adoption, crop diversification, crop husbandry, fertilizer use, seeds, and machinery.

10. Brambilla and Porto (2005).

Table 5-7. *Urban Welfare Gains from Employment Growth in Zambia, by Decile of per Capita Expenditure: Business-as-Usual Scenario*[a]
Percent

Decile	All individuals	Heads of household only
1	0.65	0.90
2	0.62	0.37
3	0.28	0.41
4	0.63	0.93
5	0.63	1.00
6	0.88	0.68
7	0.60	0.69
8	0.17	0.26
9	0.23	0.20
10	0.10	0.12
Total	0.48	0.55

Source: Authors' calculations, based on Living Conditions Monitoring Survey for 1998.

a. The "all individuals" variant assumes that any household member can enjoy the growth in employment; instead, the "heads only" variant allocates the new job openings to unemployed household heads.

After estimating the model, we use the estimated coefficients and the individual's characteristics to predict, for each unemployed individual, the probability of becoming employed (represented by a propensity score) and the imputed wage that he or she could earn in one of the new jobs. Then we rank the individuals according to their propensity scores and allocate jobs to those with a higher probability of employment until all the new jobs are filled.

We calculate the likely growth in employment in Zambia based on the estimates of exports, imports, and price changes reported by Kee, Nicita, and Olarreaga in chapter 2.[11] Under the business-as-usual scenario, we estimate that overall employment in Zambia would rise by around 0.9 percent, as the net result of increases in employment in export sectors and declines in employment in import-competing sectors. This small estimated increase in employment is in line with the small price and quantity changes noted above.

The effects of the employment growth on urban household welfare are shown in table 5-7 for two variants: the first, shown in column 1, treats every unemployed individual in the same way, and the second, shown in column 2, assumes that the new jobs are filled only by heads of households. In the "all individuals" variant, the gains would be fairly small, at around 0.48 percent of households' initial per capita expenditure, and spread more or less uniformly from the first to the seventh deciles. An explanation for this result is the correlation between new employment probabilities (as measured by the estimated propensity scores) and

11. The changes in quantities exported, imported, and consumed allow us to predict changes in output, which we link to employment using data on labor requirements.

having someone employed in the family, so that the gains are concentrated in those households with someone in employment, which tend to be richer households. This indicates the importance of peer effects: if there are employed individuals in the family, it might be easier to benefit from new job opportunities. A possible implication of this result is that well-connected individuals are more likely to enjoy new opportunities.

If the new jobs were taken only by household heads (column 2 of table 5-7), the gains would be slightly higher across the entire income distribution, with an average gain of 0.55 percent of initial household per capita expenditure. Further, the gains would be somewhat larger for the poorer half of households than for the richer. In other words, the "heads only" model would work in favor of the poorest Zambian households. Hence it seems that a policy linking employment opportunities to household heads is likely to complement trade opportunities to the benefit of the poor.[12]

Expenditures

We now investigate some of the consumption effects of the price changes that would be induced by policy reforms arising from the Doha Round. We begin by describing the structure of expenditure by household, which helps us to predict the short-run impact of a change in trade policy on consumers.

Table 5-8 reports the average budget shares spent by Zambian households on different goods and services. As expected, most of the budget is spent on food, with a national average share of 67.5 percent. The share of food is higher in rural areas (74 percent) than in urban (57 percent) and is higher among the poor (72 percent) than the non-poor (59 percent).

Other typical differences can be seen between poor and non-poor and between urban and rural households. For instance, non-poor households tend to use a larger fraction of their expenditure for clothing, personal items, housing, and transport, but the budget shares spent on education and health are not very different across poor and non-poor households. Comparing rural and urban households, we find that urban households spend larger shares of their incomes on personal items, housing, transport, and education.

Since in Zambia, as in many low-income developing countries, the largest fraction of household expenditure is spent on food, the largest impacts of trade policies and economic reforms on the consumption side will be caused by changes in the prices of food.

---

12. These results should be interpreted carefully. We are not evaluating such a policy; rather we use this example to illustrate channels by which domestic reforms can complement global trade reforms. Needless to say, the implementation of a policy like this is far from easy. See Jalan and Ravallion (2003) and Galasso and Ravallion (2004).

Table 5-8. *Composition of Household Expenditure in Zambia, by National, Rural, and Urban Area and by Income Group*
Percent

Expenditure item	National			Rural			Urban		
	Total	Poor	Non-poor	Total	Poor	Non-poor	Total	Poor	Non-poor
Food	67.5	71.8	59.3	73.6	74.6	70.3	56.6	63.1	51.2
Clothing	5.6	4.8	7.1	5.6	5.2	7.0	5.5	3.6	7.1
Alcohol and tobacco	3.6	2.9	4.9	3.7	3.0	6.0	3.3	2.3	4.1
Personal goods	7.1	6.8	7.6	5.7	6.1	4.5	9.5	9.1	9.9
Housing	4.5	4.2	5.0	2.9	3.0	2.4	7.3	7.7	6.9
Education	2.5	2.6	2.3	1.9	2.1	1.0	3.6	3.9	3.3
Health	1.4	1.3	1.6	1.3	1.3	1.5	1.7	1.5	1.7
Transport	4.2	3.2	5.9	3.4	3.1	4.3	5.5	3.6	7.1
Remittances	1.3	0.7	2.4	1.0	0.7	1.9	1.9	0.8	2.8
Other	2.4	1.7	3.9	0.9	0.8	1.2	5.1	4.2	5.9
Total	100.0	100.0	100.0	100.0	100.0	100.0	100.0	100.0	100.0

Source: Authors' calculations, based on Living Conditions Monitoring Survey for 1998.

In this section we study the impacts of the Doha-related reforms on household spending. The price changes estimated by Kee, Nicita, and Olarreaga in chapter 2 show that for food items, which account for 67.5 percent of the average Zambian household budget, the average price increase would be around 3 percent. Clearly, such a price change would not have an enormous impact on household welfare. Another 16 percent of the household budget is spent on nontraded goods, such as health, housing, education, transport, and remittances. We do not have estimated price changes for these goods.[13] The remaining 16 percent is spent on tradable goods such as clothing, alcohol and tobacco, and personal goods. Here, the prices of clothing and tobacco are each expected to increase by around 1 percent.

The estimated effects of the international price changes on consumption are reported in table 5-9, which shows the total effects (in the last column) and the effects for select individual goods. Only first-order effects are estimated; that is, we assume no substitution responses, even though in reality households would switch their consumption away from goods whose price had risen, in favor of substitutes whose price had fallen. This means that the consumption losses reported in table 5-9 are actually upper bounds.[14]

The aggregate losses are estimated at 0.98 percent of households' initial per capita expenditure. There is some evidence that the poorer households would be harder hit by the price changes. The main component among the consumption effects comes from the rise in the price of cereals, including maize, which is the main staple of Zambian households.

Total Welfare Effects of a Development Round

We now combine the results of the analyses to investigate the total impact of implementing the Doha Development Agenda on household welfare. The results are reported in table 5-10 for the business-as-usual scenario.

Model 1, shown in column 1, is the constrained model in agriculture: this simulation includes the first- and second-order effects of multilateral trade reform on agricultural production, but without the complementary reforms to encourage supply; it includes the consumption effects and the "all individuals" employment effects. Thus we estimate that the average impact on Zambia of a business-as-usual Doha outcome would be negative, but small, at 0.40 percent of household per capita expenditure. The losses are somewhat greater among the

13. In general equilibrium, the prices of the nontraded goods are likely to change if, for example, there are changes in factor prices (wages) induced by trade. Measuring these impacts, however, is very difficult and outside the scope of the present study. See Porto (2003) for an attempt to measure some of these effects for the case of Argentina.

14. However, the corrections for second-order effects in consumption are usually small and not likely to change the conclusions significantly (Porto 2005, 2006).

Table 5-9. *Effects on Household Consumption in Zambia, by Decile of per Capita Expenditure: Business-as-Usual Scenario*

Percent

Decile	Clothing	Vegetables	Fish	Cereals	Dairy	Tobacco and alcohol	Meat and poultry	Total
1	-0.03	0.01	-0.006	-1.39	-0.001	-0.02	-0.01	-1.44
2	-0.04	0.02	-0.006	-1.18	-0.001	-0.03	-0.02	-1.26
3	-0.04	0.02	-0.006	-1.14	-0.001	-0.03	-0.02	-1.22
4	-0.05	0.02	-0.006	-1.04	-0.001	-0.03	-0.04	-1.14
5	-0.05	0.02	-0.005	-0.93	-0.002	-0.03	-0.04	-1.04
6	-0.05	0.02	-0.005	-0.83	-0.003	-0.03	-0.02	-0.93
7	-0.06	0.02	-0.005	-0.76	-0.004	-0.04	-0.02	-0.87
8	-0.07	0.01	-0.005	-0.65	-0.004	-0.04	-0.02	-0.77
9	-0.08	0.01	0.004	-0.52	-0.005	-0.04	-0.02	-0.66
10	-0.08	0.01	-0.003	-0.36	-0.005	-0.06	-0.00	-0.49
Average of total	-0.05	0.01	-0.005	-0.88	-0.003	-0.03	-0.02	-0.98

Source: Authors' calculations, based on Living Conditions Monitoring Survey for 1998.

Table 5-10. *Doha Effects on Household Welfare in Zambia: Business-as-Usual Scenario and Complementary Reforms*[a]
Percent

Decile	Model 1	Model 2
1	−0.60	1.50
2	−0.48	0.58
3	−0.85	0.05
4	−0.39	0.08
5	−0.32	0.17
6	0.03	0.32
7	−0.20	0.13
8	−0.54	−0.37
9	−0.36	−0.11
10	−0.32	−0.19
Total	−0.40	0.22

Source: Authors' calculations, based on Living Conditions Monitoring Survey for 1998.

a. Model 1 includes income gains in agriculture, employment effects, and consumption effects. Model 2 adds complementary reforms in agriculture.

poorest deciles. The main forces driving these results are the small and distributionally neutral income gains in both agriculture and "all individuals" employment and the increase in the price of cereals, which hurts poor households disproportionately.

Model 2, shown in column 2 of table 5-10, is the unconstrained agricultural model in which complementary policies boost agricultural supply and income in rural areas; like Model 1, this simulation also includes consumption effects and the "all individuals" employment effects. As a result of the complementary policies in agriculture, the aggregate impact of the development round is now positive, though very small, adding 0.22 percent to initial household expenditure. There is now a distributional conflict: while the poorer seven deciles would gain—because the complementary policies would boost agricultural responses among the poorest households, particularly in rural areas—the top three deciles would lose. This suggests that a combination of the business-as-usual Doha reforms and complementary domestic policies would have some pro-poor effects.

The Ambitious Scenario

In this section, we explore the impacts of the ambitious Doha scenario that was introduced in chapter 2. The ambitious scenario entails the worldwide elimination of all tariffs, the elimination of agricultural subsidies, improvements in trade facilitation equivalent to a 2 percent increase in exports (as in business as usual), and a reduction in nontariff measures. This scenario introduces two new considerations for our analysis: first, the elimination of Zambian tariffs would cause domestic prices to decrease, and second, enhanced market access in developing countries may boost Zambian agricultural exports and employment.

We follow the same methodology as before. As table 5-11 shows, we estimate the effects on household real income, allowing for first- and second-order effects (column 1), additional gains from complementary reforms in agriculture (column 2), employment effects (column 3), and consumption gains (column 4). The total effects are shown in column 5 (the ambitious scenario) and column 6 (the ambitious scenario plus complementary reforms).[15]

The simulations show that Zambia would gain, in aggregate, from the ambitious scenario. Without complementary policies, the gains would be equivalent to 1.64 percent of average household per capita expenditure (column 5 of table 5-11). With the complementary reforms, the gains would be boosted, reaching 2.41 percent (column 6).

To understand this result, we compare the welfare gains in agriculture, the employment effects, and the consumption effects in the business-as-usual and ambitious scenarios.

Notice first that the welfare gains in agriculture in the ambitious scenario are roughly similar to those under business as usual. The first- and second-order effects in agriculture produce a gain of 0.17 in average household purchasing power, and the additional gains from the elimination of supply constraints through complementary policies are equivalent to 0.77 percent (columns 1 and 2 of table 5-11).

By contrast, the employment increases implied by the two scenarios differ significantly. Under business as usual, employment would increase slightly (by 0.9 percent), but it would decline in the ambitious scenario by nearly 4 percent. The reason is that the ambitious scenario includes the elimination of Zambian tariffs, which in practice would destroy more jobs than would be created by the global reforms. Across all households, the associated loss in wages from employment would be equivalent to 0.81 percent of average per capita expenditure. The losses would be concentrated at the top of the income distribution, and the poorest 10 percent of households would not lose from job destruction. This is because the poorest households are less likely to be employed in the first place, and better-off households (whose members have jobs before the reforms) are likely to suffer greater losses.

The major difference in the welfare impacts of the two scenarios lies in the effects on consumption. These are negative, overall, in the business-as-usual

15. Since the ambitious Doha scenario requires a significant cut in Zambia's tariffs, there is an additional effect to consider: the loss of government revenue. To deal with this, we assume transfers from consumers to compensate for revenue losses.

Table 5-11. *Effects on Household Welfare in Zambia, by Decile of per Capita Expenditure: Ambitious Scenario and Complementary Reforms*
Percent

Decile	Income gains		Employment gains	Consumption gains	Total effects	
	Doha 1	Complementary reforms			Doha ambitious scenario	Complementary reforms
1	0.38	2.15	-0.00	1.74	1.85	4.00
2	0.21	1.24	-0.48	1.78	1.51	2.75
3	0.16	1.38	-0.25	1.94	1.86	3.23
4	0.16	0.44	-0.60	2.13	1.69	2.13
5	0.16	0.68	-0.86	2.22	1.52	2.20
6	0.11	0.35	-0.91	2.36	1.56	1.91
7	0.16	0.58	-0.88	2.60	1.88	2.45
8	0.09	0.23	-0.83	2.72	1.98	2.21
9	0.11	0.46	-1.43	2.84	1.52	1.99
10	0.12	0.20	-1.88	2.79	1.03	1.23
Total	0.17	0.77	-0.81	2.29	1.64	2.41

Source: Authors' calculations, based on Living Conditions Monitoring Survey for 1998.

scenario, but they are positive overall in the ambitious scenario. The key factor driving this difference is the elimination of domestic tariffs in the ambitious scenario, which forces certain domestic prices down. The average household would gain about 2.29 percent in purchasing power as the result of this price reduction. The richest households would gain significantly more than the poorest: compare the gains of 2.84 or 2.79 in deciles nine and ten with the gains of 1.74 and 1.78 in deciles one and two. The reason is the following. Before the reform, goods such as clothing face high tariffs, of around 15–20 percent on average, but cereals (the main staple of the poor) face lower tariffs of only 5 percent. As a result of the ambitious scenario, the price of clothing declines, but the price of cereals rises: the cut in cereal tariffs is not enough to compensate for the increase in international prices that is generated by the multilateral reductions in agricultural subsidies and tariffs.

As in the business-as-usual scenario, complementary domestic reforms would augment the expected welfare gains from trade liberalization. In the ambitious scenario, the complementary reforms would raise the gains from 1.64 to 2.41 percent of current per capita household consumption. More important, these additional gains would benefit poor households, mainly by increasing their supply. As shown in the last column of table 5-11, the gains for the poorest 30 percent of households would be doubled by the complementary policies. In contrast, the increase in the gains for the richest households would be relatively small.

The important message is, once again, that domestic policies that complement multilateral trade liberalization can succeed in boosting the gains and in ameliorating eventual losses, particularly among the poor.

Conclusions

In this chapter we have investigated some of the impacts of multilateral trade reform on poverty in Zambia. Our main finding is that a business-as-usual outcome from the Doha Round is likely to have fairly small impacts on household welfare in Zambia, probably causing small losses. Complementary domestic policies matter, however. If the Doha-related reforms are accompanied by complementary domestic reforms, the losses are likely to become gains, particularly among the poorest households. Examples of complementary policies include the provision of extension services in agriculture, the privatization of marketing institutions in cotton, and the implementation of employment plans targeting household heads.

Ambitious multilateral trade liberalization would be more conducive to poverty reduction than the business-as-usual scenario. This is mainly because the elimination of Zambian tariffs associated with the ambitious reforms would cause the prices of certain consumer goods to decline, thus benefiting households as consumers. The magnitude of change, however, is fairly small, and the conclusion remains that complementary Zambian policies matter. When complemented with policies that facilitate production for the export sector, the ambitious scenario would generate bigger gains, not only at the national level but particularly among the poorest households. This result illustrates the role of these complementary policies and highlights the potential importance of aid for trade in poverty alleviation.

References

Balat, Jorge, and Guido Porto. 2005. "Globalization and Complementary Policies: Poverty Impacts in Rural Zambia." In *Globalization and Poverty,* edited by Ann Harrison. Boston, Mass.: National Bureau of Economic Research.

Brambilla, Irene, and Guido Porto. 2005. "Farm Productivity and Market Structure: Evidence from Cotton Reforms in Zambia." Growth Center Discussion Paper 919. Yale University.

Deaton, Angus. 1989. "Rice Prices and Income Distribution in Thailand: A Non-Parametric Analysis." *Economic Journal* 99, no. 395 (supplement): 1–37.

———. 1997. *The Analysis of Household Surveys: A Microeconometric Approach to Development Policy.* Baltimore, Md.: John Hopkins University Press for the World Bank.

Dehejia, Rajeev, and Sadek Wahba. 2002. "Propensity Score Matching Methods for Nonexperimental Causal Studies." *Review of Economic Studies* 84, no. 1: 151–61.

Galasso, Emanuela, and Martin Ravallion. 2004. "Social Protection in a Crisis." *World Bank Economic Review* 65, no. 2: 261–94.

Heckman, James J., Hidehiko Ichimura, Jeffrey Smith, and Petra Todd. 1996. "Sources of Selection Bias in Evaluating Social Programs: An Interpretation of Conventional Measures and Evidence on the Effectiveness of Matching as a Program Evaluation Method." *Proceedings of the National Academy of Sciences* 93, no. 23 (November): 13416–20.

Heckman, James J., Hidehiko Ichimura, and Petra Todd. 1997. "Matching as an Econometric Evaluation Estimator: Evidence from Evaluating a Job Training Program." *Review of Economic Studies* 64, no. 4: 605–54.

———. 1998. "Matching as an Econometric Evaluation Estimator." *Review of Economic Studies* 65, no. 2: 261–94.

Heltberg, Rasmus, and Finn Tarp. 2001. "Agricultural Supply Response and Poverty in Mozambique." Mimeo. University of Copenhagen, Institute of Economics.

Jalan, Jyotsna, and Martin Ravallion. 2003. "Estimating the Benefit Incidence of an Antipoverty Program by Propensity Score Matching." *Journal of Business and Economic Statistics* 21, no. 1: 19–30.

Lopez, Ramón, John Nash, and Julie Stanton. 1995. "Adjustment and Poverty in Mexican Agriculture: How Farmers' Wealth Affects Supply Response." Policy Research Working Paper 1494. Washington: World Bank.

Nicita, Alessandro. 2005. "The Price Effect of Trade Liberalization: Measuring the Impact on Household Welfare." Mimeo. Washington: World Bank.

Porto, Guido. 2003. "Trade Reforms, Market Access, and Poverty in Argentina." World Bank Policy Research Working Paper 3135. Washington: World Bank, September.

————. 2004. "Agricultural Trade, Wages, and Unemployment." Mimeo. Washington: World Bank.

————. 2005. "Estimating Household Responses to Trade Reforms: Net Consumers and Net Producers in Rural Mexico." Policy Research Working Paper 3695. Washington: World Bank.

————. 2006. "Using Survey Data to Assess the Distributional Effects of Trade Policy." *Journal of International Economics* 7, no. 1: 140–60.

Rosenbaum, Paul R., and Donald B. Rubin. 1983. "The Central Role of the Propensity Score in Observational Studies of Causal Effects." *Biometrika* 70, no. 1: 41–55.

Rubin, Donald B. 1977. "Assignment to a Treatment Group on the Basis of a Covariate." *Journal of Educational Statistics* 2, no. 1: 1–26.

WTO (World Trade Organization). 1996. *Trade Policy Review: Zambia.* Geneva.

6

Cambodia

ISIDRO SOLOAGA

C hanges in trade policies can create opportunities as well as risks for the poor.[1] This chapter assesses the likely impact of the implementation of the Doha Development Agenda on household income and expenditures in Cambodia. And, since rice plays a large role in both production and consumption for Cambodia's poor, the chapter also assesses the ability of potential domestic reforms to improve the production, processing, and trading of rice. The results shed light on priorities for poverty reduction by suggesting how different income groups of households would be affected by different reforms and what they would gain or lose in purchasing power.

The assessment is conducted in a partial equilibrium setting and provides an indication of the first-order impact on poverty of potential changes in key prices and quantities. Specifically, it explores the effects on Cambodian household income and expenditures of the following:

—Changes in world prices and exports derived from implementation of multilateral trade liberalization, under the business-as-usual and the more ambitious scenarios that were introduced in chapter 2,

—A unilateral change in Cambodia's tariff structure to a flat 7 percent rate,

—Increased demand for labor in industry, associated with a growth in demand for Cambodian textile exports, and

1. World Bank (2001).

—Key improvements in rice production, along with a reduction in trans-action costs.

The chapter is organized as follows. The first section offers a brief poverty profile of Cambodia in terms of consumption patterns and sources of income, followed by a section describing the analytical framework used in assessing the impact on household welfare of the various policy changes. A third section describes the simulation results, and a final section concludes.

People who are poor cannot afford much flexibility in their spending, so among the poor trade policies are expected to have more impact on the sources of income than on the consumption bundle.[2] Nonetheless, some of the scenarios examined assume strong changes in international prices, which do affect the real incomes of the poor. The results show that a business-as-usual Doha outcome would produce a small average loss of 0.2 percent in household purchasing power, whereas an ambitious outcome would generate a substantial gain of about 7.5 percent. Losses to producers from lower global rice prices would be more than offset by gains to consumers. If Cambodia were to act on its own, changing its tariff structure to a 7 percent flat rate, average household real income would rise by about 3.7 percent, nearly half as much as the estimated gain from ambitious global liberalization. Most of the benefit in this case would come from lower prices for food, which takes more than 70 percent of spending for all but the richest 20 percent of households. An expansion of textile exports would raise demand for labor, with potentially highly beneficial effects on the real incomes of households with at least one member switching into one of the new jobs. For these households, most of which would be in the poorer 40 percent of the income distribution, the average gain would be about 8 percent of purchasing power. The poorer half of the population also would gain if Cambodia took measures to improve the paddy-to-rice yield, to reduce post-harvest losses, and to lower transaction costs: here the average gain for the poorer 50 percent of households would range from 5 to 7.2 percent of real income. The gain for the poor could rise to more than 10 percent of real income if the rice market improvements were simultaneous with the ambitious Doha scenario.

Poverty in Cambodia

Cambodia has about 14 million people, 75 percent of them living in rural areas. Current measures of poverty are controversial since changes in survey design and in interview practices make it difficult to compare estimates of poverty rates for different years. Following Gibson, the nationwide proportion of the population in poverty was 35.9 percent in 2000.[3] The urban poverty rate was only about 18 percent, and in the capital city, Phnom Penh, it was the lowest in the country,

2. World Bank (2001).
3. Gibson (2002).

at 1.6 percent. The rural rate was much higher, at about 39 percent. In turn, the national food-poverty headcount was 11.5 percent: 9.4 percent in urban areas and 11.8 percent in rural areas.[4] This poverty line corresponds roughly to $1 per day.

In Cambodia, as in many other developing countries,

—Poverty rates are higher in rural areas and among people living in households headed by farmers,

—Poorer households tend to be larger and younger and to have more children, and

—The poor are more likely to live in households where the head is illiterate and has few years of schooling. Poverty is much lower for households where the head has a secondary or advanced education.

To assess the impact of economic policies on poor people, knowledge of how the poor obtain and spend their incomes is crucial. This chapter uses data from the Cambodia Socioeconomic Survey (CSES) for 1999, which was conducted by the Cambodian National Institute of Statistics in two rounds to take into account the seasonality of rural activities. This survey is representative at the national, rural, and urban levels and is the first attempt to collect detailed information on household incomes in Cambodia.[5]

Consumption Patterns

To investigate consumption patterns, we rank households in deciles according to their adult-equivalent per capita expenditures.[6] Table 6-1 shows the shares of key types of products and services in total household spending. Food takes about three-fourths of total spending for the poorer 50 percent of households and takes more than 70 percent for all but the richest 20 percent of households. This pattern reflects how widespread poverty is in Cambodia; in other developing countries, the share of expenditures on food decreases sharply beyond the fifth or sixth deciles.

As expected, rice is by far the most important single item of expenditure for poor households: it accounts for 28 percent of spending in the poorest deciles and about 23 percent in the second and third deciles; it still accounts for more than 20 percent of spending in the fourth and fifth deciles. Thus any policy with a large impact on rice prices is likely to have a large impact on the consumption of poor households. A simple exercise, keeping other prices and the sources of

---

4. The poverty headcount is the percentage of the population with an income below the poverty line, calculated here as the monetary value of a bundle of goods that would allow the consumer to reach a minimum caloric intake.

5. Gibson (2002) presents detailed information about the main characteristics of the survey. Following his suggestions, in what follows we use round two of the survey. Results are qualitatively similar if we use round one or the combination of both rounds.

6. Following Deaton (1997), the deciles were formed by computing the per capita adult-equivalent household consumption for each sample household as total household consumption divided by (0.5 times the number of children plus the number of adults). This was also done in previous poverty analysis for Cambodia and will make comparisons easier.

Table 6-1. *Composition of Household Expenditure in Cambodia, by Decile of per Capita Expenditure*

Percent

Consumption item	1	2	3	4	5	6	7	8	9	10	Average
Food total	75.7	76.3	76	73.7	73.7	62.6	72.0	70.3	64.4	38.6	63.5
Rice, all varieties	28.4	23.3	22.7	20.7	20.6	18.9	17.5	15.1	12.5	5.8	15.6
Fish and fish products	9.9	11.1	10.6	10.5	10.9	10.8	10.0	10.0	9.2	5.0	8.9
All other consumption items	37.4	41.9	42.7	42.5	42.2	43.0	44.5	45.2	42.7	27.8	39.0
Non-food total	24.4	23.8	24.1	26.4	26.3	27.5	28.0	29.7	35.6	61.4	36.5
Housing, fuel, and transport[a]	15.7	15.5	15.2	17.1	17.3	17.4	17.5	19.4	24.1	46.7	25.5
Clothing[b]	2.9	2.8	3.0	3.0	2.8	3.4	3.4	3.2	2.9	2.3	2.9
Other expenditures[c]	5.8	5.4	5.9	6.2	6.1	6.6	7.1	7.1	8.6	12.4	8.2

Source: Cambodia Socioeconomic Survey for 1999 (round two data).

a. Includes house rent (rental value of subsidized housing, rental value of owner-occupied housing, hotel charges), house maintenance and repair, water and fuel, medical care, transport and communications, and personal care.

b. Clothing and footwear (tailored clothes, ready-made clothes, shoes).

c. Includes furniture and household equipment and operation, expenditures on recreation, education, personal effects, and miscellaneous items.

Figure 6-1. *Share of Food in Rural and Urban Household Expenditures in Cambodia, by Decile of per Capita Expenditure*
Percent

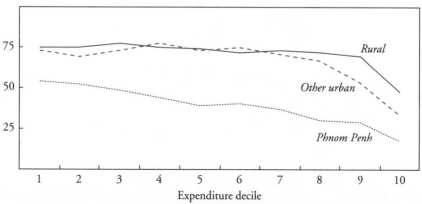

Source: Cambodia Socioeconomic Survey for 1999 (round two data).

income constant, shows that a reduction of 10 percent in the price of rice would yield an extra 3 percent of disposable income for people in the poorest decile (10 percent of 28.4 percent) and an extra 0.6 percent for people in the richest decile (10 percent of 5.8 percent).

Second in importance among food items is fish and fish products, a category that accounts for 9–11 percent of total household expenditures in deciles one to nine and for only 5 percent in the tenth decile. Regarding non-food expenditures, the major differences among deciles are in housing, fuel, and transport: this category captures 46.7 percent of total spending in the richest decile and only 15.7 percent in the poorest one.

Consumption patterns differ among Cambodia's regions: in rural as well as urban areas other than Phnom Penh, the share of food in total spending is greater than 70 percent among the first eight deciles, while in Phnom Penh this share is below 55 percent for all deciles and as low as 18 percent for the wealthiest (figure 6-1).

Sources of Income

Cambodian households depend heavily on self-employment, particularly in agriculture, and on average, earnings from self-employment supply 61 percent of total income. Activities related to cultivation—largely of rice—supply 22 percent of total income and two-thirds of self-employment income (table 6-2).

Wage employment supplies only 20.5 percent of income for the average household—slightly more than the 16.5 percent coming from rental income, interest received, and the imputed value of houses. On average, remittances supply only about 2 percent of total income.

Table 6-2. *Sources of Household Income in Cambodia, by Decile of per Capita Expenditure*
Percent

Source of income	1	2	3	4	5	6	7	8	9	10	Average
Self-employment	67.8	71.4	71.7	70.3	73.6	68.5	71.2	70.7	63.3	36.3	60.9
Cultivation	27.8	29.7	31.1	30.3	31.9	32.1	30.6	32.3	19.8	3.2	22.4
Rice	21.4	24.3	25.3	23.6	25.7	25.0	22.7	20.4	9.7	2.1	16.3
Other crops	6.4	5.4	5.8	6.7	6.2	7.1	7.9	11.9	10.1	1.1	6.1
Livestock	16.6	14.3	14.2	13.0	12.4	11.9	11.6	12.0	8.3	1.5	9.4
Fish raising and other	6.1	7.1	5.5	8.7	6.9	6.8	8.7	7.1	5.2	2.1	5.6
Forestry and hunting	8.3	10.2	9.7	7.3	7.7	7.9	8.1	6.1	4.9	0.6	5.7
Non-farming activities	8.9	10.0	11.2	10.9	14.7	9.8	12.2	13.2	25.1	29.0	17.7
Other sources	32.2	28.6	28.3	29.7	26.4	31.5	28.8	29.3	36.8	63.9	39.1
Wages	19.0	15.0	15.9	14.5	14.3	18.5	17.6	16.5	21.0	30.2	20.5
Remittances	1.2	1.9	1.6	2.8	1.3	2.4	1.6	1.7	2.3	2.6	2.1
Other (rents, dividends, and other)	12.1	11.7	10.9	12.4	10.8	10.6	9.6	11.1	13.4	31.0	16.5
Total	100	100	100	100	100	100	100	100	100	100	100

Source: Cambodia Socioeconomic Survey for 1999 (round two data).

Figure 6-2. *Share of Wages in Rural and Urban Household Income in Cambodia, by Decile of per Capita Expenditure*
Percent

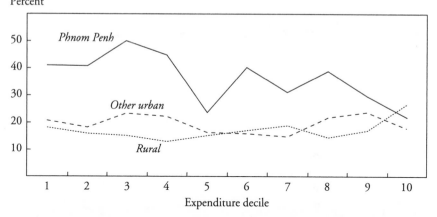

Source: Cambodia Socioeconomic Survey for 1999 (round two data).

The distribution pattern of consumption mirrors that of income: as table 6-2 shows, the sources of income are similar for deciles one to eight and differ only for the ninth and tenth deciles. Compared with poorer households, households in the top two deciles draw more of their income from non-farming activities in self-employment and from wages, and households in the tenth decile also draw on sources such as rental income, interest received, and the imputed value of houses, reflecting their higher ownership of capital stock.

Figure 6-2 shows variations in the importance of wages across different regions of the country; for deciles one to eight, wages supply about 40 percent of total income in Phnom Penh, but only about 20 percent in the rest of the country.

Most of Cambodia's households draw their living from primary production: three out of four household heads have "agriculture, hunting, and forestry" as their main occupation (figure 6-3). Employment in the public, education, and health sectors is next in importance as a main source of income (9 percent on average, 11 percent for male heads of household, and 3.5 percent for females), followed by employment in wholesale and retail trade (7.3 percent average for the whole country). The textile industry, like the hotel and restaurant industry, provides the main source of income for less than 1 percent of household heads.

Analytical Framework

The empirical methodology used here extends the one presented in Nicita, Olarreaga, and Soloaga.[7] This takes the household as the unit of analysis and estimates how the consumption and income structure of individual households would be

7. Nicita, Olarreaga, and Soloaga (2001).

Figure 6-3. *Employment of Household Heads in Cambodia, by Industry Group and Gender*
Percent

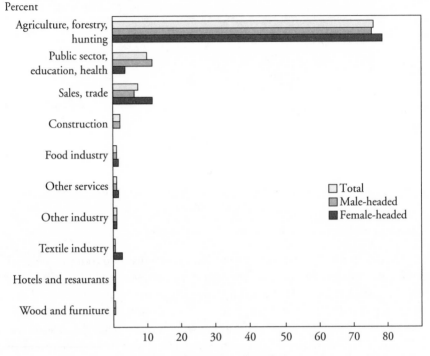

Source: Cambodia Socioeconomic Survey for 1999 (round two data).

affected by changes in the prices and quantities of goods and factors of production. The price and quantity effects of the Doha-related trade liberalization adopted for the analysis are those estimated by Kee, Nicita, and Olarreaga in chapter 2.

Total net household income (savings) is defined as the sum of total income minus the sum of total expenditures. Each household has endowments (for example, land of different quality and number of skilled and unskilled workers) that generate income. Each household also has a spending pattern (for example, allocation to food and non-food items). The general formulation is as follows:

$$
\begin{aligned}
(6\text{-}1) \quad NetIncome = &\sum_m X_m^{SRice} P_m^{Rice}\left(1 - t_m^{SRice}\right) + \sum_i X_i^{SO} P_i^{O}\left(1 - t_i^{O}\right) \\
&- \sum_j X_j^{I} P_j^{I}\left(1 + t_j^{I}\right) + \sum_k L_k^{Skilled} W_k^{Skilled}\left(1 - t_k^{Skilled}\right) \\
&+ \sum_l L_l^{Unskilled} W_l^{Unskilled}\left(1 - t_l^{Unskilled}\right) - \sum_m X_m^{DRice} P_m^{Rice}\left(1 + t_m^{DRice}\right) \\
&- \sum_n X_n^{Oth.Food} P_n^{Oth.Food}\left(1 + t_n^{Oth.Food}\right) \\
&- \sum_o X_o^{NonFood} P_o^{NonFood}\left(1 + t_o^{NonFood}\right) + \sum_p \sum_q T_p^{q},
\end{aligned}
$$

where

X_m^{SRice} = The amount of rice of quality m produced by the household;

P_m^{Rice} = The selling price of rice of quality m produced by the household (gross price); for internationally tradable varieties, this price is the border price;

t_z^w = Ad valorem tax on good z of the w sector; alternatively, t_z^w = is the tax equivalent of a distortion that affects good z of sector w;

X_i^{SO} = Output i (other than rice) produced by the household (for example, cattle, handicrafts, services);

P_i^I = Selling price of output i produced by the household (gross price); for an internationally tradable output, this price is the border price;

X_j^I = Amount of input j used by the household in production (for example, fertilizers, land rented, hired labor, hired animals);

P_j^O = Before-tax (or before a tax-equivalent domestic distortion) price of input j used by the household in production;

$L_K^{Skilled}$ = Amount of skilled labor sold by the kth member of the household;

$W_k^{Skilled}$ = Before-tax (or before a tax-equivalent transaction cost or domestic distortion) wage of skilled labor supplied by the household;

$L_l^{UnSkilled}$ = Amount of unskilled labor sold by the lth member of the household;

$W_l^{UnSkilled}$ = Before-tax (or before a tax-equivalent transaction cost or domestic distortion) wage of unskilled labor supplied by the household;

X_m^{DRice} = Amount of rice of quality m demanded by the household (including rice produced by the household and not sold in the market);

P_m^{Rice} = Buying price of rice of quality m demanded by the household (gross price);

t_m^{DRice} = Import tariff on rice imports;

$X_n^{Oth.Food}$ = Amount of non-rice food n demanded by the household;

$P_n^{Oth.Food}$ = Buying price of non-rice food n demanded by the household (gross price);

$t_n^{Oth.Food}$ = Import tariff on non-rice food n;

$X_o^{NonFood}$ = Amount of non-food good o demanded by the household;

$P_o^{NonFood}$ = Buying price of non-food good o demanded by the household (gross price).

$t_o^{NonFood}$ = Import tariff on non-food good o; and

T_p^q = Transfer received by household member p from source q (q could be public or private).

In addition, the value of paddy rice output can be expressed as a function of the value of milled rice:

$$(6\text{-}2) \quad \text{Value of Rice Output} = Q_m^{PaddyRice}\left(1 - phl_m^{PaddyRice}\right)\left(1 - t_m^{Rice}\right)P_m^{PaddyRice}$$
$$= Q_m^{PaddyRice}\left(1 - phl_m^{PaddyRice}\right)\left(1 - t_m^{Rice}\right)(1 - \alpha)\lambda P_m^{Rice},$$

where $phl_m^{PaddyRice}$ denotes post-harvest losses (for example, caused by improper handling, lack of adequate storage facilities, or loss to rodents), assumed to be about 10 percent currently; α denotes milling transformation costs; and λ is the milling yield of paddy to rice, which is assumed to be 0.62 percent on average (with some regional variation) by the Ministry of Agriculture, Forestry, and Fisheries (MAFF).[8]

Next all quantities in equation 6-1 are considered to be fixed in the short run, and the impact of a change in prices, taxes, or transaction costs is simulated. The formulation is as follows:

$$(6\text{-}3) \quad \Delta NetIncome\Big/_{all\ \overline{q}} = \sum_m P_m^{Rice}\left(1 - t_m^{SRice}\right)X_m^{SRice}\frac{\Delta\left[P_m^{Rice}\left(1 - t_m^{SRice}\right)\right]}{P_m^{Rice}\left(1 - t_m^{SRice}\right)}$$

$$+ \sum_i P_i^{O}\left(1 - t_i^{O}\right)X_i^{SO}\frac{\Delta\left[P_i^{O}\left(1 - t_i^{O}\right)\right]}{P_i^{O}\left(1 - t_i^{O}\right)}$$

$$- \sum_j P_j^{I}\left(1 + t_j^{I}\right)X_j^{I}\frac{\Delta\left[P_j^{I}\left(1 + t_j^{I}\right)\right]}{P_j^{I}\left(1 + t_j^{I}\right)}$$

$$+ \sum_k W_k^{Skilled}\left(1 - t_k^{Skilled}\right)L_k^{Skilled}\frac{\Delta\left[W_k^{Skilled}\left(1 - t_k^{Skilled}\right)\right]}{W_k^{Skilled}\left(1 - t_k^{Skilled}\right)}$$

$$+ \sum_l W_l^{UnSkilled}L_l^{UnSkilled}\frac{\Delta\left[W_l^{UnSkilled}\left(1 - t_l^{UnSkilled}\right)\right]}{W_l^{UnSkilled}\left(1 - t_l^{UnSkilled}\right)}$$

$$- \sum_m P_m^{Rice}\left(1 + t_m^{DRice}\right)X_m^{DRice}\frac{\Delta\left[P_m^{Rice}\left(1 + t_m^{DRice}\right)\right]}{P_m^{Rice}\left(1 + t_m^{DRice}\right)}$$

$$- \sum_n P_n^{Oth.Food}\left(1 + t_n^{Oth.Food}\right)X_n^{Oth.Food}$$
$$\frac{\Delta\left[P_n^{Oth.Food}\left(1 + t_n^{Oth.Food}\right)\right]}{P_n^{Oth.Food}\left(1 + t_n^{Oth.Food}\right)}$$

$$- \sum_o P_o^{NonFood}\left(1 + t_o^{NonFood}\right)X_o^{NonFood}$$
$$\frac{\Delta\left[P_o^{NonFood}\left(1 + t_o^{NonFood}\right)\right]}{P_o^{NonFood}\left(1 + t_o^{NonFood}\right)}$$

$$+ \sum_p \sum_q \Delta T_p^{q}.$$

8. MAFF (2001).

In reality, after changes in prices, producers would switch production to the more valuable crops, consumers would, in general, switch to cheaper goods away from the now relatively more expensive ones, and households would adjust their labor supply to changes in wages. Because equation 6-3 keeps quantities fixed, this formulation provides a lower bound for estimated gains and an upper bound for estimated losses.

Simulation Results

The specifications for equations 6-1 to 6-3 are flexible enough to examine the effects of measures that other authors have proposed for improving the livelihood of poor households. For instance, by introducing tax-equivalent parameters for different types of transaction costs and parameters for the milling yield of paddy rice, post-harvest losses, and milling costs, it is possible to estimate the effects of various policy reforms that might be appropriate in today's Cambodia, in addition to those stemming from multilateral trade liberalization under the Doha Round.

The following simulations adopt strong assumptions on quantities demanded and consumed and on price linkages; thus they capture only partial and extremely simplified aspects of the plausible impact of policy reforms on households. Nonetheless, the dimensions of the impacts simulated, as well as their distribution across consumption deciles, give a first approximation of the positive or negative effects of different economic policy scenarios on poor people in Cambodia.

Following common practice in the literature on poverty, the analysis is anchored on household expenditures, and all results are expressed as percentages of current per capita household expenditure, for households ordered by decile of per capita adult-equivalent expenditure. That is, the absolute change in the net real income of household i that is expected to come from a policy change is divided by the total expenditures of household i. The interpretation in terms of poverty is straightforward: a strategy is pro-poor if it provides extra spending power for households in the first five deciles.

Effects of Changes in Prices from the Doha Round

Simulations by Kee, Nicita, and Olarreaga in chapter 2 provide estimates of changes in world prices and quantities (exports and imports) that would follow from trade liberalization agreed in the Doha Round for two different scenarios:

—The baseline scenario, business as usual, includes a 40 percent reduction in bound tariffs, with applied tariffs varying accordingly; a reduction of all tariff peaks to a maximum of 50 percent, a 40 percent reduction in support for domestic agriculture; elimination of agricultural export subsidies; and an improvement in trade facilitation.

—The ambitious scenario involves full worldwide elimination of tariffs and subsidies, the same improvement in trade facilitation, and a 50 percent reduction in the restrictiveness of nontariff measures.

The following discussion traces the likely impact of these changes on Cambodian household budgets, assuming that changes in international prices are perfectly passed through to households.[9]

For products such as rice, cereals, and fish, which are produced by many households, it is assumed that the change in income is given by:

$$(6\text{-}4) \quad \Delta NetIncomechange\_from\_good\_i = P^{goodi}\left(X_m^{Sgoodi} - X_m^{Dgoodi}\right)\frac{\Delta\left[P_m^{goodi}\right]}{P_m^{goodi}}.$$

The sign (positive or negative) of the impact of a price increase on a particular household is given by the sign of $(X^{Supplygoodi} - X^{Demandgoodi})$. For instance, the impact of an increase in the price of rice would be positive for households that are net sellers of rice and negative for households that are net buyers. For all other goods not produced by the household, $X^{Supplygoodi}$ is set to 0, and an increase in prices translates into an income loss for the family.

Table 6-3 shows that a major consumption item in Cambodia—rice—is expected to experience important price changes: an increase of 4 percent under business as usual and a more important increase of 22 percent in the ambitious scenario. Other products that are expected to experience relatively large price changes (more than 4 percent) in the business-as-usual scenario are other cereals, dairy products, and fresh vegetables. In the ambitious scenario, besides the 22 percent increase in rice prices, fish and fish products, eggs, dairy products, and alcoholic beverages would see a drop in their domestic prices of more than 20 percent, mainly due to lower tariffs in Cambodia.

Although all these changes—in particular, those coming from the ambitious scenario—are important, almost 70 percent of the households grow rice only for their own consumption and hence are not affected by changes in the market price of rice.

Regarding changes in quantities, the Kee, Nicita, and Olarreaga estimates show important changes only in textile exports.[10] For Cambodia, then, in

9. With this assumption, the impact presented here is the maximum impact. It is easy to change this assumption to that of partial pass-through, taking into account regional variations in price transmission.

10. Changes in rice exports are important in percentage terms but of no relevance in absolute value: Cambodia's current rice exports amount to only $627,000. Moreover, some exported quantities increase even though domestic prices are falling. This occurs for two reasons: there are general equilibrium effects across different markets, and export increases are, by assumption, driven by changes in world prices and not changes in tariff-inclusive domestic prices.

Table 6-3. *Changes in Prices and Quantities in Cambodia: Business-as-Usual and Ambitious Scenarios*

Product or product group	Share in current expenditure (percent)	Current exports (thousands of U.S. dollars)	Domestic price changes (percent)		Export changes			
			Business as usual	Ambitious	Business as usual		Ambitious	
					Thousands of U.S. dollars	Percent	Thousands of U.S. dollars	Product
Rice	16	627	4	22	153	24	1,179	188
Other cereals	2	188	6	-9	2	1	-10	-6
Tobacco	3	206	4	2	60	29	174	84
Fish and fish products	9	17,657	-1	-26	507	3	-3,716	-21
Meat and poultry	8	555	1	0	25	5	558	101
Eggs	1	0	3	-26	0		0	
Dairy	1	1,470	-6	-34	-997	-68	-1,470	-100
Oils and fats	1	33	-1	-10	1	4	-1	-4
Fresh vegetables	3	20	4	-1	0	1	-4	-20
Tubers	1	0	0	-7	0		0	
Legumes	1	185	0	-10	1	1	-19	-11
Prepared vegetables	1	101	1	-12	7	7	5	5
Fruits	3	6	4	2	1	22	3	44
Prepared fruits	1	0	3	-4	0		0	0
Sugar	2	14	3	5	2	16	4	27
Spices	2	16	0	-13	0	1	-3	-18
Coffee, tea, cocoa	1	6	2	-15	0	3	2	28
Nonalcoholic beverages	1	0	2	-20	0		0	
Alcoholic beverages	1	270	-1	-32	-58	-21	-119	-44
Other food	5	78	1	-7	3	3	4	6
Personal care	3	22	1	-14	1	3	1	5
Clothing	3	1,319,370	2	-18	143,246	11	461,288	35
Other goods	8	143,873	0	-9	1,264	1	2,621	2
All goods	75	1,484,697	1	-8	144,218	10	460,497	31

Source: Author's calculations, based on Kee, Nicita, and Olarreaga, chapter 2 of this volume, and Cambodia Socioeconomic Survey for 1999 (round two data).

Table 6-4. *Effects of Price Changes on Household Welfare in Cambodia, by Decile of per Capita Expenditure: Business-as-Usual Scenario*

Percent

All households	1	2	3	4	5	6	7	8	9	10	Average
Total gains	−0.09	−0.14	−0.17	−0.30	−0.28	−0.26	−0.28	−0.33	−0.28	−0.27	−0.24
From food basket	−0.05	−0.09	−0.12	−0.25	−0.22	−0.21	−0.23	−0.28	−0.22	−0.22	−0.19
From other goods	−0.05	−0.05	−0.05	−0.05	−0.05	−0.05	−0.06	−0.06	−0.05	−0.04	−0.05

Source: Author's calculations, based on Kee, Nicita, and Olarreaga (chapter 2 of this volume) and Cambodia Socioeconomic Survey for 1999 (round two data).

contrast with the other countries studied in this volume, the inclusion or exclusion of changes in export quantities makes little difference to the simulation results. Accordingly, this section presents only the impacts of changes in prices. The impact on household income of changes in textile exports is better captured by examining the induced change in labor demand, as discussed later in this section.

Business-as-Usual Scenario

This simulation indicates that, all else held constant (including the amount of rice consumed and produced by each household), changes in international prices due to implementation of the Doha Development Agenda are likely to cause a small fall in purchasing power of about 0.24 percent for the average Cambodian household (table 6-4). The main reason for this reduction is a change in the food basket.[11] Prices are expected to rise 1 percent on average, although the price of rice, the main staple food, is expected to go up by 4.2 percent, reducing the real income of net buyers of rice and augmenting that of net sellers. The losses seem to be slightly larger for richer households, but the overall impacts are quite small.

Ambitious Scenario

Results for the ambitious scenario are shown in table 6-5. Following the sharp drop in almost all prices that would be associated with Cambodia's elimination of its own tariffs, the average household would gain about 7.5 percent in purchasing power. Most of this gain (7 percent out of 7.5 percent) would come from food items, reflecting their importance in overall consumption. All deciles would benefit, although the gains would be significantly higher for households in the middle of the income distribution (between the fourth and eighth deciles).

---

11. Losses are only slightly lower for households that are net sellers of rice.

Table 6-5. *Effects of Price Changes on Household Welfare in Cambodia, by Decile of per Capita Expenditure: Ambitious Scenario*
Percent

Item	1	2	3	4	5	6	7	8	9	10	Average
All households											
Total gains	6.9	7	7.4	10	8	8.6	9	8.9	6.3	3.7	7.5
From food basket	6.4	6.5	6.9	9.5	7.5	8.1	8.4	8.3	5.8	3.2	7
From other goods	0.5	0.5	0.5	0.5	0.5	0.5	0.6	0.6	0.5	0.5	0.5
By households' net participation in the rice market											
Net gains from rice only	1.4	1.0	1.0	2.6	1.5	1.7	1.7	1.8	0.3	−0.8	1.2
Net rice buyers	−1.2	−1.4	−1.3	−0.8	−0.9	−1.0	−1.1	−0.8	−1.2	−1.2	−1.1
Net rice sellers	2.6	2.4	2.3	3.4	2.4	2.7	2.8	2.6	1.5	0.4	2.3

Source: Author's calculations, based on Kee, Nicita, and Olarreaga (chapter 2 of this volume) and Cambodia Socioeconomic Survey for 1999 (round two data).

As noted, almost 70 percent of the households consuming rice are subsistence producers. The lower panel of table 6-5 shows how the average gain would be distributed among net sellers and buyers of rice. Of the overall average 7.5 percent gain in real income, net rice sellers would see a gain of 2.3 percentage points, but net rice buyers would suffer, with a fall of −1.1 percentage points. The gains associated with higher rice prices seem to be concentrated among middle-income households.

Trade Liberalization by Cambodia

Cambodia's tariff structure has important implications for the government's export-led economic development and poverty alleviation strategy. High tariffs on semiprocessed and consumer goods mean that Cambodians pay more than international prices for basic needs, unless smuggled imported goods circumvent these high prices. Of the gains shown in table 6-5, a significant share comes from the complete removal of Cambodian tariffs and nontariff barriers that forms part of the ambitious Doha scenario. The following discussion explores the implications of a more modest unilateral trade reform: Cambodia's potential adoption of a 7 percent uniform tariff.

Table 6-6 shows the current tariff structure for the main categories for which detailed information is available on household consumption. Although for rice (the single largest consumption item in Cambodia's household budgets) the tariff is only 7 percent, for meat, dairy products, and prepared and preserved vegetables the tariff is higher than 30 percent. Among non-food items, the average unweighted tariff for clothing and footwear is 28 percent. For fish the tariff is 18 percent, but an export tax of 10 percent plays in the opposite direction. Since no detailed infor-

Table 6-6. *Current Tariff Rates for Main Consumer Items in Cambodia*
Percent

Consumption item	Share in total consumption, average for Cambodia	Current tariff level
Food and beverages		
Rice (all varieties)	15.6	7.0
Other cereals and preparations (bread, maize, other grains, rice or wheat flour, noodles, biscuits)	2.6	19.0
Fish (fresh fish, shrimp, crab, fermented, salted, and dried fish, canned fish)	8.9	18.0[a]
Meat (pork, beef, buffalo, mutton, dried meat, innards)	5.0	35.0
Poultry (chicken, duck, other fresh bird meat)	3.2	35.0
Eggs (duck egg, chicken egg, quail egg, fermented and salted egg)	1.4	33.0
Dairy products (condensed milk, powdered milk, fresh milk, ice cream, cheese, other dairy products)	0.9	33.0
Oil and fats (vegetable oil, pork fat, rice bran oil, butter, margarine, coconut or frying oil)	1.3	7.0
Fresh vegetables (*trakun,* cabbage, eggplant, cucumber, tomato, green gourd, beans, onion, shallot, chili)	4.3	7.0
Tuber (cassava, sweet potato, potato, *traov, jampada*)	1.4	7.0
Pulses and legumes (green gram, dhall, cowpea, bean sprout, other seeds)	1.0	7.0
Prepared and preserved vegetables (cucumber pickles, other pickles, tomato paste)	0.8	34.0
Fruit (banana, mango, orange, pineapple, lemon, watermelon, papaya, durian, grape, apple, canned and dried fruit)	2.8	7.0
Other fruits and seeds (coconut, cashew nut, lotus seed, peanut, gourd seed, other nuts)	1.2	12.0
Sugar, salt (sugar, jaggery, sugar products, including candy, and salt)	1.4	11.0
Spices and seasoning (fish sauce, soy sauce, vinegar, garlic, ginger, coriander, red pepper, monosodium glutamate)	1.7	16.0
Tea, coffee, cocoa	0.8	24.5
Nonalcoholic beverages (drinking water, sugar cane juice, syrup with ice, bottled soft drink, fruit juice)	0.8	35.0
Alcoholic beverages (rice wine, other wine, beer, whisky, palm juice)	1.6	35.0
Tobacco products (cigarettes, mild tobacco, strong tobacco)	2.2	26.0
Other food products (fried insects, peanut preparations, flavored ice, ice, other food products)	1.0	22.0
Food taken away from home (meals at work, school, restaurants, snacks, coffee, soft drinks purchased outside the home)	2.9	[b]
Prepared meals bought outside and eaten at home	0.8	[b]
Total food	64.0	17.0
Textiles and footwear	2.9	28.0

Source: World Bank (2004).
a. There is also an export tax of 10 percent on fish.
b. The effect will be indirect, through the tradable contents of these mostly nontradable final goods.

mation is available on the consumption of different types of fish, for this exercise it is assumed that there is no change in the tariff rate for fish and fish products.[12]

Following equation 6-3, the simulated change in household real income after the tariff reform is given by:

$$(6\text{-}5) \quad \Delta NetIncome\Big/_{all\ \overline{q}} = \sum_m P_m^{Rice}\left(1+t_m^{DRice}\right)\left(X_m^{DRice}-X_m^{SRice}\right)$$

$$\frac{\left[P_m^{Rice}\left(t_{m1}^{DRice}-t_{m0}^{DRice}\right)\right]}{P_m^{Rice}\left(1+t_m^{DRice}\right)}$$

$$+\sum_n P_n^{Oth.Food}\left(1+t_n^{Oth.Food}\right)\left(X_n^{D.Oth.Food}-X_n^{S.Oth.Food}\right)$$

$$\frac{\left[P_n^{Oth.Food}\left(t_{n1}^{Oth.Food}-t_{n0}^{Oth.Food}\right)\right]}{P_n^{Oth.Food}\left(1+t_n^{Oth.Food}\right)}$$

$$+\sum_o P_o^{NonFood}\left(1+t_o^{NonFood}\right)X_o^{NonFood}$$

$$\frac{\left[P_o^{NonFood}\left(t_{o1}^{NonFood}-t_{o0}^{NonFood}\right)\right]}{P_o^{NonFood}\left(1+t_o^{NonFood}\right)},$$

where t_{ij}^z is the tariff level i of good z (rice, other food, and non-food consumption items), in moment j (0 = before tariff reform, 1 = after tariff reform). Since this simulation does not imply a change in the tariff on rice—which is already at 7 percent—the first term on the right-hand side is 0. The second term on the right captures the fact that, although most households are net consumers of other food and therefore benefit from lower tariffs, some households may be net producers of other food and may therefore lose as tariffs decline.

The results for this simulation underestimate instantaneous gains (because in reality demand would increase for those goods that are now relatively cheaper), and it overestimates instantaneous losses (because production would diminish after a price fall). Thus applying the framework that is described in equation 6-3 obtains a lower bound for the changes that may favor poor people and an upper bound for the changes that may negatively affect them.

Further, other potential positive or negative income effects are not accounted for in this simple formulation. For instance, jobs can be lost due to the contraction of an import-competitive sector, and for many Cambodian households the loss of a job may outweigh the gains in consumption. Moreover, lower tariffs

12. The ambitious scenario assumes that the 18 percent tariff is eliminated, and therefore the contribution of Cambodia's own liberalization to the domestic price is a reduction of around 18 percent.

Table 6-7. *Effects of Price Changes on Household Welfare, by Decile of per Capita Expenditure in Cambodia: Flat Cambodian Import Tariff of 7 Percent*

Expenditure item	1	2	3	4	5	6	7	8	9	10	Average
Total gains	2.2	2.9	3.3	3.6	3.8	3.9	4.2	4.4	4.5	4.1	3.7
From food basket	1.8	2.5	2.8	3.1	3.3	3.4	3.6	3.9	4.0	3.7	3.2
From other goods	0.4	0.4	0.4	0.5	0.5	0.5	0.5	0.5	0.5	0.4	0.5

Source: Author's calculations, based on Cambodia Socioeconomic Survey for 1999 (round two data).

could mean a decrease in tariff revenues for the government, and this may affect the level of transfers to the poor.

As shown in table 6-7, the lower prices due to tariff reduction imply an improvement of 3.7 percentage points in the average household's purchasing power. This gain is nearly half of what is obtained on average under the ambitious Doha scenario. Most of the impact comes from a reduction in the prices of food items, which releases 3.2 percent of household spending, and a smaller part comes from reduced prices of clothing and footwear (releasing 0.5 percent of household spending).

Growth in Demand for Labor in Industry

The two multilateral trade liberalization scenarios imply a significant expansion in textile exports from Cambodia, which in turn may raise the demand for labor. The following simulations throw light on which income groups of households would benefit from such an expansion and by how much.

For each household, the sources of income are identified according to the sector of principal occupation of all household members, and those household members who work for a wage are selected. There is assumed to be surplus labor in the informal sector and in subsistence agriculture, so that a marginal loss of labor in these sectors implies minimal or no loss of output.[13]

For each wage worker, the probability of finding a job in industry is estimated, considering age, education, family composition, and location, among other factors. The wages being earned inside and outside industry are compared for workers who have similar human capital characteristics. Those workers outside industry who are earning less than they could earn in industry are selected and ranked in descending order according to their probability of finding a job in industry. In other words, a queue of potential entrants to the industrial labor market is constructed.

13. For the rationale underlying this approach, see Magnac (1991); Dickens and Lang (1985).

As the industrial sector grows, workers from outside the sector are assigned to jobs in industry according to their probability of finding employment there. The first to be incorporated is the worker with the highest probability and so on. This adapts the literature of "matching methods" to this particular case.[14]

The impact on household income of the expansion of industrial employment comes from the wage premium that is paid by the industrial sector. This is calculated as the difference between the actual wage of the worker and the expected wage of this worker in the industrial sector (that is, the fitted wage for each individual) times the total number of working days. The econometric estimations used to estimate the probabilities and to impute wages are detailed in Nicita, Olarreaga, and Soloaga.[15]

Table 6-8 shows the number of workers who are likely to switch jobs (that is, who are in the queue), the average wage these workers are earning currently, their expected wage after they switch to the industrial sector, and the size of the wage premium in industry.

The exercise indicates that about 220,000 workers would probably be willing to switch into the industrial sector. Almost 80 percent (174,439) of them are currently working in services (trade, restaurants, hotels, the public sector), and the rest are working in the primary sector (agriculture, mining, and fishing). Among the workers (45,536) likely to switch from the primary sector, more than half (57 percent) are women, while among those switching from the service sector, only 23 percent are women. The average gain for workers switching from the primary sector is equivalent to 22 percent of current wages, and for those switching from the services sector, it is 39 percent.

Table 6-9 shows the impact on household welfare, by deciles, of an increase of 50,000 and of 125,000 jobs in the industrial sector. These increases correspond roughly to what would be expected to happen under the business-as-usual and the ambitious scenarios, respectively.[16] The first and third panels of the table show the average impact of adding 50,000 and 125,000 workers to the industrial sector, respectively, and take account of all households including those whose members are not expected to switch occupations. The second and fourth panels show the simulated impact only on those households with at least one member who switches into the industrial sector.

Overall, the changes in average household purchasing power would be modest, at only 0.2 and 0.5 percent, respectively, in the two scenarios. Nonetheless, the results are important for those households with at least one member who switches into an industrial job: if labor demand in industry were to increase by 50,000 employees, for households with switchers the average expected gain

---

14. See, for instance, Cochran and Rubin (1973); Heckman, Ichimura, and Todd (1997).

15. Nicita, Olarreaga, and Soloaga (2001).

16. These estimates were computed using the method described for Ethiopia in chapter 3.

Table 6-8. *Number of Workers in Cambodia Likely to Switch Jobs if Demand for Labor Rises in Industry, by Decile of per Capita Expenditure*

Indicator	1	2	3	4	5	6	7	8	9	10	Total
Primary sector											
Number of workers expected to switch jobs	5,171	7,218	3,821	4,108	3,672	7,407	4,218	3,794	3,345	2,782	45,536
Percent of workers expected to switch jobs who are women	50	74	8	62	74	51	52	55	54	92	57
Current wage earned in the sector (riels per day, average)	3,165	2,901	4,751	3,056	3,260	3,951	4,435	4,390	3,895	5,834	3,818
Expected wage to be earned in industry (riels per day, average)	4,154	3,427	5,138	3,758	3,636	5,142	5,463	5,347	5,178	6,948	4,671
Difference (expected minus current)	989	526	386	702	376	1,191	1,028	957	1,283	1,114	853
Difference as percent of current wage	31	18	8	23	12	30	23	22	33	19	22
Services sector											
Number of workers expected to switch jobs	20,417	16,072	12,331	10,381	6,594	15,804	14,984	11,803	31,042	35,011	174,439
Percent of workers expected to switch jobs who are women	29	28	24	25	25	12	15	9	26	27	23
Current wage earned in the sector (riels per day, average)	3,734	3,583	3,676	4,288	3,499	4,642	4,345	5,065	4,335	5,340	4,394
Expected wage to be earned in industry (riels per day, average)	4,994	4,654	5,306	5,834	4,975	6,005	6,251	6,972	6,221	7,492	6,087
Difference (expected minus current)	1,261	1,071	1,630	1,546	1,476	1,363	1,906	1,906	1,886	2,152	1,693
Difference as a percent of current wage	34	30	44	36	42	29	44	38	44	40	39

Source: Author's calculations based on Cambodia Socioeconomic Survey for 1999 (round two data).

Table 6-9. *Effects on Household Welfare in Cambodia, by Decile of per Capita Expenditure: Increase in Industrial Employment*
Percent

Level of increase and type of household	1	2	3	4	5	6	7	8	9	10	Average
Increase of 50,000 new employees in the industrial sector											
All households											
Urban	1.69	0.16	0.17	0.19	0.82	0.21	0.51	0.21	0.33	0.22	0.35
Rural	0.42	0.27	0.11	0.07	0.17	0.14	0.12	0.18	0.21	0.15	0.19
Total	0.52	0.26	0.11	0.07	0.22	0.15	0.15	0.19	0.24	0.19	0.21
Households with at least one member switching to industry											
Urban	16.1	27.5	15.7	6.9	15.0	6.7	17.0	4.5	6.2	4.0	7.2
Rural	12.1	11.3	5.3	9.8	9.4	8.2	6.4	13.6	6.0	4.4	8.7
Total	12.9	11.6	5.8	9.2	10.4	8.0	7.5	10.3	6.1	4.1	8.3
Increase of 125,000 new employees in the industrial sector											
All households											
Urban	2.5	0.7	0.9	0.2	1.4	0.4	1	0.7	0.9	0.7	0.8
Rural	1.1	0.6	0.4	0.5	0.4	0.5	0.2	0.3	0.4	0.5	0.5
Total	1.2	0.6	0.4	0.5	0.4	0.5	0.3	0.4	0.5	0.6	0.5
Households with at least one member switching to industry											
Urban	15.3	10.8	13.9	5.6	11.6	7.7	10.4	5.8	7.3	4.3	6.8
Rural	15.3	11.3	8.8	12.7	10.2	9.7	6.3	8.4	6.6	6.5	10.0
Total	15.3	11.2	9.4	12.3	10.5	9.6	6.9	7.5	6.9	4.9	9.0

Source: Author's calculations based on Cambodia Socioeconomic Survey for 1999 (round two data).

in purchasing power from switching would be about 8.3 percent (second panel in table 6-9). The gain would be a little larger (8.7 percent) for the households of laborers coming from rural areas. Results would be broadly similar for an increase of 125,000 employees.

Improvements in the Rice Sector

A high proportion of Cambodia's households produce rice, but most do so largely for their own consumption and hence would be unlikely to benefit directly from the higher rice prices caused by a Doha deal. It seems that in Cambodia, the greatest efficiency gains are likely to stem from reforming domestic production, processing, and trading systems rather than from reforms at the border.

This section investigates the results of three potential reforms that would affect the domestic rice sector: the introduction of better varieties of seeds, which would improve the paddy-to-rice yield; reductions in post-harvest losses; and reductions in transaction costs, broadly defined so as to capture the impact of bad roads on net revenues and that of bribes needed to be allowed to do business.[17] The two first elements are key components of the rice production system and are often indicated as avenues for improving household revenues.[18] Broadly defined transaction costs were identified during fieldwork in Cambodia as impediments to the development of the rice sector.

To assess the combined impact of these three potential reforms, equation 6-2 offers a useful decomposition of the value of the m quality of paddy rice output and is reproduced here for convenience:

$$(6\text{-}2) \quad \textit{Value of Rice Output} = Q_m^{PaddyRice}\left(1 - phl_m^{PaddyRice}\right)\left(1 - t_m^{Rice}\right)\left(1 - \alpha\right)\lambda P_m^{Rice},$$

where, again, $phl_m^{PaddyRice}$ denotes post-harvest losses, assumed to be about 10 percent currently; α denotes milling transformation costs; and λ is the milling yield of paddy to rice, assumed to be 0.62 percent on average (with some regional variation), by the MAFF. The term t_m^{Rice} adopts here the form of tax-equivalent "transaction costs," assumed to be 10 percent.

This simulation assesses the impact of a plausible change in $phl_m^{PaddyRice}$ from its current level of 10 percent to 5 percent, due, for instance, to an improvement in handling and packaging; in λ from its current level of 0.62 to 0.64, due, for instance, to a plausible and attainable improvement in rice variety; and in t_m^{Rice} from its current 10 percent to 5 percent, due, for instance, to an improvement in infrastructure or a reduction in other transaction costs.

17. Porto (2005).
18. Nesbitt (1997); JICA (2001).

The impact on total household income is:

(6-6) $\Delta Value\ of\ Rice\ Output = Q_m^{PaddyRice}\left(1-\alpha\right)P_m^{Rice}\left[\lambda_2\left(1-phl_{m,2}^{PaddyRice}\right)\right.$

$$\left.\left(1-t_{m,2}^{Rice}\right)-\lambda_1\left(1-phl_{m,1}^{PaddyRice}\right)\left(1-t_{m,1}^{Rice}\right)\right],$$

where subscripts 1 and 2 denote the current value and the simulated new value, respectively.

(6-7) $\Delta Value\ of\ Rice\ Output = P_0Q_0*[0.64*(1-0.05)(1-.05)$

$$-0.62(1-0.10)(1-010)]$$

$$= P_0Q_0*[0.5776-0.5022]$$

$$= P_0Q_0*0.0754.$$

In other words, the combined simulated effect of a 5 percentage point improvement in post-harvest management, a 2 percentage point improvement in the milling yield of paddy, and a 5 percentage point reduction in broadly defined transaction costs produces an increment of 15 percent (0.5776/0.5022) in the total value of rice production. The gains are linked directly to the amount of rice produced.

To calculate the welfare impact at the household level, the change in the value of rice output is divided by total household expenditures. The average gain in this simulation is 4.6 percent of real income, with net sellers gaining 9.1 percent and net buyers gaining 1.7 percent (table 6-10). The average gain for households in the poorer five deciles ranges from 5 to 7.2 percent.

Conclusions

The changes in prices and quantities that are likely to take place under a business-as-usual implementation of the Doha Development Agenda would have only a small impact on Cambodia's poor. Losses would be almost negligible, at about 0.2 percent of consumption per capita on average and slightly less than this for households that are net producers of rice, as they see the price of rice increase.

Much larger gains would follow from a more ambitious outcome from Doha. In this scenario, changes in international prices, coupled with the elimination of all Cambodian tariffs, would raise the purchasing power of the average Cambodian household by about 7.5 percent. Most of the gains would be felt by producers of rice and consumers of important categories of food, whose prices decline. Households in the poorest deciles would gain by 7–10 percent of purchasing power, although larger gains would accrue to the middle-income group. (Although the sharp increase in rice prices would benefit net producers

Table 6-10. *Effects on Household Welfare in Cambodia, by Decile of per Capita Expenditure: Improvements in the Rice Market*
Percent

Improvement	1	2	3	4	5	6	7	8	9	10	Average
Total	7.2	5.9	5.4	6.0	5.0	4.8	4.6	4.2	2.6	0.7	4.6
Reducing post-harvest losses by 5 percentage points	2.7	2.2	2.0	2.2	1.9	1.8	1.7	1.5	1.0	0.2	1.7
Increasing yield by 2 percentage points	1.6	1.3	1.2	1.3	1.1	1.0	1.0	0.9	0.6	0.1	1.0
Reducing transaction costs by 5 percentage points	2.7	2.2	2.0	2.2	1.9	1.8	1.7	1.5	1.0	0.2	1.7
Total for net sellers of rice	12.3	11.2	9.9	10.2	8.5	8.7	8.4	7.0	6.4	6.5	9.1
Reducing post-harvest losses by 5 percentage points	4.6	4.1	3.7	3.8	3.1	3.2	3.1	2.6	2.4	2.4	3.4
Increasing yield by 2 percentage points	2.6	2.4	2.1	2.2	1.8	1.9	1.8	1.5	1.4	1.4	2.0
Reducing transaction costs by 5 percentage points	4.6	4.1	3.7	3.8	3.1	3.2	3.1	2.6	2.4	2.4	3.4

Source: Author's calculations, based on Cambodia Socioeconomic Survey for 1999 (round two data).

of rice, at the aggregate level its impact would be softened because only a relatively small percentage of households actually sell rice.)

If Cambodia were to change its tariff structure unilaterally to a 7 percent flat rate, the purchasing power of the average household would rise by about 3.7 percent, or by nearly half as much as would be obtained under the ambitious Doha reforms. Almost all of this improvement would stem from reduced prices of foods.

These estimates do not include the expansion of employment in the textile industry that would be associated with a significant increase in exports. Among Cambodia's nonindustrial working population, there is a pool of about 220,000 underemployed laborers who would most likely be willing to switch to jobs in the industrial sector. For them, the potential wage gains would be large: the average gain would be equivalent to 22 percent of current wages for people switching from the primary sector and 39 percent for those switching from the services sector. If labor demand in industry were to rise by 50,000 employees (roughly what would be expected under the business-as-usual scenario), the average gain in per capita real income for those households with at least one member switching jobs would be about 8.3 percent, and the gain would be greater in the poorest four deciles of the income distribution. For Cambodia's population at large, this switch of 50,000 workers out of agriculture or the service sector and into industry would produce a small average gain of 0.2 percent in real income.

Finally, improvements in two key elements of rice production technology (paddy-to-rice yield and post-harvest losses) and in transaction costs would produce noticeable gains for poor Cambodians: households in the poorer five deciles would add 5–7 percent to their real income. And, if these policy changes were combined with the multilateral trade reforms of the ambitious Doha scenario, these households could gain more than 10 percent.

References

Cochran, William, and Donald B. Rubin. 1973. "Controlling Bias in Observational Studies." *Sankhya* 35, no. 4 (series A): 417–46.

Deaton, Angus. 1997. *The Analysis of Household Surveys: A Microeconometric Approach to Development Policy.* Baltimore, Md.: Johns Hopkins University Press.

Dickens, William T., and Kevin Lang. 1985. "A Test of Dual Labor Market Theory." *American Economic Review* 75, no. 4: 792–805.

Gibson, John. 2002. "A Poverty Profile of Cambodia." Mimeo. Washington: World Bank.

Heckman, James J., Hidehiko Ichimura, and Petra E. Todd. 1997. "Matching as an Econometric Evaluation Estimator: Evidence from Evaluating a Job Training Program." *Review of Economic Studies* 64, no. 4: 605–54.

JICA (Japanese International Cooperation Agency). 2001. "Study on Improvement of Rice Marketing System and Post-Harvest Quality Control of Rice in Cambodia." Tokyo.

MAFF (Cambodia Ministry of Agriculture, Forestry, and Fisheries). 2001. *Agricultural Statistics, 1999–2000.* Statistics Office, Department of Planning and International Cooperation.

Magnac, Thierry. 1991. "Segmented or Competitive Labor Markets." *Econometrica* 59, no. 1: 165–87.

Nesbitt, H. J. 1997. "Rice Production in Cambodia." Phnom Penh: International Rice Research Institute (IRRI).

Nicita, Alessandro, Marcelo Olarreaga, and Isidro Soloaga. 2001. "A Simple Methodology to Assess the Poverty Impact of Economic Policies Using Household Data." Mimeo. Washington: World Bank.

Porto, Guido. 2005. "Informal Export Barriers and Poverty." *Journal of International Economics* 66, no. 2: 447–70.

World Bank. 2001. "Trade Policy and Poverty." In *Poverty Reduction Strategy Paper Sourcebook*. Washington.

7

Vietnam

AYLIN IŞIK-DIKMELIK

V ietnam took big unilateral steps in trade liberalization during the last
decade and is now one of the most open economies in Southeast Asia. It
continues to emphasize trade reforms, as evidenced by the negotiations for its
accession to the World Trade Organization, the ratification of the Bilateral
Trade Agreement with the United States, and the new round of talks under the
Doha Development Agenda (DDA).

The debate surrounding the Doha talks is that trade reforms will not be effective in reducing poverty in developing countries. It is clear that multilateral trade
reforms will have differing effects on individual countries depending on a number of factors (notably the commodities produced, how protected the commodities are, and how well the markets are integrated, to name a few). In chapter 2
above, Kee, Nicita, and Olarreaga showed that the DDA is expected to have a
substantial impact on Vietnam. This chapter will shed light on the distribution
of this impact among Vietnamese households, estimating the impact on household welfare under a limited trade liberalization scenario and a more ambitious
scenario for both the short and long run.

To investigate the short-run effects, the analysis uses the methodology outlined in Nicita, Olarreaga, and Soloaga (2001), where the impact of trade policy

The author would like to thank Ataman Aksoy, Alessandro Nicita, and Marcelo Olarreaga for
valuable discussions and comments.

changes on welfare makes itself felt through changes in prices of commodities (quantities are assumed to be fixed in the short term). To calculate the long-term impact, a model of the farm household (Singh, Squire, and Strauss 1986) is used, following Winters (2002) in tracking changes in prices and production and the effect on households through changes in employment. The analysis does not take account of the productivity changes that might take place in response to higher prices in some commodities,[1] and thus the results from the simulations are conservative estimates of potential gains and overestimates of potential losses.

The changes in prices and production are obtained from chapter 2, in which Kee, Nicita, and Olarreaga use a partial equilibrium model to estimate the changes that would result from implementing the Doha Development Agenda. As detailed in their chapter, these changes are estimated for two scenarios: limited multilateral trade liberalization, termed business as usual, and deeper trade liberalization, termed the ambitious scenario. By coupling the changes in exports from Kee, Nicita, and Olarreaga with input-output tables and employment statistics from the Global Trade Analysis Project database, we also obtain an estimate of the effect on employment in Vietnam under both scenarios.

The chapter is organized as follows. The first section provides an overview of the poverty profile in Vietnam, presenting income and spending patterns across deciles of households, ranked by consumption per capita. The second section explains the methodology used for calculating the impact of policy changes on household welfare. The third section provides the price and production changes for Vietnam that would be associated with the implementation of the Doha Development Agenda. The fourth section discusses the results for the scenarios considered, and a final section concludes.

The results suggest that implementation of the Doha Development Agenda will likely have only a minor impact on the overall poverty rate in Vietnam. However, an important redistribution of purchasing power takes place, from urban to rural households and from net rice buyer households to net rice seller households.[2] In Vietnam 90 percent of the poor are rural, and rural households gain under both the Doha scenarios considered. If expected gains in productivity are also taken into account, the gains to net seller households (and to rural households) are likely to be larger, creating a more positive effect on poverty.

Poverty Profile of Vietnam

The poverty rate in Vietnam has declined dramatically in the last decade with rapid economic growth (table 7-1). However, poverty is still prominent,

---

1. It is very hard to quantify the potential productivity changes.
2. This is consistent with the theoretical literature (for example, see Deaton 1997), which predicts that net sellers will benefit while net buyers will suffer.

Table 7-1. *Poverty Trends (Headcount Measure) in Vietnam, 1993–2002*[a]
Percent

Indicator	1993	1998	2002
$1 a day			
Poverty rate	14.63	3.80	1.95
Poverty gap	2.55	0.48	0.14
$2 a day			
Poverty rate	58.16	39.68	33.44
Poverty gap	20.13	10.55	8.31

Source: PovcalNet, World Bank.

a. The poverty rate, measured by the headcount index, is the percentage of the population whose total consumption falls below the poverty line. The poverty gap measures the depth of poverty. It is the average of the differences of incomes from the poverty line as a percent of the poverty line. The average is taken over the whole population and those above the poverty line are assumed to have zero distance.

especially in rural areas. According to the $1 a day benchmark, only 2 percent of the population is poor, but the rate jumps to 33 percent when the $2 a day benchmark is used (World Bank 2004). Some 45 percent of the rural population is below the national poverty line (World Bank 1999) and 90 percent of the poor live in rural areas.

Although Vietnam's poverty rates are lower than previously, the fact that 80 percent of the poor are farmers underscores the importance of agriculture for poverty reduction. About 60 percent of the population list agriculture as their principal occupation. Education levels are low among poor farmers and access to information and functional skills is limited.

Rural areas responded positively to previous trade liberalization, suggesting that further liberalization may help to reduce poverty more. A major decline in poverty occurred in the five-year period 1993–98, during which Vietnam liberalized its rice quota to a nonbinding level (table 7-1). This liberalization, coupled with the lifting of internal trade restrictions on rice (in 1997), led to average income growth of approximately 60 percent during the five-year period for households in the rural areas (Işık-Dikmelik 2006).

If the Doha Development Agenda is implemented, multilateral trade liberalization in some of Vietnam's main agricultural products (particularly rice, coffee, and corn) may lead to gains for farmers, thus alleviating some of the poverty. The extent of the effect will depend on which products are important income sources for the poor and which products the poor consume extensively.

Sources of Income

Poor rural households draw 58 percent of their income from agriculture (crop cultivation, livestock rearing, fisheries, and crop processing) (figure 7-1). Poor urban households, by contrast, rely mainly on self-employment and wage employment

Figure 7-1. *Sources of Income for Rural Households in Vietnam,*
by Decile of per Capita Expenditure

Percent

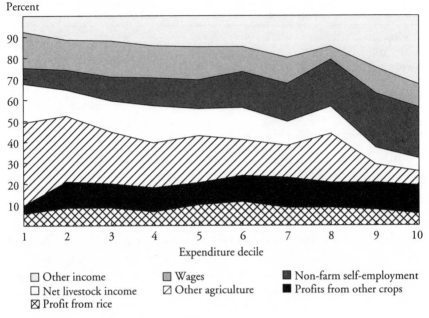

Source: Author's calculations using 1998 VLSS.

in services and manufacturing (figure 7-2); some engage in agriculture, consuming
half of what they produce. (For more details on the sources of income, see the
appendix to this chapter.)

Although most of the rice produced in Vietnam is consumed by the producer households themselves, rice still provides a significant source of cash
income for poor rural families. Figure 7-3 illustrates that rice production is
mainly a rural phenomenon, and emphasizes that any change in the rice price
will affect all rural households, especially net sellers of rice, from the income
side. Rural non-poor households get most of their crop income from cash
crops (such as coffee, cashews, tobacco) and are mostly involved in non-farm
self-employment.

The sources of income offer an idea of how the incomes of the poor will be
affected by policy changes. However, to obtain the complete picture we also
need to consider what households spend their incomes on.

Expenditure Patterns

Rice is a major staple throughout Vietnam. Food items account for a large share
of total spending for both rural and urban households (63 and 58 percent,

Figure 7-2. *Sources of Income for Urban Households in Vietnam, by Decile of per Capita Expenditure*
Percent

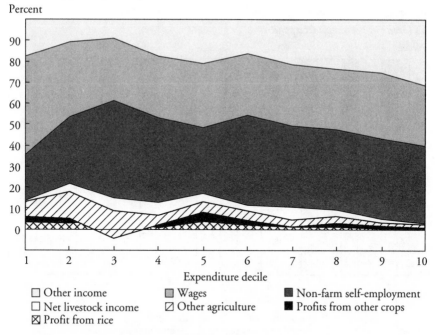

Source: Author's calculations using 1998 VLSS.
Note: "Other agriculture" includes the imputed value of income from subsistence production and income from sources such as agricultural by-products and processing of home-produced goods. "Profits from other crops" include profits from both food and cash crops.

Figure 7-3. *Share of Rice Income in Total Income of Rural and Urban Households in Vietnam, by Decile of per Capita Expenditure*[a]
Percent

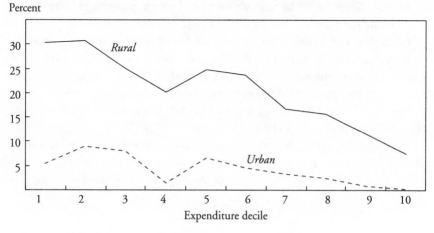

Source: Author's calculations using 1998 VLSS.
Note: Rice income includes the value of rice produced for the family's own consumption.

Figure 7-4. *Composition of Rural Household Expenditure in Vietnam,*
by Decile of per Capita Expenditure
Percent

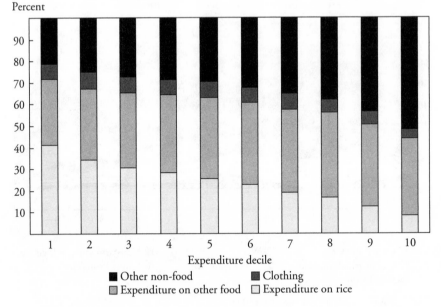

Source: Author's calculations using 1998 VLSS.

respectively), and among the rural poor, half of food spending goes for rice
(figures 7-4 and 7-5).[3] Since rice accounts for such a large share of spending,
any policy that significantly affects the price of rice will clearly affect household
welfare. Among the poor in rural areas, as was noted earlier, most of the rice
consumed comes from the family's own production, whereas in urban areas,
even among the poor, 95 percent of the rice consumed is purchased.

Education and health account for a smaller share of spending among the
poor than among the rich. This difference is more pronounced in rural areas,
where on average the poor (lowest three deciles) devote only 9 percent of their
expenditure to education and health, and the rich (highest three deciles) spend
18 percent. This may be because the poor are less able to afford health care, and
also less likely to send their children to school.

Figure 7-6 illustrates that the consumption of home-produced food is more
widespread in rural than in urban areas. This is not surprising, as urban households engage in agriculture less often. It also shows that poorer households are
more likely to be subsistence farmers.

3. See tables A-3 and A-4 in the appendix to this chapter for more detailed expenditure patterns.

Figure 7-5. *Composition of Urban Household Expenditure in Vietnam, by Decile of per Capita Expenditure*

Percent

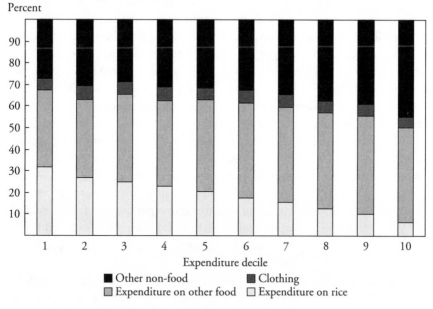

Expenditure decile

- ■ Other non-food   ■ Clothing
- ▨ Expenditure on other food   □ Expenditure on rice

Source: Author's calculations using 1998 VLSS.

Figure 7-6. *Share of Home-Produced Food in Total Expenditure in Vietnam, by Decile of per Capita Expenditure*

Percent

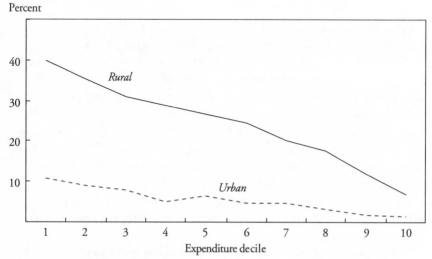

Expenditure decile

Source: Author's calculations using 1998 VLSS.

Methodology

Following Winters (2002), the analysis below takes the perspective that trade policies mainly operate through price, production, and factor (that is, labor market) links. In Vietnam as in most developing countries, most households are simultaneously consumers and producers of the same goods. To capture this duality we use a farm household model of the type introduced by Singh, Squire, and Strauss (1986), in which the household is the unit of analysis. As is custom-ary, for the short-run analysis we track only the changes in prices,[4] and calculate the effect on household welfare by feeding the new prices into the model. For the long-run analysis, we track changes in prices, changes in production quanti-ties (by way of increased international demand for Vietnamese products), and changes in employment, in order to measure the impact on household welfare.

The effects of policy changes on household welfare are calculated in terms of percentages of current household income and expenditures, for households ordered by decile of per capita adult equivalent expenditure, as outlined below. Hence a policy change is pro-poor if it enhances the real income, or purchasing power, of households in the first five deciles.

The data used for the analysis come from the Vietnam Living Standards Survey (VLSS) for 1998. For this survey, 6,001 households were surveyed by the Vietnamese General Statistics Office between December 1997 and December 1998. The survey is stratified, multistaged, and clustered. It includes detailed data on household composition, education, employment, expenditure, land holdings, and agricultural activities.

Short-Run Analysis: Price Changes

For the short-run analysis we use the simple partial equilibrium model devel-oped by Nicita, Olarreaga, and Soloaga (2001). This model takes the house-hold as the unit of analysis, and estimates the first-order effects of a policy change, assuming that in the short run households cannot change their con-sumption and production activities in response to a price change. Income is defined as the sum of the household's own production (including non-farm self-employment), wage employment, and transfers (pensions, remittances, and government transfers). Different households have different sources of income and different expenditure patterns. Total net household income is defined as total income minus total expenditure.

Given the fixed quantities assumption, the first-order effect of a price shock will be given by the change in price times the quantity of the commodity produced

4. We assume that there is perfect pass-through of prices from the border to producers. With this assumption the effects presented here will provide an upper bound. However, Seshan (2005) reports that in Vietnam farm-gate prices are 80 percent of border prices (especially for rice). Thus this assumption does not greatly compromise the results of our analysis.

and consumed. Formally, the income and the expenditure of a household can be written as:

$$(7\text{-}1) \qquad Income = \sum_i X_i^O P_i^O - \sum_j X_j^I P_j^I + \sum_k L_k W_k + \sum_m \sum_n T_{mn}$$

$$(7\text{-}2) \qquad Expenditure = \sum_l X_l^c P_l^c,$$

where P_i^O is the price of output i, X_i^O is the quantity produced of output i, P_j^I and X_j^I are the price and quantity of input j, respectively W_k is the wage rate for factor k, L_k is the supply of factor k by the household, T_{mn} is the net transfer received by the household, P_l^c is the consumer price of commodity l, and X_l^c is the quantity consumed of commodity l. We can then compute the percentage change in welfare in response to price changes as follows (assuming quantities remain fixed):

$$(7\text{-}3) \qquad dWelfare = \underbrace{\left[\sum_i IS_i^O dP_i^O - \sum_j BS_j^I dP_j^I \right]}_{Income\ Effect} - \underbrace{\sum_l BS_l^c dP_l^c}_{Consumption\ Effect},$$

where IS (BS) indicates the shares of income from (budget shares for consumption of) the respective commodities and inputs, and d refers to the percentage change.

Since the households are assumed not to adjust their activities, this approach underestimates the gains and overestimates the losses. In reality, households will substitute away from consuming commodities whose prices have risen, while moving into the production of such commodities.

Long-Run Analysis

For the long-run analysis, we relax our assumption of fixed quantities and allow the households to respond to changed international demand for Vietnamese goods by changing their production quantities. In addition, we estimate the impact of changed employment (due to increased demand for Vietnam's exports, resulting from Doha-related multilateral liberalization) on household welfare. The following discussion explains how we estimate which households would benefit from the changed employment and to what extent.

Impact on Employment. Using the expected export changes for different commodities given by Kee, Nicita, and Olarreaga in chapter 2, along with the GTAP input-output tables and employment statistics,[5] we estimate that approximately

---

5. To obtain our estimates, we assume that in each industry the increase in employment is proportional to the increase in production.

36,000 jobs will be created under the business-as-usual scenario. Under the ambitious scenario, the increase will be around 96,000 jobs. Most of the jobs arise from increased export production in industry, particularly textiles.[6]

To determine the effect of the newly created jobs on households, we need to establish who will get the new jobs and how much their income will be affected. With this in mind, we split the labor market into two sectors: formal and informal. Since most of the increase in employment is due to expansion in industry, we assume that the new jobs are in the formal sector. Clearly, the impact of the increased employment on poverty will depend on whether the poor are able to get these jobs and also on the size of the wage difference between the formal and informal sector.

To determine who will obtain the new jobs, we use the propensity score matching method (Heckman, Ichimura, and Todd 1998). In this context, the propensity score for an individual is the probability of his or her being employed in the formal sector, as a function of observed characteristics such as age, education, and location. The propensity scores are estimated using the following probit model:

$$(7\text{-}4) \qquad\qquad F_i = \beta_0 + \beta_1 C_i + \beta_2 H_i + \varepsilon_i,$$

where F_i is the formal sector indicator and takes the value 1 only if individual i is employed in the formal sector, C_i is composed of variables of individual characteristics, and H_i of household characteristics. (Results from this estimation are shown in the appendix to this chapter.)

Once we obtain the propensity scores for each individual, we rank the individuals who are working in the informal sector according to their probability of being employed in the formal sector. The highest-ranking individuals are switched to the formal sector until all new jobs are filled. This accomplishes our goal of determining who will get the new jobs.

To identify the wage difference between the formal and the informal sector, we estimate a wage equation of the Mincerian form.[7] The dependent variable is the logarithm of wages. Independent variables are workers' characteristics such as gender, age, education, location, and a set of industry dummies. The coefficient of the industry dummies captures the wage premium of an industry over the omitted industry—the informal sector. Formally:

$$(7\text{-}5) \qquad\qquad \ln w_i = \alpha_0 + \alpha_1 C_i + \alpha_2 F_i + \eta_i.$$

---

6. According to UNIDO statistics, the number of workers (jobs) in Vietnam's textile industry in year 2000 was about 608,500, and the number of workers in all manufacturing was about 1,541,000.

7. The Mincerian wage equation relates an individual's characteristics (most importantly education) with his wage earnings. See Mincer (1974) for a detailed analysis.

The results of this regression (detailed in the appendix to this chapter) show that individuals working in the formal sector earn a premium of 7 percent more than individuals with the same characteristics who are working in the informal sector. Thus we raise by 7 percent the observed wage incomes of the individuals who get the new jobs, to calculate their new incomes.

Impact on Household Welfare. Having estimated the impact of new employment on workers' wages, we can now turn our attention to the impact of multilateral trade liberalization on household welfare as a whole. The three major links are as follows. The change in prices will affect both income (through the price effect) and expenditure (through the consumption effect). The change in employment will affect the income as outlined above. The change in exports of Vietnamese products will affect income (through production) and will be allocated to households according to their market participation.

The percentage change in welfare in this case (using the farm household model) can formally be expressed as:

$$
(7\text{-}6) \qquad dWelfare^h = \underbrace{\left[\sum_i IS_i^{Oh} dP_i^O - \sum_j BS_j^{Ih} dP_j^I \right]}_{\text{Price Effect (from goods produced)}} - \underbrace{\sum_l BS_l^{ch} dP_l^c}_{\text{Consumption Effect}}
$$

$$
+ \underbrace{IS_h^w dW_h}_{\text{Employment Effect}} + \underbrace{\sum_i dExp_i \pi_i^h + \sum_i dP_i^O \Delta X_i^h}_{\text{Export Effect}}
$$

and

$$
(7\text{-}7) \qquad \Delta X_i^h = \Delta EXP_i \frac{\pi_i^h}{\sum_h \pi_i^h},
$$

where $dExp_i$ is the percentage change in exports of good i, ΔX_i^h is the change in production of good i by household h due to the change in international demand, π_i^h is the profit[8] obtained by household h producing good i, and ΔEXP_i is the total change in exports for Vietnam in good i, and:

$$
(7\text{-}8) \qquad dW_h = \frac{\sum_i w_i^h S_i z_i}{\sum_i w_i^h},
$$

8. The profit is defined as income from sales minus expenses associated with the production of the good. According to this definition, only households who sell good i can obtain profit from it. Hence only the households who participate in the market experience a change in production.

where w_i^h is the initial wage income of individual i in household h, S_i is an indicator variable for the switch and takes the value 1 if the individual i switched to the formal sector, z_i is the wage premium for individual i as estimated by equation (5), and d refers to the percentage change.

The export effect can be decomposed into two parts. The first part takes into account the change in profit from adjusted production.[9] The second part recognizes the fact that the changed production will be sold at the new prices, hence accounting for the change in income through that link.

Price Changes for Vietnam from the Doha Development Agenda

Given the commodities Vietnam exports, the implementation of a Doha agreement on multilateral trade reforms is likely to have a substantial impact on the Vietnamese economy. As already noted, Vietnam's main agricultural product is rice, which is produced by 70 percent of households and is also widely traded. Rice is the major export product and Vietnam has been one of the largest exporters of rice in the last decade. Coffee and textile products are other key exports, and seafood is gaining an important share.

In the short run, the impact on poverty will be determined by the change in the prices of commodities produced or consumed by the poor. In the long run, the change in exports of goods that affect the incomes of the poor, and—if the poor can get the newly created jobs—the extent of growth in employment will also be significant.

For commodities important to Vietnam, table 7-2 presents the expected changes in international prices in the short run, in response to limited and more extensive multilateral trade liberalization. The price changes are those estimated in chapter 2.

The short-run effect of multilateral trade liberalization on the rice price is an increase of 8 percent under business as usual and an increase of 20 percent in the ambitious scenario. Other major exports of Vietnamese households are also significantly affected: the price of corn rises by 16 percent under business as usual and by 29 percent in the ambitious scenario, whereas the prices of coffee, seafood, and "other agriculture" products decrease. The ambitious scenario is expected to create more significant changes in prices.

Table 7-3 shows the expected long-run changes in prices, along with changes in exports and jobs, under the two scenarios. Again the underlying price and quantity changes are taken from Kee, Nicita, and Olarreaga in chapter 2. They assume an improvement in trade facilitation corresponding to an increase of 2 percent in world trade in both scenarios. Hence, an improvement in trade

---

9. An implicit assumption is that the prices of inputs will also change proportionally, so that the profit margin changes by the same ratio.

Table 7-2. *Short-Run Changes in International Prices in Vietnam: Business-as-Usual and Ambitious Scenarios*
Percent change in prices

Products	Business as usual	Ambitious
Rice	8.0	20.0
Corn	16.6	29.0
Grains (other cereals)	1.2	−5.4
Fruit	12.7	27.0
Vegetables	−1.5	−12.8
Coffee	−0.5	−2.1
Cashews	0.0	0.0
Other industrial crops	−0.3	−2.4
Livestock	2.4	6.2
Seafood	−0.6	−2.8
Other agriculture	−0.8	−3.3
Food industry	1.0	2.8
Textiles	−3.4	−7.3

Source: Author's calculations, based on VLSS for 1998.

Table 7-3. *(Long-Run) Changes in International Prices and Exports in Vietnam: Business-as-Usual and Ambitious Scenarios*

Products	Price changes (percent)		Changes in exports (thousands of U.S. dollars)	
	Business as usual	Ambitious	Business as usual	Ambitious
Rice	6.0	19.0	74,993	237,479
Corn	7.3	11.8	3,663	5,774
Grains (other cereals)	6.5	13.6	231	−182
Fruit	0.0	−1.7	375	−1,938
Vegetables	2.7	24.2	1,475	1,046
Coffee	−0.5	−2.1	3,132	−28,053
Cashews	0.0	0.0	2,817	2,233
Other industrial crops	0.3	1.1	11,609	18,971
Livestock	−0.1	1.1	500	2,717
Seafood	0.5	1.3	87,927	525,005
Other agriculture	−2.0	−9.2	3,434	−23,452
Food industry	2.0	3.9	11,851	63,873
Textiles	1.5	4.3	336,717	898,026
New jobs			36,000	96,000

Source: Author's calculations, based on VLSS for 1998.

facilitation can compensate for a decrease in the world price of a commodity, causing a positive change in exports. In general, as table 7-3 shows, the price changes are smaller in the long run than in the short run (as adjustments take place), and in the ambitious scenario, the changes are more pronounced than with more limited liberalization.

The long-run effects of the business-as-usual and ambitious scenarios on important commodities in Vietnam are as follows. The increase in the price of rice is 6 percent with the limited liberalization and 19 percent with deeper liberalization. Other cereals also experience a large impact, of 6.5 percent under business as usual and 13.6 percent under the ambitious scenario. The impact on "other agriculture" is more pronounced in the long run: a decline of 2 percent and 9.2 percent with the limited and full liberalization respectively. For textiles the long-run impact is relatively small: a price increase of 1.5 percent under business as usual and of 4.3 percent under the ambitious scenario.

Looking at the effects on exports, under business as usual the impact on exports is most significant in rice, among agricultural products. Rice exports grow by around U.S.$75 million, and this increased demand will be a large factor, especially for rice-selling households, in determining household welfare. Increased demand for seafood is estimated at U.S.$88 million, for corn U.S.$3.6 million, and for coffee U.S.$3 million. In the industrial sector, textiles will have the biggest increase, with U.S.$337 million. In the ambitious scenario, the increases in export demand are more significant. Demand for rice will increase by U.S.$237 million and that for seafood by U.S.$525 million. Textiles will face an increase of U.S.$898 million. By contrast, coffee exports are expected to decline—by U.S.$28 million.

The price, export, and employment changes are used to measure the effects of trade liberalization on household welfare. The following section presents the simulation results for the two Doha scenarios in both the short and long run.

Simulation Results

Short Run

We consider the short-run effects first. In this case, the only effect on the welfare of households is through the changes in the short-run prices of the goods they produce and consume.

Business as Usual. As figure 7-7 illustrates, the price changes resulting from limited multilateral liberalization lead to a decline of 0.2 percent in real income for the average Vietnamese household. Rural households gain by 0.1 percent on average, whereas urban households lose by 1.5 percent. The greatest losses are for the poorest 40 percent of urban households.

As figure 7-8 illustrates, the losses in welfare come from the consumption side. The effects of trade liberalization on consumption are negative for all

Figure 7-7. *Short-Run Effects on Welfare of Rural and Urban Households in Vietnam, by Decile of per Capita Expenditure: Business as Usual*

Percent

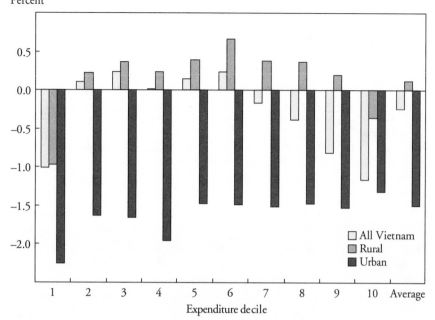

Expenditure decile

Source: Author's calculations using 1998 VLSS.

Figure 7-8. *Short-Run Effects on Household Consumption and Income in Vietnam, by Decile of per Capita Expenditure: Business as Usual*

Percent

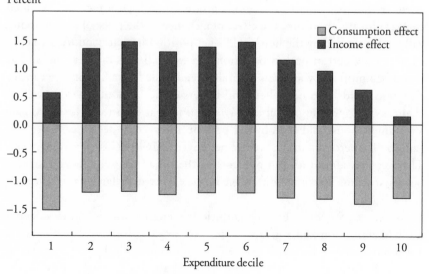

Expenditure decile

Source: Author's calculations using 1998 VLSS.

Table 7-4. *Short-Run Effects on Net Sellers and Net Buyers of Rice in Vietnam,
by Decile of Total Household per Capita Expenditure: Business-as-Usual
and Ambitious Scenarios*

Percent

Scenario and buyer or seller	1	2	3	4	5	6	7	8	9	10	Average
Business as usual											
All Vietnam	−1.0	0.1	0.2	0.0	0.1	0.2	−0.2	−0.4	−0.8	−1.2	−0.2
Net buyers of rice	−2.0	−0.9	−0.8	−0.8	−0.9	−0.9	−1.0	−1.3	−1.3	−1.3	−1.2
Net sellers of rice	1.2	1.4	1.4	1.0	1.3	1.5	1.0	1.2	1.6	0.7	1.3
Ambitious											
All Vietnam	−2.3	0.0	0.5	−0.1	0.4	0.6	−0.4	−0.9	−1.9	−2.8	−0.6
Net buyers of rice	−4.7	−2.7	−2.2	−2.3	−2.4	−2.4	−2.5	−3.1	−3.1	−3.1	−3.0
Net sellers of rice	3.0	3.2	3.3	2.6	3.5	3.9	2.5	3.2	3.8	1.3	3.2

Source: Author's calculations, based on VLSS for 1998.

households (an average loss of 1.3 percent), but more so for the poorest and the richest. These consumption effects are overestimates of the potential losses, since we have assumed that in the short run, households cannot change their behavior in response to price changes.

Since the quantities of the goods produced and consumed are assumed constant for the short run, the effect of a change in the price of a commodity will be determined by the household's net position in that good. As rice constitutes a big part of both production and expenditures in Vietnam, and as it will be significantly affected by multilateral trade liberalization, we categorize households into net sellers and buyers of rice and analyze the welfare changes correspondingly (table 7-4). We find that even though the average Vietnamese household loses by 0.2 percent, the average net seller household gains by 1.3 percent and the average net buyer household loses by 1.2 percent. The fact that almost all (94 percent) of the urban households are net rice buyers helps to explain the difference in the expected welfare changes in rural and urban areas.

Ambitious Scenario. For the ambitious scenario, which features deeper trade liberalization and a greater impact on world prices, the overall results are summarized in figure 7-9. The pattern of change is broadly similar to that in the business-as-usual case but the magnitudes are larger. In this scenario, where the price of rice is expected to increase by 20 percent, the pur-

Figure 7-9. *Short-Run Effects on Welfare of Rural and Urban Households in Vietnam, by Decile of per Capita Expenditure: Ambitious Scenario*
Percent

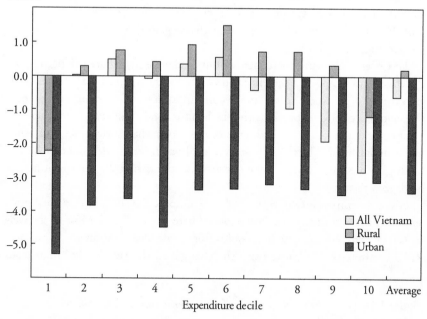

Source: Author's calculations using 1998 VLSS.

chasing power of the average Vietnamese household declines by 0.6 percent. Rural households gain on average (by 0.2 percent), while urban households lose by 3.4 percent. The largest losses are again among the poorest 40 percent of urban households.

Households that are net sellers of rice gain (by 3.2 percent). Households that are net buyers lose (by 3 percent, and by more than they did in the business-as-usual scenario) (table 7-4).

Long Run

In addition to changes in prices, the long-run analysis considers changes in international demand for Vietnamese products and changes in employment. It is assumed that the increase in international demand for Vietnam's exports will be matched by increased production, to which households will contribute in proportion to their current market participation. Increased demand for exports, especially in labor-intensive sectors, will cause an increase in labor demand which in turn will create additional employment and help to raise household income. The change in household welfare through the change in employment is incorporated using the method described in the second section above.

Business as Usual. Under the business-as-usual scenario, the average Vietnamese household gains by about 0.9 percent of real income. The gains are
unevenly distributed across rural and urban households. While urban households
are expected to lose by 0.9 percent, on average, rural households gain by 1.4 percent. In rural areas, middle-income households gain the most, and the poorest
10 percent gain the least.

To better understand the contributions to change in welfare, we decompose
the effect on income and the effect on consumption (figure 7-11). Households
gain from the income effect, but the consumption effects are uniformly negative, and more so for urban households than for rural. This reflects the fact that
most urban households are net buyers of the goods whose prices rise, and hence
will be more affected by an increase in price. In addition, middle-income households gain the most from income effects while the richest 20 percent of households gain the least.

Given the importance of rice, we also decompose the effect of rice (total price
and export effects of rice) on household welfare (figure 7-12). Most of the welfare changes for Vietnamese households from trade liberalization are due to rice.
Rural consumers gain more from the changes in the rice market than from

Figure 7-10. *Long-Run Effects on Welfare of Rural and Urban Households
in Vietnam, by Decile of per Capita Expenditure: Business as Usual*

Percent

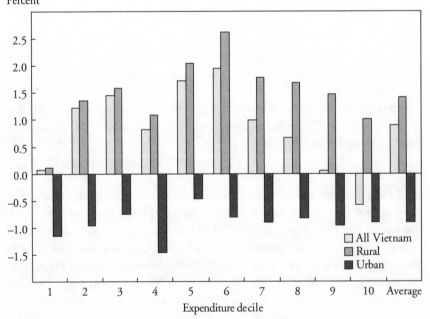

Expenditure decile

Source: Author's calculations using 1998 VLSS.

Figure 7-11. *Long-Run Effects on Household Income and Consumption in Vietnam, by Decile of per Capita Expenditure: Business as Usual*[a]

Percent

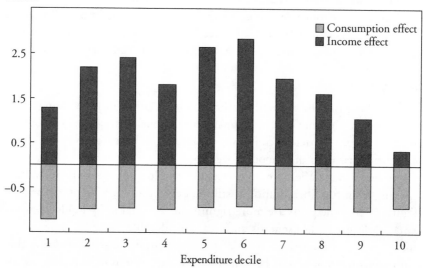

Source: Author's calculations using 1998 VLSS.

a. The consumption effect represents the change in welfare due to changes in prices of consumed goods. The income effect represents the change in income due to changes in prices of produced goods (price effect), changes in production of the household (export effect), and changes in wage income of the household (employment effect).

Figure 7-12. *Effect of Rice in Total Change in Welfare in Vietnam, by Decile of per Capita Expenditure: Business as Usual*

Percent

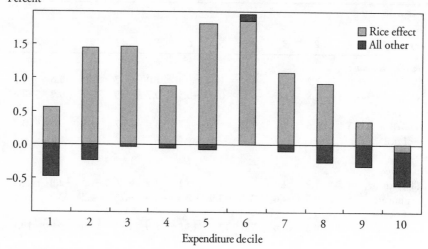

Source: Author's calculations using 1998 VLSS.

changes in other goods, and the losses urban consumers face are due to rice (since hardly any of them are net sellers of rice).

This prompts us to look at the changes in welfare for net rice seller and net rice buyer households. As table 7-5 shows, net sellers gain by 3.7 percent while net buyers lose by 0.8 percent. Net buyers lose slightly less in rural areas (0.6 percent), and net sellers gain slightly more in urban areas (3.8 percent).

Ambitious Scenario

Over the long run the deeper liberalization leads to larger price changes and hence to larger income effects, compared to the business-as-usual case. But it also has a bigger impact on consumption, leading to losses for the poorest and the richer households and a modest overall gain.

For the average Vietnamese household the long-run change in welfare resulting from full liberalization is still modest, at an increase of 1.1 percent (figure 7-13). The gains are more significant for rural households (2.5 percent) while urban households suffer a considerable loss (3.9 percent). A closer look into the distribution of gains for rural households shows that middle-income households benefit the most (by around 4.5 percent), while poor households gain the least (by 1.3 percent) with the poorest decile losing by 1.0 percent.

Table 7-5. *Long-Run Effects on Net Sellers and Net Buyers of Rice in Vietnam, by Decile of Total Household per Capita Expenditure: Business-as-Usual and Ambitious Scenarios*

Percent

Scenario and buyers or sellers	1	2	3	4	5	6	7	8	9	10	Average
Business as usual											
All Vietnam	0.1	1.2	1.4	0.8	1.7	1.9	1.0	0.7	0.0	−0.6	0.9
Net buyers of rice	−1.3	−0.8	−0.7	−0.7	−0.6	−0.5	−0.7	−0.9	−0.9	−0.9	−0.8
Net sellers of rice	3.1	3.6	3.8	2.7	4.3	4.7	3.4	3.7	4.7	3.5	3.7
Ambitious											
All Vietnam	−1.2	1.2	2.4	1.3	3.7	5.1	1.2	−0.6	−1.3	−2.9	1.1
Net buyers of rice	−5.4	−5.5	−4.6	−3.3	−3.9	−2.5	−4.3	−6.3	−4.2	−3.9	−4.5
Net sellers of rice	8.4	9.3	10.0	7.0	12.2	13.8	8.9	10.3	13.0	9.9	10.1

Source: Author's calculations, based on VLSS for 1998.

Figure 7-13. *Long-Run Effects on Welfare of Rural and Urban Households
in Vietnam, by Decile of per Capita Expenditure: Ambitious Scenario*
Percent

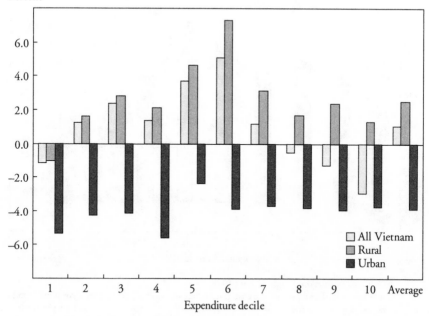

Source: Author's calculations using VLSS for 1998.

The changes are larger when we categorize households as net sellers and net buyers of rice: the ambitious liberalization brings net seller households a long-term welfare gain of 10 percent, while net buyers face a long-term loss of 4.5 percent (table 7-5).

Once again, the income effects from the ambitious scenario are all positive (figure 7-14). However, for the poorest and the richest households they are not large enough to outweigh the negative consumption effects, which are much more pronounced than under business-as-usual. This may be due to the large changes in the prices of rice, grains (other cereal), corn, fruit, and textiles, which are important consumption items for both poorer and richer households.[10]

The contribution of rice to the overall long-run change in welfare indicates that rural households gain more than the average household, as they tend to be net rice sellers, while urban households lose, since they tend to be net rice buyers (table 7-6).

10. The expected increase in demand for Vietnam's textile exports does not have a large direct impact on household income, though it is expected to create new jobs. Households produce some cotton, but apparel and finished textile products are largely produced by firms, and hence these products do not constitute a major source of income in our model.

Figure 7-14. *Long-Run Effects on Household Income and Consumption in Vietnam, by Decile of per Capita Expenditure: Ambitious Scenario*[a]
Percent

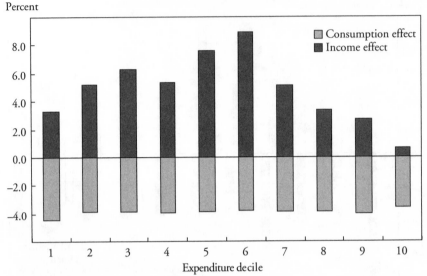

Expenditure decile

Source: Author's calculations using VLSS for 1998.
a. The consumption effect represents the change in welfare due to changes in prices of consumed goods. The income effect represents the change in income due to changes in prices of produced goods (price effect), changes in production of the household (export effect), and changes in wage income of the household (employment effect).

Table 7-6. *Vietnam: Effect of Rice in Total Change in Welfare, by Decile of per Capita Expenditure: Ambitious Scenario*
Percent

Item	Effect from rice	All other effects	Overall effect
All Vietnam	3.5	−2.4	1.1
Rural	4.8	−2.4	2.5
Urban	−1.3	−2.6	−3.9

Source: Author's calculations using VLSS for 1998.

Conclusions

The findings of this chapter suggest that implementing the Doha Development Agenda would have only a minor impact on the overall poverty rate in Vietnam, due to offsetting effects on different groups of households.[11] However, a significant redistribution of wealth would take place, from urban to rural and from net rice buyer households to net rice seller households.

11. As explained earlier, given the limitations of data and methodology, the results probably underestimate welfare gains and overestimate welfare losses.

In the short run, neither the business-as-usual nor the ambitious scenario has more than a modest effect on the welfare of the average Vietnamese household (declines of −0.2 percent and −0.6 percent in purchasing power, respectively). The long-run effects are more significant (gains of 0.9 percent and 1.1 percent, respectively) as they also take changes in export demand and employment into account.

In all cases, however, the estimated distribution of gains is highly unequal. Urban households almost always lose, while rural households—which include 90 percent of the country's poor—gain much more than the average. Full liberalization (the ambitious scenario) yields a considerable loss (3.9 percent) of real income for urban households, while rural households gain by 2.5 percent. A closer look at the distribution of gains for rural households shows that middle-income households benefit the most (by around 4.5 percent), while poor households gain the least (by 1.3 percent), and those in the poorest decile lose by 1.0 percent.

Most of the gains from multilateral liberalization would come from rice, benefiting rice producers and sellers while hurting rice buyers. For example, in the ambitious scenario over the long run, sellers increase their real income by 10 percent, while buyers lose by 4.5 percent. Nearly all (94 percent) of the urban poor are net buyers, but only 60 percent of the rural poor are net buyers. If productivity gains are also taken into account, the gains to net seller households (and to rural households) are likely to be larger, creating a more positive effect on poverty.

Implementation of the Doha Development Agenda is also expected to significantly raise demand for Vietnam's textile exports, and with it, employment in the textile industry.

References

Deaton, A. 1997. *The Analysis of Household Surveys: A Microeconometric Approach to Development Policy.* Baltimore: Johns Hopkins University Press.

Heckman, J., H. Ichimura, and P. Todd. 1998. "Matching as an Econometric Evaluation Estimator." *Review of Economic Studies* 65: 261–94.

Işık-Dikmelik, Aylin. 2006. "Trade Reforms and Welfare: An Ex Post Decomposition of Income in Vietnam." Policy Research Working Paper 4049. Washington: World Bank.

Mincer, J. 1974. *Schooling, Earnings, and Experience.* New York: Columbia University Press.

Nicita, A., M. Olarreaga, and I. Soloaga. 2001. "A Simple Methodology to Assess the Poverty Impact of Economic Policies Using Household Data." Mimeo. Washington, DC: World Bank.

Seshan, G. 2005. "The Impact of Trade Liberalization on Household Welfare in Vietnam." World Bank Policy Research Working Paper No. 3541. Washington, DC: World Bank.

Singh, I., L. Squire, and J. Strauss. 1986. *Agricultural Household Models, Extensions, Applications, and Policy.* Washington and Baltimore: World Bank and Johns Hopkins University Press.

Winters, L. A. 2002. "Trade Liberalization and Poverty: What Are the Links?" *World Economy* 25 (9): 1339–67.

World Bank. 2004. PovcalNet. http://iresearch.worldbank.org/PovcalNet/jsp/index.jsp.

———. 1999. "Vietnam Development Report 2000: Attacking Poverty." Country Economic Memorandum. Washington: World Bank.

Details on Sources of Income and Expenditures and Regression Results

Table 7A-1. *Detailed Sources of Income for Rural Households in Vietnam, by Decile of per Capita Expenditure*

Percent

Sources of income	1	2	3	4	5	6	7	8	9	10	Average
Profit from rice	6	9	9	6	10	11	9	9	8	6	8
Net own consumption rice	25	22	16	14	15	12	8	7	4	2	16
Profits from other food crops	0	6	6	6	6	6	7	7	5	3	5
Profits from cash crops	4	6	5	6	5	6	7	5	7	10	5
Net own consumption all other food	10	9	8	7	6	4	6	15	4	4	8
Net livestock income	19	12	15	18	13	15	11	13	8	6	14
Other agriculture income (by-products, rent)	4	0	1	1	2	1	1	1	1	1	1
Non-farm self-employment profit	8	9	11	13	14	18	18	22	26	24	14
Wages from agriculture	10	8	7	5	5	3	3	2	3	2	6
Wages from other	8	7	10	10	11	9	10	4	10	9	9
Remittances	2	3	3	3	3	3	5	5	8	13	3
Other income	6	8	9	11	11	12	16	10	17	20	10
Total	100	100	100	100	100	100	100	100	100	100	100

Table 7A-2. *Detailed Sources of Income for Urban Households in Vietnam, by Decile of per Capita Expenditure*

Percent

Sources of income	1	2	3	4	5	6	7	8	9	10	Average
Profit from rice	3	3	4	1	4	2	1	1	1	0	1
Net own consumption rice	2	6	4	1	3	2	2	1	0	0	1
Profits from other food crops	1	1	−9	1	1	1	1	1	1	0	1
Profits from cash crops	2	2	0	0	3	1	−1	0	0	1	1
Net own consumption all other food	5	5	2	2	3	2	1	2	1	1	2
Net livestock income	1	4	6	6	4	3	6	3	2	0	3
Other agriculture income (by-products, rent)	0	2	8	2	0	0	0	0	0	0	0
Non-farm self-employment profit	22	32	46	40	31	43	39	38	38	37	38
Wages from agriculture	4	6	1	1	2	0	1	0	1	0	1
Wages from other	43	30	29	28	29	29	29	28	30	28	29
Remittances	5	2	4	6	6	4	7	7	9	12	8
Other income	13	9	5	12	15	13	15	16	17	19	16
Total	100	100	100	100	100	100	100	100	100	100	100

Table 7A-3. *Detailed Composition of Expenditure for Rural Households in Vietnam, by Decile of per Capita Expenditure*
Percent

Consumption items	1	2	3	4	5	6	7	8	9	10	Average
Expenditure on rice	41	34	31	28	26	23	19	17	13	8	28
From own consumption	29	26	23	20	19	17	13	12	7	3	21
Expenditure on other food	31	33	35	36	38	38	38	39	38	35	35
From own consumption	11	9	8	8	8	7	7	6	5	3	8
Clothing	7	8	7	7	7	7	7	6	6	4	7
Utilities	1	1	1	2	2	2	2	2	3	2	2
Fuel and transport	5	5	5	5	5	5	5	6	6	6	5
Education and health	8	9	10	10	11	12	13	14	18	21	11
Other non-food	7	10	11	12	12	13	15	15	18	22	12
Total share	100	100	100	100	100	100	100	100	100	100	100

Table 7A-4. *Detailed Composition of Expenditure for Urban Households in Vietnam, by Decile of per Capita Expenditure*
Percent

Consumption items	1	2	3	4	5	6	7	8	9	10	Average
Expenditure on rice	32	27	25	23	21	17	15	13	10	6	14
Expenditure on rice from own consumption	5	6	6	3	4	3	3	1	1	0	2
Expenditure on other food	35	36	41	40	42	44	44	45	45	44	44
Expenditure on other food from own consumption	6	3	2	2	2	2	2	2	1	1	2
Clothing	5	6	6	6	5	6	6	5	5	5	5
Utilities	3	3	4	4	5	4	5	6	6	7	5
Fuel and transport	5	5	5	6	5	5	6	5	6	6	6
Education and health	12	10	12	11	12	11	12	15	15	16	14
Other non-food	7	13	8	11	9	12	12	12	13	16	13
Total share	100	100	100	100	100	100	100	100	100	100	100

Table 7A-5. *Propensity Score Estimation (PROBIT) for Vietnam*

Dependent variable: $F_i = 1$ if individual i is employed in formal sector

Regressors	Coefficient	Standard error
Age (years)	−0.019***	0.004
Gender dummy (male = 1)	−0.311***	0.061
Education (years)	0.228***	0.038
Education squared	−0.015***	0.002
Computer dummy (received computer training = 1)	−0.494**	0.197
Urban dummy (urban = 1)	0.476***	0.087
Region 1 dummy	0.647***	0.211
Region 2 dummy	0.233*	0.128
Region 3 dummy	0.2	0.169
Region 4 dummy	0.471***	0.149
Region 5 dummy	−0.72**	0.328
Region 6 dummy	0.793	0.127
Marital status (married = 1)	−0.291***	0.087
Constant	−1.026***	0.177
Number of regions	7	
Number of observations	3,285	
$F(13, 340)$	21.22	
Prob > F	0	

***Significant at .01 percent; **significant at .05 percent; *significant at .10 percent.

Table 7A-6. *Wage Premium Estimation for Vietnam*

Dependent variable: log of wages

Regressors	Coefficient	Standard error
Age (years)	0.057***	0.007
Age squared	−0.001***	0.000
Gender dummy (male = 1)	0.247***	0.022
Formal industry dummy (formal = 1)	0.069**	0.031
Education (years)	0.009**	0.004
Computer dummy (received computer training = 1)	0.124*	0.064
Region 2 dummy	−0.034	0.049
Region 3 dummy	−0.098	0.064
Region 4 dummy	0.174***	0.053
Region 5 dummy	0.252**	0.104
Region 6 dummy	0.43***	0.054
Region 7 dummy	0.203***	0.053
Marital status (married = 1)	−0.020	0.030
Urban dummy (urban = 1)	0.155***	0.038
Constant	3.313***	0.107
Number of observations	3,249	
R-squared	0.2038	

***Significant at .01 percent; **significant at .05 percent; *significant at .10 percent.

8

Bolivia

GABRIEL LARA AND ISIDRO SOLOAGA

Bolivia is one of the poorest countries in Latin America and suffers from widespread income inequality and unemployment. This chapter evaluates how Bolivia's households would be affected by multilateral trade reforms arising from the Doha Round. Besides the probable impacts on commodity prices and quantities, including export quantities, these reforms are likely to augment the demand for labor. Thus we evaluate the income that subsistence producers would gain by switching into wage employment in agriculture and the income that urban households would gain from an expansion of labor demand in the manufacturing sector.

We adopt the expected changes in international prices and trade volumes estimated in chapter 2 by Kee, Nicita, and Olarreaga and explore the two Doha scenarios that were introduced in that chapter. The base case scenario, referred to as business as usual, involves a 40 percent reduction in bound tariffs, with applied tariffs varying accordingly; a reduction in all tariff peaks to a maximum of 50 percent; a 40 percent reduction in support for domestic agriculture; elimination of agricultural export subsidies; and an improvement in trade facilitation. The ambitious scenario entails much deeper global trade liberalization: full elimination of tariffs and subsidies, the same improvement in trade facilitation, and a 50 percent reduction in the restrictiveness of nontariff measures.

This chapter is organized as follows. The first section provides an overview of Bolivia's consumption patterns and sources of income, poverty, agriculture, and

174

commerce, followed by a section outlining the analytical framework used for the study. The third section explains the methodology followed for each simulation and presents the results. A final section concludes.

The results show that with limited multilateral trade liberalization—the business-as-usual scenario—very little change would take place in household welfare in Bolivia. But a more ambitious freeing of international trade policies could produce an average gain of 4.5 percent in real income; households at all levels of the income distribution would benefit in this scenario, and those in the middle range would gain by more than 5 percent. Further, if the reforms stemming from the Doha Round were to raise the demand for Bolivian exports and with it the number of wage jobs in Bolivia, the gains could be greater than these first-order effects. Assuming that business-as-usual changes take place in the international trade regime, an expansion in agricultural wage employment could yield an average gain of 7 percent in household purchasing power, nationwide, because many households would switch out of subsistence production and into wage jobs. Job growth in manufacturing would produce an average welfare gain, across all households, of 2 percent.

Poverty and the Economy in Bolivia

Bolivia is a landlocked country almost in the center of South America. In 2002 its population numbered 8.5 million, 62 percent of whom lived in urban areas. The country is geographically divided into three regions: the Altiplano (plateau), between two towering Andean ranges to the west of the country, has the least fertile soils and the least rain but is home to 60 percent of Bolivia's farmers. The Valley, east of the Andes, with comparatively wet and fertile land, was the site of most of Bolivia's coca production during the 1980s; today, farmers in this region grow crops ranging from sugarcane and tropical fruits to wheat and rye. The Plain comprises the northern and eastern lowlands and supplies Bolivia's agricultural exports.

Poverty

Bolivia's per capita gross national income is $920—half as large as income in Peru and a third as large as income in Argentina, Brazil, or Chile. The recent trend in poverty rates is not clear. Government reforms such as macro stabilization and policies to encourage private investment, beginning in the later 1980s, have not outweighed the effects of the global economic slowdown and internal economic and social crises. In 2002 almost two-thirds of the population (64.3 percent) were living in poverty and just over one-third (36.6 percent) were in extreme poverty (table 8-1). While the urban poverty rate is 53.5 percent, the rural poverty rate is as high as 80 percent.

Table 8-1. *Poverty and Extreme Poverty Rates in Bolivia, Urban and Rural, 1999–2002*

Percent

Area	November 1999	November 2000	November 2001	November 2002
Poverty rate				
Bolivia	62.0	65.4	64.3	64.2
Urban	51.3	54.4	54.2	53.6
Rural	80.1	84.5	81.0	82.0
Extreme poverty rate				
Bolivia	35.8	39.1	37.2	36.6
Urban	23.6	28.0	26.1	25.4
Rural	56.8	58.7	55.6	55.0

Sources: Landa Casazola (2003) and Bolivian National Institute of Statistics (INE).

Bolivia's poor have broadly similar attributes to the poor in other countries (table 8-2).[1] Data from the 2002 household survey, *Mejoramiento de Encuestas de Condiciones de Vida* (MECOVI), of the National Institute of Statistics (INE), show that, compared with non-poor households, Bolivia's poor households have:

—Less education: on average, household heads in poor families have fewer than half as many years of schooling as non-poor household heads,

—Higher unemployment rates,

—Larger families,

—Much less access to basic services such as electricity, clean water, or sanitation,

—Less access to formal health centers,[2] and

—A greater propensity to work in agriculture.[3]

There are regional disparities as well, related to the economic activities and opportunities that the three ecological regions offer. The Altiplano has the highest concentration of poor households, followed by the Valley and the Plain.

Consumption Patterns

Distinguishing the consumption patterns of households categorized by decile of per capita household expenditure[4] reveals which parts of the population would

1. Wodon (2000).

2. Access to health care is a general problem in Bolivia. In 2002 only 44 percent of the population sought help from qualified personnel in case of sickness or accident. Most people choose self-medication or go to *curanderos*. This result is probably related to the problem of general poverty in the country. Landa Casazola (2003).

3. For a deeper study of poverty in Bolivia, see Landa Casazola (2003), Arias and Sosa Escudero (2004), or World Bank (2000).

4. Per capita refers to the members of the household. Employees who live in the household and their relatives are not taken into account. We use per capita terms instead of adult equivalency to avoid further discussion of the validity of the potential equivalencies selected (see Székely and others 2000).

Table 8-2. *Characteristics of Poor and Non-Poor Households in Bolivia*[a]

Characteristic	Poor	Non-poor
Household size	5.56	3.90
Consumption per capita (2002 Bolivianos a month)	97.49	584.29
Household head's years of schooling	4.20	7.92
Access to electricity (percent)	34	72

Source: Authors' calculations, based on MECOVI for 2002.

a. A household is considered poor if it is below the poverty line.

feel the greatest impact of the economic shocks to be studied. As expected, food takes a large share of household spending in the poorer deciles: among the poorer 60 percent of the population, its share is greater than 60 percent (table 8-3). The share of food declines as household income rises, and for the richest decile it is only 33 percent—less than half that for the first decile. Among the most important food items for poor Bolivian households are cereals, potatoes, and meat; potatoes are important mainly for the poorest two deciles. Looking at non-food expenditure, we find that housing, fuel, and communications dominate, accounting for 22 percent of an average household's total spending. Education comes next in importance, representing just over 6 percent of spending by the average household.

As expected, consumption patterns differ between urban and rural areas. Food takes a smaller share of spending for urban households than for rural, across all deciles (figure 8-1). For rural households, food takes more than 60 percent of spending until the eighth decile, unlike for urban households, where only the first three deciles spend such a high proportion on food. Although the share of food drops in both rural and urban areas as income rises, the drop is sharper in urban areas, where the richest decile's food share is about half that of the poorest.

Sources of Income

Bolivia's labor force is concentrated in the primary sector (figure 8-2), and about 38 percent of household heads work in agriculture. Next in importance are manufacturing and commerce, each with around 13 percent of the labor force.

As expected, employment patterns differ between urban and rural areas. The most important urban activities are manufacturing and commerce, each one providing almost one in five urban jobs. Other important activities are construction (12 percent) and transport and communications (11 percent). In rural areas, agriculture absorbs more than 80 percent of the labor force, and all other activities have shares smaller than 4 percent.

Self-employment supplies 42 percent of total income for the average Bolivian household and more than 45 percent for households in the poorest four deciles

Table 8-3. *Composition of Household Expenditure in Bolivia, by Decile of per Capita Expenditure*
Percent

Consumption item	1	2	3	4	5	6	7	8	9	10	Average
Food total	69.5	70.4	66.2	64.3	62	60.2	55.8	50.9	45.7	33.2	57.8
* Rice	4.4	4.6	4.7	3.7	3.1	2.8	2.1	2.1	1.2	0.7	2.9
* Bread and cereals	12.1	12.4	11.7	11.1	9.6	8.6	7.4	5.4	4.5	2.6	8.5
* Poultry	1.1	2.1	2.9	3.0	3.1	3.7	3.5	3.1	2.6	1.7	2.7
* Meat (except poultry)	5.9	7.8	8.6	8.9	9.1	9.2	8.7	7.9	6.9	4.5	7.7
* Dairy products	1.8	2.6	3.2	2.8	3.7	3.8	3.6	3.9	3.7	3.0	3.2
* Fresh vegetables	4.9	6.0	5.9	6.0	5.7	5.0	4.5	4.1	3.2	2.0	4.7
* Potatoes and chuño	12.4	7.4	4.6	4.2	3.4	2.8	2.6	1.6	1.3	0.6	4.1
* Other consumption items	27.0	27.4	24.5	24.7	24.2	24.4	23.5	22.8	22.3	18	23.9
Non-food total	30.5	29.6	33.8	35.7	38.0	39.8	44.2	49.1	54.3	66.8	42.2
* Housing, fuel, and communications[a]	11.5	14.7	17.0	18.4	19.9	21.8	23.3	27.6	30.3	35.4	22.0
* Education	5.9	4.7	4.8	4.9	6.0	6.5	7.4	7.3	8.0	9.1	6.5
* Clothing and foot wear	2.9	2.4	2.4	2.2	2.4	2.5	2.6	2.4	2.6	2.3	2.5
* Other expenditures[b]	10.1	7.9	9.7	10.3	9.7	9.0	10.9	11.9	13.5	20.0	11.3

Source: Authors' calculations, based on MECOVI for 2002.
a. Includes house rent (or rental value of owner-occupied housing), house maintenance, transport, fuel, and communications.
b. Includes furniture and household equipment, health, personal effects, and transfers.

Figure 8-1. *Share of Food in Urban and Rural Household Expenditure in Bolivia, by Decile of per Capita Expenditure in Rural and Urban Areas*
Percent

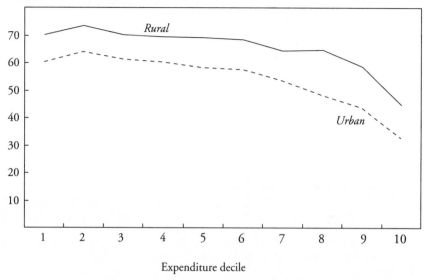

Expenditure decile

Source: Authors' calculations, based on MECOVI for 2002.

(table 8-4). The composition of self-employment income differs across deciles: farming activities and own-consumption income (from subsistence agriculture and some small businesses) are more important for the poorest households than for richer ones.

Agriculture supplies 66 percent of income for households in the poorest decile, and 42 percent for households in the next poorest, compared with less than 5 percent for the richest households.

Another difference between rich and poor comes from the share of wages in household income: wages supply only 4 percent of total income for households in the poorest decile and more than 40 percent for those in the richest decile. Wages are more important for urban than for rural households in all deciles, although the rural-urban gap diminishes as income rises (figure 8-3).

Agriculture

Agriculture has long been an important economic activity in Bolivia.[5] Most households undertake some agricultural activities, especially home production of food crops for their own consumption.[6] In the 1970s, more than half the labor force was working in agriculture, but by the end of the 1980s this share

5. We do not consider the production of coca leaves.
6. About 45 percent of the population produces at least partly for its own consumption, and 15 percent derive a third or more of their income from home production.

Figure 8-2. *Employment of Rural and Urban Household Heads in Bolivia, by Sector*

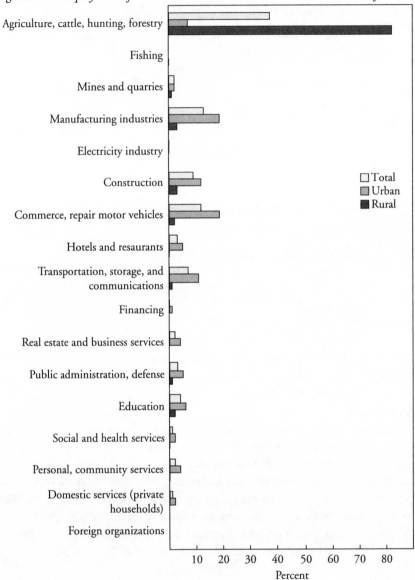

Table 8-4. *Sources of Household Income in Bolivia, by Decile of per Capita Expenditure*

Percent

Sources of income	Decile										Average
	1	2	3	4	5	6	7	8	9	10	
Self-employment	73.7	61.6	49.3	45.7	40.9	37.8	36.5	28.4	29.3	23.8	42.7
From farming activities[a]	22.5	18.5	16.4	10.8	10.1	6.7	7.1	3.5	2.7	3.6	10.2
Own consumption[b]	44.0	23.3	14.7	9.7	7.0	5.6	4.8	3.5	2.8	1.3	11.7
From non-farming activities	7.2	19.8	18.2	25.2	23.8	25.5	24.6	21.4	23.8	18.9	20.8
Other sources:	26.4	38.4	50.8	54.3	59.1	62.2	63.5	71.6	70.6	76.3	57.3
From wages	4.0	16.8	25.8	32.0	34.4	38.9	37.6	45.3	38.5	40.5	31.4
From remittances	2.4	5.1	6.6	5.7	6.8	5.3	5.9	6.0	6.6	7.0	5.7
Other kinds of income[c]	20.0	16.5	18.4	16.6	17.9	18.0	20.0	20.3	25.5	28.8	20.2
Total	100	100	100	100	100	100	100	100	100	100	100

Source: Authors' calculations, based on MECOVI for 2002.

a. Income from sales (production costs already subtracted).

b. Goods taken from own production (may contain some products from small businesses other than agriculture).

c. Income from all other sources (rental, interests, dividends, and gifts).

Figure 8-3. *Share of Wages in Total Income in Bolivia, by Decile of per Capita Expenditure in Rural and Urban Areas*
Percent

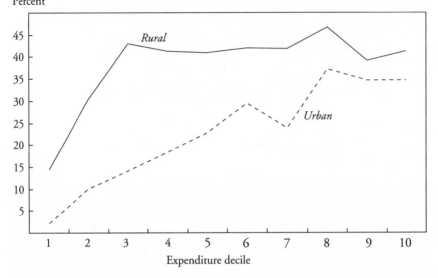

Source: Authors' calculations using 2002 MECOVI.

had dropped to 47 percent. Since the later 1990s, it has been steady at 44 percent. Agriculture's share of GDP has remained constant, too, at roughly 13 percent in the past five years.

Of Bolivia's area of 108.5 million hectares, only 2.9 million hectares are arable, and only 4.5 percent of that is irrigated. Fertilizer use varied widely in the last decade, but in the last few years it has risen steadily, reaching 5 kilograms of nutrients per hectare in 2002.[7] Bolivia's main cash crops are soybeans and Brazil nuts, and the most important food crop is potatoes, followed by maize and wheat. Cropping patterns and land productivity vary by region. Farmers in the Altiplano confine themselves to food crops: with small plots and an adverse climate, practically all their production is for subsistence. The country's most productive farmers, who produce cash crops, are located in the Plain and own larger farms.

Poverty and agriculture are closely related. A significant proportion of Bolivian farmers face several problems that undermine their ability to overcome poverty. Poor roads, and therefore poor access to markets, are one of the most difficult. Farmers in the Altiplano and the Valley rely on truckers to get their products to the cities. Lack of appropriate agricultural research and low levels of

7. This level is still far below that of other countries in the region, such as Peru or Colombia, that grow similar crops, and it is only a tenth of that of Paraguay, a neighboring country with a similar income level.

farming technology seriously hinder agricultural development. In addition, poor infrastructure makes farmers prone to yearly floods or droughts. Farming families in the Altiplano and Valley are among the worst-positioned groups in the country. Thus it is important to assess what kind of economic reforms could improve their welfare.

Manufacturing and Services

In 2002 manufacturing accounted for 13 percent of Bolivia's GDP and employed 11 percent of the labor force. Over the past five years, these shares remained quite stable, but they represent a high rate of job creation: about 10,000 people entered the manufacturing sector every year, equivalent to a growth rate of about 4.7 percent a year in manufacturing employment.[8]

Bolivia's main industries, ranked by their contribution to GDP, are food products, oil-refining products, beverages and tobacco, and textiles. In terms of the number of people employed, textiles are the most important.[9] The textile industry has increased its share of people employed in the last decade despite the crises that have affected it since 1997. Projections for the next two years by the National Institute of Statistics and the U.S. Embassy show investment opportunities for manufacturing in Bolivia, mainly because of the country's receptivity to U.S. brands and its trading status with South American markets.[10] This argument supports our decision to simulate the expansion of the manufacturing sector.

The services sector employed around 55 percent of Bolivia's labor force in 2002. Between 1992 and 2001, employment in the sector grew by 4.3 percent annually, led by commerce (growing at 10.1 percent) and hotels and restaurants (growing at 19.7 percent).

Trade

In 2002 Bolivia's exports were worth around $1.3 billion, and imports were around $1.7 billion. Minerals (zinc, silver, tin, and gold) are the largest source of export earnings, followed by soybeans, natural gas, and wood. Imports include mainly capital goods, raw materials and semimanufactures, chemicals, and petroleum; major agricultural imports are soybeans, wheat, and wheat flour.

For almost two decades, Bolivia has maintained a relatively open trade regime, with few restrictions on imports and no subsidies on exports. Tariffs are low, at 10 percent. Exceptions are capital equipment, with a 5 percent tariff, and books and publications, with a 2 percent tariff. In a 1999 review of Bolivia's trade policies, the World Trade Organization highlighted the benefits of the

8. Andersen, Osvaldo, and te Velde (2004).
9. Andersen, Osvaldo, and te Velde (2004).
10. Gottret (2004).

country's unique tariff regime in terms of its predictability, transparency, and promotion of an efficient allocation of resources.[11]

Implications of the Doha Development Agenda for Bolivia

Within our analytical framework, the implications of the Doha Development Agenda for Bolivia's economy, and particularly for the poor, depend on three factors:

—Impact on prices of goods produced and consumed by the poor,

—Impact on world demand for Bolivian products produced and sold by the poor, and

—Impact on employment levels, linked directly to poor people.

Within a partial equilibrium setting, we simulate changes in the price and quantity of commodities and the increase in labor demand derived from the expansion of agricultural and textile exports.

Changes in Prices and Quantities

Using the probable changes in prices and quantities estimated by Kee, Nicita, and Olarreaga in chapter 2, we investigate both the business-as-usual and the ambitious Doha scenarios.

Table 8-5 shows the expected changes in prices and quantities (weighted by Bolivia's total trade in each product) for the main products and product groups of importance in Bolivia. The changes were estimated using the shares of these products in Bolivia's total household spending or income (see table 8-5).

Looking first at prices, in the business-as-usual scenario, changes of 2 percent or more would take place for fresh vegetables (5.4 percent), cereals other than rice or corn (2.9 percent), and sugar (2 percent). The ambitious scenario would produce greater—and negative—price changes, mainly because of the elimination of Bolivian tariffs and the reduction in nontariff barriers. Of importance for Bolivian households, the ambitious scenario would entail a reduction in the prices of potatoes (−12.6 percent), clothing and footwear (−6.6 percent), and cereals other than rice or corn (−5.1 percent).

As for quantities, Bolivia's total exports would increase by between 3.2 percent under business as usual and 23.4 percent in the ambitious scenario.

---

11. Bojanic (2001). Bolivia has actively negotiated trade agreements with its neighboring countries, and this policy could be behind its growing trade with these countries. Bolivia belongs to the Andean Community and enjoys nominally free trade with Colombia, Ecuador, Peru, and Venezuela. Bolivia began to implement an association agreement with Mercosur in March 1997 and has signed agreements with Mexico (free trade), Chile (preferential), and the United States. The Andean Trade Preference and Drug Enforcement Act signed with the United States allows numerous Bolivian products (such as alpaca and llama products) to enter the United States free of duty on a unilateral basis. Cotton textiles are part of this agreement, too, but are subject to a quota.

Table 8-5. *Changes in International Prices and Exports in Bolivia: Business-as-Usual and Ambitious Scenarios*

Product or product group	Share in expenditures	Share in income	Current exports (thousands of U.S. dollars)	International price change[a] Business as usual	International price change[a] Ambitious Doha[b]	Export changes (thousands of U.S. dollars) Business as usual Absolute	Business as usual in %	Ambitious Doha Absolute	Ambitious Doha in %
Clothing and footwear	2.5	—	34,177	1.1	−6.6	3,817	11.2	23,491	68.7
Dairy	3.2	1.3	8,450	1.1	−2.4	1,190	14.1	15,717	186.0
Fresh vegetables	4.7	0.7	128	5.4	−1.0	13	9.8	142	110.4
Meat	7.7	3.0	987	1.2	−1.9	104	10.5	3,127	316.9
Other cereal	8.5	1.7	6,881	2.9	−5.1	413	6.0	1,324	19.2
Potatoes	4.1	2.1	186	−1.2	−12.6	−2	−0.9	−31	−16.7
Rice	2.9	0.8	1	0.1	−8.5	1	65.3	5	380.7
Sugar	2.0	0.3	16,229	2.0	0.4	707	4.4	36,212	223.1
All goods	—	—	1,475,269	0.6	−6.1	47,789	3.2	344,539	23.4
Employment						50,000			

Source: Authors' calculations, based on MECOVI for 2002.
a. Changes in prices from Kee, Nicita, and Olarreaga (chapter 2 of this volume), weighted by Bolivia's total trade.
b. In the ambitious scenario, the change in domestic prices reflects Bolivia's removal of all its remaining import tariffs.

Exports would increase even though some domestic prices would decline, because exports are assumed to be driven by changes in world prices rather than domestic prices. Among the changes in export levels under the business-as-usual scenario, those with the greatest impact on households would come from increases in exports of clothing and footwear as well as sugar. In the ambitious scenario, by contrast, the biggest impacts would come from greater exports in the meat and dairy industries.

Simulation Results

To assess the effects of changes in commodity prices and quantities on household welfare, we calculate the shares of specific commodities in household income and expenditure using a farm household model.[12] These shares are then used to trace how changes in prices and quantities of commodities would affect the welfare of households at different levels of wealth.

A large proportion of Bolivia's households own farms. How they are affected by price changes depends on their status as net buyers or net sellers of particular commodities. Since net seller households are affected by changes in the level of exports, we also evaluate the impact of simultaneous changes in prices and export levels for several commodities. Household income is defined as the sum of own production (including non-farm self-employment), wage employment, and transfers (pensions, remittances, government transfers). Households in different deciles have different sources of income and different patterns of expenditure. Total net household income is defined as total income minus total expenditure. Changes in welfare are defined as percentage changes in households' original per capita expenditure.

We first examine the direct effects on household welfare of the changes in prices and quantities associated with the two scenarios. However, besides its effects on prices and quantities, implementation of the Doha agenda is also expected to affect households through the expansion of labor markets. Thus later in this section we also simulate this "second-round" effect—first evaluating the expected income gain that subsistence farmers would achieve by switching from subsistence production to wage jobs in agriculture and then evaluating the impact on household welfare of an expansion of the manufacturing sector.

Changes in Prices and Quantities from Implementation of the Doha Development Agenda

By estimating the share of net income that households spend on particular goods or groups of goods, we can assess the impact of percentage changes in the prices and quantities of these goods on household welfare. The net income

12. Singh, Squire, and Strauss (1986).

shares, and whether a household is a net buyer or a net seller of the goods in question,[13] will determine whether positive or negative changes in prices will be beneficial or prejudicial for a specific household. Regarding the effects of changes in quantities (coming from changes in export levels), we assume that households meet the increased demand for Bolivian products by raising their production and increasing their market participation. Thus supply responses are only correlated with marketed quantities, and the increase in exports will only affect net sellers.

Our estimates constitute lower bounds (for gains) and upper bounds (for losses) on the probable effects of the Doha-related reforms on households. There are two main reasons for this. First, we exclude from the estimation possible changes in the behavior of the economic actors (farmers and consumers).[14] Second, we allocate the full extent of the increase in exports to households. This means that the increase in supply is assumed to be produced at zero costs or by a better allocation of assets.[15] Despite these somewhat optimistic assumptions, the analysis gives a useful general idea of what could be expected from implementation of the Doha agenda.

Results for the business-as-usual and ambitious scenarios are shown in table 8-6.

Business-as-Usual Scenario. In the business-as-usual scenario, shown in the first and third panels of table 8-6, the Doha reforms would not significantly affect household welfare, producing an average gain equivalent to 0.02 percent of household expenditure. The first panel of the table shows the results of the changes in prices alone. The impact of the price changes would be less than 1 percent on average and be broadly similar for all income deciles. As can be expected for a country where food takes more than half of household spending for 80 percent of the population, most of the impact would come from changes in food prices. The third panel of table 8-6 shows the results, including changes in quantities. Impacts on household welfare would still be smaller than 1 percent, but the difference now is that they would be positive for practically half of the population. The poorest three deciles would fare better than the rest. The results are driven by the large expected increase in exports of the majority of products and by the fact that households in poorer deciles are net sellers of several of these products. Prices of commodities

13. A positive sign on net income defines a household as a net seller; a negative sign defines it as a net buyer.

14. For example, in reality, a rise in prices will encourage a farmer to increase the production of a particular good, furthering his gains from the price change. This change in behavior could be assessed by including price elasticities of supply in the calculations.

15. This assumption is based on the fact that Bolivia's agriculture has been identified as having low productivity, with scope for improvements (USAID 2005). Lacking reliable estimates of the links between tariffs and prices, we assume perfect pass-through in our scenarios.

Table 8-6. *Effects on Household Welfare in Bolivia, by Source of Impact and Decile of per Capita Expenditure: Business-as-Usual and Ambitious Scenarios*

Percent

Item	Deciles										Average
	1	2	3	4	5	6	7	8	9	10	
International price changes: Business-as-usual simulation											
Total impact on household	-0.43	-0.70	-0.77	-0.77	-0.80	-0.75	-0.68	-0.73	-0.65	-0.43	-0.67
Total impact from food products	-0.40	-0.65	-0.72	-0.72	-0.75	-0.71	-0.64	-0.69	-0.61	-0.40	-0.63
From income	0.29	0.12	0.09	0.17	0.15	0.09	0.14	0.04	0.01	0.02	0.11
From consumption	-0.68	-0.78	-0.81	-0.89	-0.90	-0.80	-0.77	-0.73	-0.62	-0.41	-0.74
Total impact from non-food products	-0.03	-0.04	-0.05	-0.05	-0.05	-0.05	-0.04	-0.04	-0.04	-0.04	-0.04
From income	0.00	0.00	0.00	0.00	0.00	0.00	0.00	0.00	0.00	0.00	0.00
From consumption	-0.03	-0.04	-0.05	-0.05	-0.05	-0.05	-0.04	-0.04	-0.04	-0.04	-0.04
International price changes: Ambitious Doha scenario											
Total impact on household	-0.59	-0.16	1.08	1.96	1.73	2.18	1.97	1.06	1.55	1.38	1.22
Total impact from food products	-0.99	-0.60	0.62	1.48	1.27	1.71	1.54	0.64	1.15	1.05	0.79
From income	-2.94	-2.76	-1.74	-1.04	-1.13	-0.52	-0.64	-1.33	-0.65	-0.07	-1.28
From consumption	1.95	2.16	2.35	2.52	2.39	2.22	2.18	1.98	1.80	1.11	2.07
Total impact from non-food products	0.40	0.44	0.47	0.48	0.46	0.47	0.43	0.42	0.40	0.34	0.43
From income	0.00	0.00	0.00	0.00	0.00	0.00	0.00	0.00	0.00	0.00	0.00
From consumption	0.40	0.44	0.47	0.48	0.46	0.47	0.43	0.42	0.40	0.34	0.43

International price and quantity changes: Business-as-usual simulation

Total impact on household	0.43	0.49	0.78	−0.05	0.05	−0.32	−0.03	−0.28	−0.60	−0.30	0.02
Total impact from food products	0.46	0.54	0.83	0.00	0.09	−0.27	0.01	−0.24	−0.56	−0.27	0.06
From income	1.30	1.41	1.69	0.94	1.04	0.55	0.80	0.51	0.06	0.15	0.85
From consumption	−0.83	−0.88	−0.86	−0.94	−0.95	−0.83	−0.79	−0.75	−0.62	−0.42	−0.79
Total impact from non-food products	−0.03	−0.04	−0.05	−0.05	−0.05	−0.05	−0.04	−0.04	−0.04	−0.04	−0.04
From income	0.00	0.00	0.00	0.00	0.00	0.00	0.00	0.00	0.00	0.00	0.00
From consumption	−0.03	−0.04	−0.05	−0.05	−0.05	−0.05	−0.04	−0.04	−0.04	−0.04	−0.04

International price and quantity changes: Ambitious Doha scenario

Total impact on household	2.89	4.13	9.16	6.26	6.02	4.87	6.33	2.18	1.11	2.62	4.56
Total impact from food products	2.50	3.69	8.70	5.79	5.56	4.40	5.90	1.77	0.71	2.29	4.13
From income	1.40	2.10	6.54	3.52	3.43	2.37	3.83	−0.13	−1.03	1.21	2.32
From consumption	1.10	1.59	2.16	2.27	2.13	2.03	2.07	1.89	1.74	1.08	1.81
Total impact from non-food products	0.40	0.44	0.47	0.48	0.46	0.47	0.43	0.42	0.40	0.34	0.43
From income	0.00	0.00	0.00	0.00	0.00	0.00	0.00	0.00	0.00	0.00	0.00
From consumption	0.40	0.44	0.47	0.48	0.46	0.47	0.43	0.42	0.40	0.34	0.43

Source: Authors' calculations with MECOVI 2002 Bolivian Survey.

Note: Quantity changes refer to a change in the level of exports of the country.

would rise almost across the board, and this is the reason for the negative impacts from consumption estimated for all deciles. Although the rise in prices benefits households that are net sellers, the net impact would remain negative. When changes in quantities are taken into account, their impact on welfare—a rise in income due to higher exports—would more than offset the negative effect of the rise in prices.

Ambitious Scenario. The ambitious scenario, shown in the second and fourth panels of table 8-6, would yield a relatively large positive impact, adding 4.56 percent to average household purchasing power. The impact of changes in prices alone would be 1.22 percent on average, and only the poorest 20 percent of households would experience a negative effect. This result is driven by sharp drops in the prices of products of which households in the poorest deciles are net sellers: legumes (−38 percent), potatoes (−13 percent), and jams (−13 percent). When quantities are simulated as well (panel 3), the larger welfare gains again would come from food products. In this exercise, the gains for some deciles would be bigger than 5 percent.

As noted, our model does not include any restrictions on the amounts that farmers could produce. Hence these results should be interpreted as an upper bound of the possible effects of the implementation of Doha reforms.

Impact on Employment in Agriculture

If the Doha Development Agenda were implemented, Bolivia's main agricultural exports would likely expand (table 8-7).[16] With this expansion, demand would rise for labor in agriculture.[17] In this simulation, we estimate the expected change in real income for people who switch from subsistence production to wage jobs in agriculture. The methodology used follows Balat and Porto.[18]

We estimate a probit model of participation in the agricultural labor market. To define the dependent variable, we include only those households that derive at least one-third of their total income from each activity: agricultural wage work or home production. Independent variables include characteristics of the household head, family size and structure, and regional dummies, among others. Using matching methods with the resulting propensity scores, subsistence farmers are matched with agricultural employed workers. A test of the balancing property suggests that returns to agricultural wage labor and subsistence are independent of labor market participation and thus that households in subsistence agriculture

16. We report results from the business-as-usual simulation. The ambitious simulation suggests greater changes: tobacco, 168 percent; dairy products, 186 percent; fruits, 6 percent; sugar, 223 percent; clothing, 69 percent; and soybean oil, 52 percent (see chapter 2).

17. This effect would be direct and indirect. For example, when exports of dairy products rise, demand for inputs like animal feed would rise as well.

18. Balat and Porto (2005).

Table 8-7. *Expected Changes in Exports in Bolivia: Business-as-Usual*
Percent

Product	Change in percent
Tobacco	29.3
Dairy products	14.0
Fruits	3.9
Sugar	4.3
Clothing	11.1
Soybeans	7.8
Cake of soybean	2.2
Oil of soybean	2.6
Brazil nuts	2.1

Source: Kee, Nicita, and Olarreaga (chapter 2 of this volume).

and those that work for a wage are comparable. The income differential between subsistence farmers and wage workers is estimated with kernel methods. The estimation is based on the difference between the average monthly wages of workers employed in agriculture and the value of home produce consumed per household member working in subsistence agriculture.[19]

The results are presented in tables 8-8 and 8-9. The first of these tables shows the results of the probit estimation of participation in the agricultural labor market. From this estimation we calculate the propensity scores for all subsistence farmers and agricultural wage workers. After testing that the balancing property is satisfied, we estimate the income differential using kernel methods.

The estimated gain in household welfare from a switch to agricultural wage employment is $b477 per month (about $64). Using bootstrap standard errors, we find that this impact is statistically significant. This is an important result in terms of poverty alleviation: on average, the gains that farmers would achieve by switching to wage work in agriculture represent more than 68 percent of their current household spending.

If Bolivia's exports were to expand sufficiently, most or all of the households that derive most of their income from home production would switch to wage employment (provided the expected gains are in fact significant). We assess the impact that such an expansion would have on the welfare of households in different expenditure deciles.[20]

19. Provided we focus on the differential, the estimation refers to the "constrained" model in Balat and Porto (2005)—that is, the person switching into the labor market loses his or her income from home production.

20. Specifically, we impute the expected gains to the households that were included in the probit estimation as nontreated.

Table 8-8. *Probit Estimates for Bolivia: Selection into Wage Employment in Agriculture*[a]

Variable	Estimate	Standard error
Constant	−0.375	(0.033)
Married	−0.368	(0.006)
Male	−0.247	(0.012)
Age	−0.022	(0.001)
Age sq.	0.000	(0.000)
Elementary completed	0.349	(0.024)
Household head		
Males	0.274	(0.015)
Age 8–12	−0.543	(0.028)
Age 13–18	−0.183	(0.024)
Age 19–45	0.606	(0.021)
Age 46+	0.113	(0.020)
Ill	−0.386	(0.011)
Transport	−0.947	(0.008)
Rental	−0.281	(0.024)
Number of observations	892	
Treated	303	
Nontreated	589	
Pseudo *R*-squared	0.369	

Source: Authors' calculations, based on MECOVI for 2002.

a. Probit estimates of the probability of working for a wage in agriculture. Regression includes regional dummies not shown. Standard errors are in parentheses. Married, male, age, and education dummies refer to the household head. Household males and ages variables refer to the share of males and people in each age group in the household. Transport and rental are dummies indicating whether the producer paid for transport of products or rental of land. The numbers of treated and nontreated observations are the ones included in the matching method.

The results are shown in table 8-10. The expected gains would be greater than 10 percent for the first three deciles and greater than 5 percent for the fourth and fifth; they would keep decreasing to a level just over 1 percent for the richest decile. These results—large gains for poorer deciles and small gains for richer ones—are expected and relate directly to the proportion of households for which we imputed the impact in each consumption decile. The proportion of households with expected gains—that is, households with home production as their main source of income that would switch to wage labor—would drop as income rises:[21] in the first decile, this share would be 25 percent, whereas in the tenth decile, it would be only 1.1 percent.

Impact on Employment in Manufacturing

Although we do not have a model that relates export outcomes to labor demand, the expansion in manufacturing, including the clothing and footwear

21. See also the structure of income across deciles in table 8-4.

Table 8-9. *Differential Income from Agricultural Wage Employment in Bolivia*[a]

	ATT	Percemt of expenditure
Differential	476.8	68.5
	(98.2)	

Source: Authors' calculations, based on MECOVI for 2002.

a. Results of the propensity score matching of subsistence farmers with wage employees in agriculture. The average effect of treatment on the treated (ATT) is expressed in monthly 2002 bolivianos. Standard error (in parentheses) was calculated using bootstrap methods.

Table 8-10. *Welfare Gain of Households That Switch from Subsistence Production to Agricultural Wage Employment in Bolivia*
Percent of per capita household expenditure

Decile	All households	Urban	Rural
1	18.0	0.0	20.7
2	14.3	0.0	19.2
3	10.8	0.8	18.0
4	7.7	0.2	16.6
5	5.3	0.0	12.7
6	4.3	0.3	12.3
7	2.7	0.2	8.6
8	2.0	0.4	10.2
9	1.2	0.3	6.6
10	1.1	0.2	17.0

Source: Authors' calculations, based on MECOVI for 2002.

industry, is expected to raise labor demand by roughly 50,000 employees in the business-as-usual scenario. This increment represents 15 percent of the current labor force in manufacturing; the sector would take five years to absorb this number of workers at its current rate of absorption. In this section, we assess which households are expected to benefit from a Doha-related expansion in manufacturing and by how much.

First, we estimate a Mincer equation for those individuals working for a wage in manufacturing.[22] Second, we use a probit equation to calculate the probability of working for a wage in manufacturing, among all the persons working for a wage. These workers are then ranked in descending order according to their propensity score calculated with the probit. When the manufacturing sector expands its labor demand by 50,000 workers, the person working for a wage (outside manufacturing) with the highest propensity score is considered. The

22. The Mincerian wage equation is a popular model showing how an individual's characteristics affect his or her wage (Mincer 1974).

Mincer equation is used to assess whether or not a worker would earn more than his or her current wage by switching into the manufacturing sector. If the wage premium in manufacturing is positive and bigger than $1 a day, the worker is considered a "switcher." If not, the person is kept in his or her actual income level, and the person with the next highest propensity score is considered. For the switchers, the simulation imputes his or her new wage. This procedure is followed until 50,000 switchers are found.

Table 8-11 shows the potential switchers (that is, workers who would earn higher wages by moving into manufacturing jobs). Out of a labor force in the primary sector of 129,000, about 76,000 would earn a higher wage by moving into manufacturing. And out of a labor force of 832,000 in the services sector, about 500,000 would earn a higher wage by moving into manufacturing.

Table 8-12 shows that, if the demand for labor in manufacturing were to rise by 50,000 workers as a consequence of increased exports, the average Bolivian household would augment its total income by 1.6 percent. The gain would be greater in urban areas (2.7 percent). And for those households with at least one member switching into a manufacturing job, the gains would be considerably bigger (second panel of table 8-12).

Conclusions

This chapter has simulated the impact on Bolivia of a successful implementation of the Doha Development Agenda. Our results, summarized in table 8-13, show that the indirect impact of trade liberalization—whereby an increase in exports raises the demand for labor—is likely to be greater than the direct impact on prices and quantities.

Under the business-as-usual scenario, the almost general rise in prices yields small and negative effects on household income. When changes in quantities are simulated too, the overall effect would be small and positive. The reforms would have a positive redistributive effect, with the poorest deciles benefiting from the expansion in exports and from their status as net sellers of several exported products. By contrast, the ambitious scenario would produce an average gain equivalent to 4.5 percent of household spending. Households in all deciles would gain, and those in the middle of the income distribution would benefit by 5 percent or more.

More significant gains can be expected if an increase in exports were to raise the demand for labor. In the industrial sector, the estimated increase of 50,000 employees in manufacturing would lead to an average gain in household real income of 2 percent that benefits the three richest deciles the least (by less than 1 percent). Meanwhile, an expansion in the agricultural sector could yield an average gain of 7 percent in household real income, a larger gain than the one in the ambitious scenario of changes in prices and quantities. Subsistence farmers

Table 8-11. *Number of Workers Likely to Switch Jobs in Bolivia if Demand for Labor Rises in Manufacturing, by Decile of per Capita Expenditure*

Item	Decile										Total
	1	2	3	4	5	6	7	8	9	10	
From primary sector											
Number of workers likely to switch jobs	5,277	8,366	9,269	11,467	10,082	4,533	7,077	9,921	6,696	3,280	75,968
Percentage of the above that are women	22.0	11.8	23.4	10.5	19.6	5.8	14.7	6.8	24.4	0.0	14.6
Current wage earned in the sector (bolivianòs per day, average)	16.1	22.8	20.1	21.8	22.0	20.9	26.6	19.6	34.5	29.6	22.88
Expected wage to be earned in the manufacture industry (bolivianòs per day, average)	27.4	33.7	30.6	34.1	39.0	35.4	39.9	31.9	51.1	38.0	35.76
Difference (expected – current)	11.3	10.9	10.5	12.2	17.0	14.5	13.3	12.3	16.7	8.4	12.9
Difference, as percent of current wage	70.59	47.93	52.32	56.05	77.17	69.51	49.85	62.53	48.41	28.36	56.29
From services sector											
Number of workers likely to switch jobs	8,723	17,498	32,587	32,820	38,100	57,087	62,740	73,843	92401	86,303	502,102
Percentage of the above that are women	34.4	43.5	28.4	35.0	34.8	33.3	36.1	38.2	40.7	52.1	39.2
Current wage earned in the sector (bolivianòs per day, average)	17.6	19.4	21.5	21.5	26.3	27.9	29.8	37.5	48.1	66.0	38.32
Expected wage to be earned in the manufacture industry (bolivianòs per day, average)	31.0	32.8	35.4	33.8	42.5	46.3	49.3	71.6	79.8	107.1	64.4
Difference (expected – current)	13.4	13.4	13.9	12.3	16.3	18.4	19.5	34.0	31.7	41.1	26.08
Difference, as percent of current wage	75.9	69.2	64.8	56.9	61.9	65.8	65.4	90.7	65.9	62.2	68.1

Source: Authors' calculations, based on MECOVI for 2002.

Table 8-12. *Effects on Household Welfare in Bolivia, by Decile of per Capita Expenditure: Increase of 50,000 Jobs in Manufacturing*[a]

Percent

					Decile						
Item	1	2	3	4	5	6	7	8	9	10	Average
Estimated impacts of all households											
Total	1.20	1.88	2.79	1.79	3.2	1.94	2.2	0.9	0.32	0.09	1.63
Urban	3.46	4.58	5.61	2.91	4.78	1.88	2.77	0.8	0.3	0.09	2.72
Rural[b]	1.04	1.02	1.1	0.57	0.9	2.06	0.21	1.29	0.48	0	0.96
Estimated impacts for households that have at least one member switching to the industry sector											
Total	48.3	63.6	86.6	61.7	84.1	50	55	45.8	21.5	48.3	56.49
Urban	31.4	68.8	97.7	59.8	95.9	47	57.2	43.7	19.6	48.3	56.94
Rural[b]	55.3	57.5	64.3	73.7	43	57.5	20.6	51.7	35.3	0	50.99

Source: Authors' calculations, based on MECOVI for 2002.

a. Impacts calculated on an increase of 50,000 new employees in the industrial sector.

b. Does not take into account the tenth decile because this contains no people switching jobs.

Table 8-13. *Summary of Results of Different Simulations for Bolivia*

| Decile | Price and quantity changes | | Labor demand in sectors | |
	Business as usual	Ambitious Doha	Manufacture	Agricultural
1	0.43	2.89	1.2	18.0
2	0.49	4.13	1.88	14.3
3	0.78	9.16	2.79	10.8
4	−0.05	6.26	1.79	7.7
5	0.05	6.02	3.2	5.3
6	−0.32	4.87	1.94	4.3
7	−0.03	6.33	2.2	2.7
8	−0.28	2.18	0.9	2.0
9	−0.60	1.11	0.32	1.2
10	−0.30	2.62	0.09	1.1

Source: Authors' calculations based on MECOVI for 2002.

who switch to agricultural wage employment would capture gains equivalent to about 68 percent of their total household expenditure, on average. Strengthening Bolivia's agriculture is thus a particularly important strategy for poverty reduction and is feasible in view of the increasing share of nontraditional products such as soybeans and Brazil nuts in the country's exports. Implementation of the Doha Development Agenda would further increase these exports, expanding the labor market in agriculture with corresponding positive effects on household income.

The results of this study make clear that Bolivia will reap the most benefit from the Doha Round if an increase in exports leads to an expansion of employment. In the most likely scenario—business as usual—changes in prices and quantities per se are expected to have only minor effects on Bolivian household welfare.

References

Andersen, Lykke, Nina Osvaldo, and Dirk te Velde. 2004. "Trade, FDI, Growth, and Poverty in Bolivia." La Paz: Grupo Integral, July.

Arias, Omar, and Walter Sosa Escudero. 2004. "Subjective and Objective Poverty in Bolivia: A Binary Quantile Regression Approach." Mimeo. Washington: World Bank.

Balat, Jorge, and Guido Porto. 2005. "Globalization and Complementary Policies: Poverty Impacts in Rural Zambia." NBER Working Paper 11175. Cambridge, Mass.: National Bureau of Economic Research, March.

Bojanic, Alan. 2001. "Bolivia's Participation in International Trade Negotiations." London: Overseas Development Institute, October.

Gottret, Jorge. 2004. "Industry Sector Analysis: Bolivia; Textile and Apparel Sectors." U.S. Embassy in La Paz (lapaz.usembassy.gov/commercial/IndSectAnalTexFV.pdf [February 2007]).

Landa Casazola, Fernando. 2003. "Pobreza y distribución del ingreso en Bolivia: Entre 1999 y 2002." La Paz: Unidad de Análisis de Políticas Sociales y Económicas (UDAPE).

Mincer, Jacob. 1974. *Schooling, Earnings, and Experience.* Columbia University Press.

Singh, Inderjit, Lyn Squire, and John Strauss. 1986. "Agricultural Household Models, Extensions, Applications, and Policy." Washington and Baltimore: World Bank and Johns Hopkins University Press.

Székely, Miguel, Nora Claudia Lustig, José Antonio Mejía-Guerra, and Martin Cumpa. 2000. "Do We Know How Much Poverty There Is?" IADB Research Working Paper 437. Washington: Inter-American Development Bank, December (ssrn.com/abstract=258949 [February 2006]).

USAID (U.S. Agency for International Development). 2005. *Complete Bolivia Program.* Washington.

Wodon, Quentin. 2000. "Poverty and Policy in Latin America and the Caribbean." Washington: World Bank.

World Bank. 2000. *Bolivia: Poverty Diagnostic 2000; Executive Summary.* Washington.

9

Nicaragua

ANIA I. GÓMEZ AND ISIDRO SOLOAGA

This chapter assesses the expected impact of a successful implementation of the Doha Development Agenda on households in Nicaragua, differentiating between urban and rural areas and presenting results by deciles of household per capita expenditure to identify effects on the distribution of income. We also investigate the implications for poverty of some potential domestic policy changes, to help in showing other avenues for improving welfare in Nicaragua.

The empirical approach follows that of Winters, in which changes in international prices and quantities are mapped onto household data.[1] Key elements are the changes in international prices, imports, and exports that are estimated in chapter 2 by Kee, Nicita, and Olarreaga for two different scenarios. The base case scenario, referred to as business as usual, involves a 40 percent reduction in bound tariffs, with applied tariffs varying accordingly; a reduction in all tariff peaks to a maximum of 50 percent; a 40 percent reduction in support for domestic agriculture; elimination of agricultural export subsidies; and an improvement in trade facilitation. The ambitious scenario entails much deeper global trade liberalization: full elimination of tariffs and subsidies, the same improvement in trade facilitation, and a 50 percent reduction in the restrictiveness of nontariff measures.

---

1. Winters (2002).

This chapter is organized as follows. The first section provides a brief introduction to poverty in Nicaragua, including an analysis of the composition of
income and consumption for households at different levels of wealth. The second explores the implications of multilateral trade liberalization for prices and
quantities in Nicaragua under the two scenarios. The third simulates the impact
of the two Doha scenarios on household consumption and income, tracing the
implications for poor producers and consumers; it then explores the poverty
implications of potential domestic policy changes in agriculture and infrastructure. A final section concludes.

The results show that under business as usual, multilateral trade liberalization
would produce a small average loss equivalent to 0.2 percent of household per
capita expenditure, with poorer households losing more than richer ones. More
ambitious trade liberalization would produce a small average gain. In the ambitious scenario, the average household would gain 0.9 percent in purchasing
power; prices of several important foods fall and the gains would be greater in
rural areas, where the share of food in total spending is higher. The expansion in
labor demand coming from an increase in manufactured goods, in response to
higher demand for Nicaraguan exports, would raise the purchasing power of the
average household by about 1.5 percent. Further simulations show that improvements in Nicaragua's agricultural extension services and in road infrastructure
would help substantially to raise the income of poorer families.

Poverty and the Economy in Nicaragua

Data for 2002 show Nicaragua's population at 5.3 million, with 43 percent living in rural areas. The labor force is estimated at about 2 million, growing at
3.8 percent a year. Gross national income per capita is about $710. By this stan-
dard, Nicaragua is one of the poorest countries in Latin America and the world.

Manufacturing represents 24.7 percent of GDP and, like agriculture, absorbs
about 20 percent of the labor force. The main subsectors are food processing
(about 45 percent of manufacturing valued added), beverages (16 percent),
petroleum products (14 percent), and nonmineral metals (8 percent).

Agriculture supplies 18 percent of GDP, largely from beans, coffee, corn,
and cattle. Only 2 million hectares out of Nicaragua's area of 12.1 million
hectares are arable land, and on average, farm productivity is low. Only
94,000 hectares are irrigated, fertilizer usage in 2002 was only 28 kilos of
nutrients per hectare, and the average ratio of tractors to arable land was 1.5 per
1,000 hectares. Both these ratios are below the Central American average. Crop
and livestock production grew at an average rate of more than 8 percent a year
between 1994 and 2001, but their expansion was based less on enhanced productivity than on expansion of the cultivated area, a trend that cannot be sustained for long.

Figure 9-1. *Exports in Nicaragua, 1979–81 to 2002*

Millions of U.S. dollars

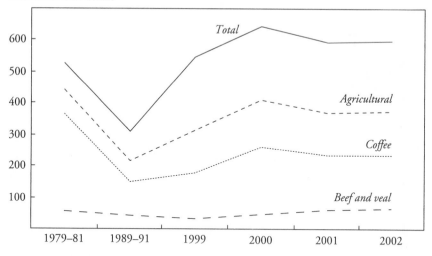

Source: FAOSTAT.

Nicaragua runs huge trade deficits, with annual imports during 1999–2002 of about $1.8 billion and exports of only $0.6 billion. Agriculture supplied more than 63 percent of total exports in 1999–2002. Major agricultural export items are coffee and beef, each representing 18 percent of agricultural exports (figure 9-1).

Poverty

Although Nicaragua remains one of the poorest and least developed countries in Latin America, its poverty levels have declined consistently in the last ten years or so.[2] Overall poverty fell by 4.5 percentage points between 1993 and 2001 (from 50 to 46 percent of the population), while extreme poverty declined from 19 to 15 percent (table 9-1). These lower poverty rates reflect the extraordinary levels of investment that followed Hurricane Mitch and declines in the relative prices of rice and beans—key food staples in Nicaragua—in spite of drought and declining coffee prices.

Data from the latest survey of the World Bank's Living Standards Measurement Study for Nicaragua—*Encuesta Nacional de Hogares sobre Medición del Nivel de Vida (ENMV) 2001*—show that, as in many other developing countries, low income levels are associated with low levels of schooling, particularly for females; large family sizes; and heavy dependence on agriculture. Households in

2. World Bank (2003).

Table 9-1. *Poverty Trends (Headcount Index), 1993–2001*
Percent

	National			Urban			Rural		
Year	Incidence[a]	Change	Annual change[b]	Incidence[a]	Change	Annual change[b]	Incidence[b]	Change	Annual change[c]
All poor[c]									
1993	50.3	. . .	. . .	31.9	. . .	. . .	76.1	. . .	. . .
1998	47.8	−2.4	−1.0	30.5	−1.4	−0.9	68.5	−7.6	−2.1
2001	45.8	−2.1	−1.5	28.7	−1.8	−2.0	64.3	−4.2	−2.1
Extremely poor									
1993	19.4	. . .	. . .	7.3	. . .	. . .	36.3	. . .	. . .
1998	17.3	−2.1	−2.3	7.6	0.3	0.8	28.9	−7.4	−4.5
2001	15.1	−2.2	−4.4	6.1	−1.5	−7.1	24.7	−4.2	−5.1

Source: World Bank (2003).

a. Incidence refers to the poverty headcount index, which is the share of the population whose total consumption falls below the poverty line.

b. The annual change is calculated as the geometric mean for three and five years, respectively.

c. Refers to extreme poor plus poor.

extreme poverty have limited access to basic services: four-fifths have no access to safe drinking water, 37 percent lack sanitation, and 70 percent lack electricity.

Poverty is substantially greater in rural than in urban areas; by 2001, 68 percent of the rural population was below the poverty line, compared with only 30 percent of the urban population. In rural areas, high poverty levels are associated with traditional family farms, producing mainly corn, beans, and sorghum. Of the households living in extreme poverty, 61 percent are dedicated to farming, particularly in the central region. Among farm households, only 60 percent own land, while about 34 percent work on rented land. Most poor rural families lack access to the technical assistance, financial services, and institutions needed to make them productive farmers. Moreover, in a region prone to natural disaster, most poor people also lack access to formal insurance mechanisms or social safety nets.

Those rural families who achieved larger declines in poverty between 1998 and 2001 had family members working for wages in nonagricultural jobs. And families who worked for wages both inside and outside agriculture achieved the largest increases in their incomes, whether or not they owned land. This pattern suggests that mixing wage labor sources is among the most successful welfare-increasing strategies.[3]

Consumption Patterns

Food takes more than half of total spending for the poorer half of households, but its importance in the consumption basket declines as household incomes rise (table 9-2). Rice is the most important item for the poorest households: it takes 15 percent of total spending in the poorest expenditure deciles, nearly 14 percent in the second, and more than 11 percent in the third and fourth deciles. Other important items for the poor are beans, vegetables, sugar, and corn, which together take more than one-fourth of total spending in the lower deciles. Among non-food items, expenditures on "household services" (water, fuel and power, wood fuel, transport and communications, medical care and personal care) are by far the most important items at all levels of wealth. Expenditures on education are also important.

In Nicaragua, unlike more urbanized countries, the share of food in total spending differs very little between rural and urban areas: throughout the country, the share of food is greater than 50 percent for the first five deciles and decreases to about 35 percent for the wealthiest decile.

Sources of Income

Earnings from self-employment supply about 31 percent of income for the average household and more than 28 percent for all but the fourth decile (table 9-3).

3. World Bank (2003).

Table 9-2. *Composition of Household Expenditure in Nicaragua, by Decile of Per Capita Expenditure*

Percent

Consumption item	Decile										Average
	1	2	3	4	5	6	7	8	9	10	
Food total	56.3	57.3	54.3	52.9	52.6	49.8	49.0	46.2	44.0	35.1	49.8
Rice	15.0	13.7	12.3	11.6	8.8	8.6	7.5	6.3	5.3	4.0	9.3
Beans	12.2	9.4	7.8	6.7	5.8	5.4	4.2	3.8	3.2	2.3	6.1
Vegetables	7.3	9.5	11.5	11.4	12.9	12.4	12.8	14.2	13.1	13.0	7.7
Sugar	10.7	7.9	7.3	6.4	5.6	5.2	5.5	4.3	4.4	3.3	7.7
Oils	6.3	5.7	4.9	4.5	4.0	4.3	3.6	2.9	2.9	2.8	4.2
Corn	11.3	6.8	5.8	4.7	4.0	2.9	3.3	1.8	1.4	0.9	4.3
Poultry	2.4	4.3	4.2	5.4	5.3	5.7	5.5	5.9	6.4	6.8	5.2
Milk	4.8	6.2	6.8	6.2	8.8	8.1	9.8	8.4	9.8	8.5	7.7
Eggs	4.7	4.3	4.4	3.7	3.5	3.3	3.5	2.9	2.9	2.1	3.5
Tortillas	4.5	4.5	3.8	4.0	3.4	3.6	4.0	3.2	3.2	2.1	3.7
Fruit	4.3	2.7	3.6	3.5	3.5	3.5	4.1	4.0	4.0	3.9	3.7
Coffee	4.1	3.6	2.6	2.9	2.0	2.1	1.7	1.6	1.6	1.2	2.3
Cheese and cream	3.0	4.9	5.0	5.6	5.9	6.2	5.9	6.5	6.3	5.8	5.5
Other food	8.9	14.2	17.6	18.6	21.1	22.8	22.4	26.0	27.4	34.3	21.3
Non-food total	43.7	42.7	45.7	47.1	47.4	50.2	51.0	53.8	56.0	64.9	50.2
Household services[a]	26.6	26.1	26.5	27.6	28.2	29.6	29.1	30.7	33.8	41.1	29.9
Health	4.5	3.6	4.0	4.5	4.7	5.0	5.5	5.9	4.9	5.4	4.8
Education	5.8	5.7	5.2	6.6	6.0	6.2	6.1	6.8	7.3	7.2	6.3
Other	6.8	7.3	9.9	8.4	8.4	9.4	10.3	10.4	9.9	11.2	9.2

Source: ENMV 2001.

a. Household services include water, fuel and power, wood fuel, transport and communications, medical care, and personal care.

Table 9-3. *Sources of Household Income in Nicaragua, by Decile of Per Capita Expenditure*

Percent

Sources of income	Decile										Average
	1	2	3	4	5	6	7	8	9	10	
Self-employment	31.3	30.9	31.2	22.5	33.7	29.6	37.3	28.8	29.5	36.8	31.2
Farming activities	21.9	21.3	19.6	16.6	9.4	12.4	12.9	8.6	11.6	6.9	14.1
Income	12.1	12.0	9.0	9.2	4.3	6.7	7.1	4.4	7.1	4.0	7.6
Beans	4.2	4.2	4.1	3.1	3.0	3.6	2.9	2.9	1.0	0.7	3.0
Corn	2.4	2.4	2.6	2.4	2.8	3.1	2.5	1.8	0.9	0.6	2.1
Coffee	2.5	4.5	0.6	0.9	0.5	1.7	2.7	1.4	2.2	2.0	1.9
Own consumption	9.8	9.3	10.7	7.4	5.1	5.7	5.8	4.2	4.4	2.9	6.5
Beans	1.4	1.8	1.6	1.2	0.6	0.8	0.5	0.3	0.2	0.1	0.8
Corn	0.7	1.1	0.9	0.8	0.7	0.5	0.8	0.4	0.3	0.1	0.6
Non-farming activities	9.4	9.6	11.6	5.9	24.4	17.2	24.4	20.2	17.9	30.0	17.1
Other sources											
Wages	42.0	42.8	39.5	42.2	38.2	35.4	34.4	36.6	31.7	28.8	37.2
Remittances	3.4	3.1	2.8	2.7	2.8	4.6	3.1	3.9	3.2	2.9	3.3
Transfers	3.2	4.0	3.3	3.4	3.1	6.5	4.3	6.7	4.2	4.6	4.3
Other income	20.2	19.1	23.3	29.2	22.0	24.0	20.9	24.0	31.4	26.9	24.1

Source: Authors' calculations, based on ENMV for 2001.

Figure 9-2. *Share of Wages in Urban and Rural Household Income in Nicaragua,
by Decile of per Capita Expenditure*
Percent

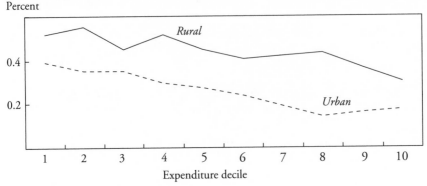

Source: Authors' calculations using 2001 ENMV.

Within the category of self-employment, income from farming activities is more
important for the poorer deciles—coffee being the main cash crop for the two
poorest deciles—while income from non-farming activities dominates in the
higher deciles. Wages supply almost 40 percent of income for the average
household, providing between 38 and 43 percent for deciles one to five and
about 30 percent for wealthier households.

As expected, wages are a less important source of income for rural than for
urban families. For the richest rural households, wages supply less than 20 percent of total income, but for the richest households in urban areas, wages supply
more than 30 percent (figure 9-2).

Agriculture and fisheries are the most important source of income for household heads, employing about 33 percent of them (figure 9-3). The sales sector
comes next, providing work for about 14 percent of household heads, followed
by manufacturing, with 9 percent—of whom a third are in the food industry.
About 5 percent of household heads work in construction.

Implications of the Doha Development Agenda for Nicaragua

For Nicaragua's economy in general, and the Nicaraguan poor in particular, the
implications of the multilateral trade liberalization proposed in Doha depend
on three factors:

—Impact on prices of goods produced and consumed by the poor,

—Impact on world demand for Nicaraguan products produced and sold by
the poor, and

—Impact on employment and the extent to which this affects the poor.

The changes in world prices and demand that might follow from implementation of the Doha Development Agenda are estimated in chapter 2 for the

Figure 9-3. *Employment of Household Heads in Nicaragua, by Sector*

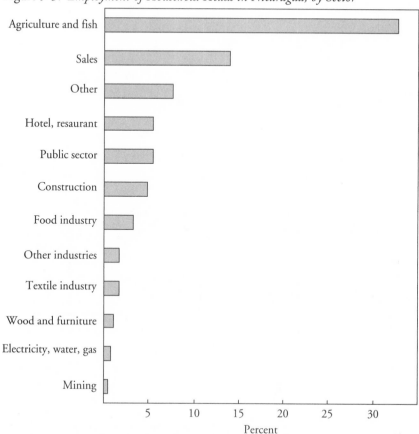

Source: Authors' calculations, based on ENMV for 2001.

business-as-usual and ambitious scenarios. Table 9-4 reports these expected changes in prices and quantities, weighted by Nicaragua's total trade in each product, for the main products and product groups in Nicaragua. The first and second columns of the table show the importance of those products in total expenditures and in total income.

In the business-as-usual scenario, the price of rice is expected to rise 3 percent, and the prices of corn, plantain, meat, and poultry are also expected to rise more than 2 percent. More ambitious multilateral trade liberalization would produce greater price changes: of special importance, because of their large shares in household spending, are the price declines for rice (−19.6 percent), beans (−13.5 percent), and clothing (−8.2 percent).

As for quantities, there are major differences between the two scenarios. Nicaraguan exports are expected to increase only 3.2 percent under business

Table 9-4. *Doha Effects on Prices and Quantities in Nicaragua: Business-as-Usual and Ambitious Scenarios*

| Product or product group | Share in expenditures | Share in income | Current exports (thousands of U.S. dollars) | Domestic price change[a] | | Export changes (thousands of U.S. dollars) | | | |
| | | | | Business as usual In percent | Ambitious Doha[b] In percent | Business as usual | | Ambitious Doha[b] | |
						Absolute	In percent	Absolute	In percent
Beans	6.3	3.5	23	-0.50	-13.50	-1	-2	-15	-66
Coffee	1.8	2.1	84,422	-0.50	-12.40	1,483	2	-37,647	-45
Corn flour	0.3	0.1	91	-0.20	-6.60	2	2	-1	-1
Corn grain	4.1	2.3	311	6.40	0.30	83	27	725	233
Mango	1.1	0.01	3,050	-3.50	-35.90	-56	-2	-5,082	-167
Manioc	0.2	0.2	145	-0.10	-13.50	1	1	-10	-7
Meat	4.1	2.9	107,591	2.30	3.50	2,590	2	275,118	256
Plantain	1.1	0.3	12,519	2.70	-13.00	3,628	29	250	2
Poultry	3.9	0.2	229	2.20	-28.60	34	15	5	2
Rice	9.0	0.8	1,032	3.00	-19.60	-307	-30	-4,589	-455
Sugar	5.2	0.004	34,315	1.00	-26.50	-229	-1	58,907	172
Taro (tuber)	…	0.02	2,247	-0.10	-14.00	39	2	-388	-17
Tomatoes	0.9	0.1	357	0.90	-13.00	38	11	7	2
Clothing	14.7	…	2,184	1.40	-8.20	157	7	1,419	65
All goods			599,152	0.50	-4.00	21,551	4	429,757	72

Source: Authors' calculations, based on ENMV for 2001.

a. Changes in prices taken from chapter 2 in this volume, weighted by Nicaragua's total trade.

b. In addition, for the ambitious scenario, all Nicaragua's tariffs were set to 0.

as usual, but 72 percent under more far-reaching multilateral liberalization. The major negative impact on households would come from the expected decrease in coffee prices (−45 percent in the ambitious scenario) and in the volume of coffee exports; as noted, coffee is the main cash crop for the poorest 20 percent of households. By contrast, positive overall impacts are expected from major increases in the price and exports of meat (a price rise of 256 percent) and of sugar (a price rise of 172 percent). As for clothing, Nicaragua's current exports are so small, at only $2 million, that even the 65 percent increase that is expected in the ambitious scenario would barely affect household welfare.

Given the estimated changes in prices and quantities, the impact on employment in Nicaragua is calculated using input-output tables and employment statistics from the Global Trade Analysis Project. A net increase of about 25,000 jobs is expected under the ambitious scenario.

Simulation Results

In this section, we present the results from simulations under the business-as-usual and the ambitious Doha scenarios. Subsequently, we investigate the impact of potential changes in Nicaraguan policies designed to improve agricultural extension and road infrastructure. As in the other case studies in this volume, the changes in household welfare are reported as percentages of current per capita household spending.

Business-as-Usual Scenario

Table 9-5 shows the expected impact on per capita expenditures of implementing the Doha Development Agenda in the business-as-usual scenario. When only changes in prices are considered, the probable losses would be small, at an average of −0.6 percent, of which −1.1 percent would come from increased expenditures and +0.6 from increased income. The impact in urban areas would be negative, as might be expected, because the opportunities are fewer there for subsistence production. While urban households would lose an average of 1.1 percent, rural ones would gain 0.3 percent. Losses would be bigger in the lower income deciles.

When changes in quantities are considered together with changes in prices, the impact on expenditures would be almost the same, although now there are clear winners in the rural areas, and the overall average effect is a gain of 3.2 percent in household purchasing power. The main negative impact here comes from the expected reduction in rice exports, but there are few net producers of rice in Nicaragua (most rice producers consume their harvest themselves). Positive impacts would come from the increases in coffee and corn production and, for the highest income decile, higher meat and milk prices.

Table 9-5. *Effects on Household Welfare in Nicaragua, by Decile of Per Capita Expenditure: Business-as-Usual Scenario*
Percent

Impact of Doha Development Agenda, Business-as-Usual Scenario	Decile										
	1	2	3	4	5	6	7	8	9	10	Average
Changes in prices—Business-as-usual scenario											
Total	-1.0	-1.0	-0.8	-0.7	-0.6	-0.6	-0.1	-0.4	-0.4	0.1	-0.6
Expenditure	-1.5	-1.4	-1.4	-1.3	-1.2	-1.2	-1.0	-1.0	-0.8	-0.6	-1.1
Income	0.4	0.4	0.6	0.6	0.6	0.6	0.9	0.6	0.4	0.8	0.6
Urban	-1.4	-1.4	-1.5	-1.3	-1.0	-1.3	-0.7	-1.0	-0.7	-0.3	-1.1
Rural	-0.9	-0.8	-0.3	-0.1	-0.1	0.3	0.8	0.9	0.6	2.2	0.3
Changes in prices and quantities—Business-as-usual scenario											
Total	0.6	2.1	1.9	3.2	2.6	4.9	4.7	2.4	4.2	5.4	3.2
Expenditure	-1.6	-1.3	-1.3	-1.3	-1.2	-1.1	-1.1	-0.9	-0.8	-0.6	-1.1
Income	2.1	3.4	3.3	4.5	3.8	6.0	5.8	3.3	5.0	6.1	4.3
Urban	-1.2	-1.2	-1.1	-0.2	-1.2	0.2	-0.5	-0.7	1.1	1.3	-0.4
Rural	1.1	4.2	4.8	7.8	8.1	11.5	15.2	9.6	14.8	24.2	10.1

Source: Authors' calculations, based on ENMV for 2001.

Ambitious Scenario

Table 9-6 shows the expected impact on per capita expenditure of implementing the Doha Development Agenda in the ambitious scenario. As noted, prices of many important consumer goods would go down, some of them by sizable amounts (rice by almost 20 percent and sugar by almost 27 percent). In a country where many farmers produce mostly for their own consumption, these changes would be beneficial to poor families, raising their purchasing power. In this scenario, the larger the share of food in a household's total expenditures, the greater the gain: the poorest two deciles would gain by 2.5 and 1.8 percent, respectively, whereas the two richest deciles would gain by 0.5 and 0.04 percent, respectively.

When changes in quantities are considered along with changes in prices, the results are slightly negative on average. For coffee producers, the impact would be large and negative, whereas for cattle producers, it would be high and positive.

Impact on Employment

If there is an expansion in demand in the industrial sector (for example, in food processing and textiles), labor demand in this sector would likely increase,[4] and household income would grow, whether through increased employment, higher wages, or both.[5] This section assesses the expected impact on poverty of an increase in labor demand by the industrial and (non-public) services sector. We do not have a model that maps the effects of changes in Nicaragua's exports onto demand for labor, but based on estimates for the other countries in this volume, we assume that the likely expansion in the manufacturing sector resulting from multilateral trade liberalization would increase labor demand by roughly 25,000 employees in the ambitious scenario. This increment represents 6 percent of Nicaragua's current labor force in manufacturing, and at the current rate of job creation in that sector (about 15,000 per year), it would take almost two years to be absorbed.

Table 9-7 shows the number of workers working in Managua who are likely to switch jobs, the average current wage they earn, their expected wage when they switch to the industrial sector, and the size of the difference.[6] This exercise

---

4. For a similar argument regarding the impact of the Central American Free Trade Agreement (CAFTA), see MIFIC (2004).

5. A 2005 study on labor markets in Central American countries points to recent legal changes in labor regulations in Nicaragua, following recommendations from the International Labor Organization, that would ease the functioning of the labor market. See Working Group of the Vice Ministers Responsible for Trade and Labor in the Countries of Central America and the Dominican Republic (2005).

6. The simulation was done only for Managua, the capital city of Nicaragua. Hence it only covers workers already living in the capital and excludes workers who might switch out of rural areas and into jobs in Managua.

Table 9-6. *Effects on Household Welfare in Nicaragua, by Decile of per Capita Expenditure: Ambitious Scenario*

Percent

Impact of Doha Development Agenda,						*Decile*					
Ambitious Doha	1	2	3	4	5	6	7	8	9	10	*Average*
Changes in prices—Ambitious Doha scenario											
Total	5.6	5.7	4.1	5.5	5.0	4.8	4.5	4.2	4.0	3.0	4.6
Expenditure	6.7	6.6	6.6	6.5	5.8	5.8	5.4	5.0	4.4	3.64	5.6
Income	-1.1	-0.9	-2.5	-1.0	-0.8	-1.0	-0.9	-0.7	-0.4	-0.69	-1.0
Urban	7.0	6.8	7.2	7.0	6.1	6.1	5.3	5.2	4.8	3.2	5.9
Rural	5.2	5.1	1.9	3.8	3.6	2.9	3.4	2.1	1.8	1.7	3.1
Changes in prices and quantities—Ambitious Doha scenario											
Total	6.0	2.8	6.6	4.6	4.7	5.2	6.0	5.1	4.7	4.1	5.0
Expenditure	6.6	6.6	6.6	5.8	5.8	4.5	5.0	4.5	3.8	3.2	5.2
Income	-0.6	-3.5	0.0	-1.1	-0.9	0.3	1.1	0.6	0.8	1.1	-0.2
Urban	6.7	7.3	9.4	6.1	5.6	3.7	5.3	4.9	4.9	2.5	5.6
Rural	5.8	-0.2	3.8	2.6	3.5	7.2	7.3	5.4	4.0	11.6	5.1

Source: Authors' calculations, based on ENMV 2001.

Table 9-7. *Number of Workers Likely to Switch Jobs if Demand for Labor Rises in Industry in Nicaragua, by Decile of per Capita Expenditure*

	Decile										Total
	1	2	3	4	5	6	7	8	9	10	
From the primary sector											
Number of workers who are expected to switch jobs	1,013	1,415	1,500	2,191	1,280	1,056	1,000	0	925	997	11,377
Percent of women who switch	0.0	0.0	0.0	26.00	0.0	0.0	0.0	0.0	0.0	0.0	0.0
Current wage earned in the sector (cordobas per day, average)	23.3	27.6	33.5	21.3	40.9	32.0	54.4	0.0	30.8	14.5	27.8
Expected wage to be earned in industry (cordobas per day, average)	40.6	54.7	50.9	31.9	51.7	41.9	73.6	0.0	45.4	54.0	44.5
Difference (expected—current)	17.3	27.1	17.4	10.5	10.8	9.9	19.2	0.0	14.6	39.5	16.6
Difference, as percent of current wage	74	98	52	49	26	31	35	0.0	47	0	41.3
From the services sector											
Number of workers who are expected to switch jobs	1,069	2,261	4,843	6,783	14,448	15,414	16,140	24,445	31,245	43,763	160,410
Percent of women who switch	66.7	56.3	33.3	31.6	27.0	45.7	20.7	32.6	59.4	45.3	41.9
Current wage earned in the sector (cordobas per day, average)	9.7	11.7	17.4	13.4	19.1	22.9	23.5	22.9	25.5	31.2	19.7
Expected wage to be earned in industry (cordobas per day, average)	25.7	33.8	47.6	40.8	45.5	51.0	51.7	48.6	52.9	57.5	45.5
Difference (expected—current)	16.0	22.2	30.2	27.4	26.4	28.1	28.2	25.7	27.4	26.4	25.8
Difference, as percent of current wage	265	290	274	303	238	223	220	212	207	185	241.6

Source: Authors' calculations, based on ENMV for 2001.

indicates that, from a pool of 300,000 people working for a wage in Managua, just over 170,000 laborers would earn higher wages if they switched into the industrial sector.[7] More than 90 percent of them currently work in services (trade, restaurants, hotels, or public services), and some 7 percent are in the primary sector. Of the likely switchers from the service sector, 42 percent are women. The average gain for workers switching from the primary sector would be equivalent to 41 percent of their current wage, and for workers switching from the services sector it would be more than 100 percent.

Table 9-8 shows the impact on household welfare of an increase of 25,000 in the number of workers demanded by the industrial sector in Managua. The first panel of the table shows the average impact, considering all households in the city (including those not expected to switch occupations). The impact for all households on average would be 1.5 percent. The second panel shows the impact only for those households with at least one member switching into the industrial sector.[8] For households with switchers, the average expected gain would be about 43 percent of current per capita expenditure.

Improvements in Agricultural Extension Policies

Insufficient access to—or straightforward absence of—technical assistance is known to hinder efforts to improve welfare and reduce poverty among rural Nicaraguans.[9] To gain a clearer picture of the impact of extension services on farm productivity, we estimate a model of coffee productivity where the dependent variable is the log of gross income per hectare in coffee production.[10] We control for demographic variables, such as the age and gender of the household head, and determinants of agricultural output, such as the use of pesticide per hectare and farm size. "Extension services" is a dummy variable that indicates whether the household received these services or not. Among the country's 30,000 coffee growers, the average-size coffee farm (owned or managed) is about 2.4 hectares for small

---

7. 11,377 workers from the primary sector and more than 160,419 from the services sector.

8. The threshold used to switch a worker out of his or her current job and into the industrial sector is an expected salary in the manufacturing sector of $1 a day greater than his or her current wage.

9. World Bank (2003: table 1). ENMV for 2001 indicates that the most frequent technical assistance received by farmers was for chemical usage (23 percent) and seed improvements (14 percent). Of the technical assistance provided in Nicaragua, almost 33 percent is supplied by nongovernmental organizations, and 30 percent is supplied by the government.

10. In the data, some expenditures on agricultural production are bundled, not allowing us to calculate net value per hectare for specific crops. A government agency has estimated average production costs to be about 70 percent of gross sales (Dirección General de Política Sectorial Agrícola 2004), and we use this estimate to assess the average impact of technical assistance.

Table 9-8. *Effects on Household Welfare in Managua, by Decile of per Capita Expenditure: Increase in Industrial Employment*
Percent

Impact of increase of 25,000 new employees in the industrial sector	*Decile*										
	1	*2*	*3*	*4*	*5*	*6*	*7*	*8*	*9*	*10*	*Average*
All households	0.72	1.02	1.12	1.26	1.56	1.41	1.60	0.81	4.13	1.51	1.5
Household with at least one member switching to industry	82.39	57.90	50.20	41.60	58.69	45.85	30.41	29.96	45.80	34.04	43.2

Source: Authors' calculations, based on ENMV for 2001.

Table 9-9. *Extension Services and Market Agricultural Productivity in Nicaragua*

Gross income per hectare	Coefficient	Standard error	P value	Coefficient	Standard error	P value
Head age	0.06	0.065	0.35	0.014	0.076	0.86
Head age (sq)	−0.001	0.001	0.31	0.000	0.001	0.80
Head male	0.116	0.536	0.83	−0.001	0.627	1.00
Pesticide per ha	0.0004	0.0001	0.00	0.0005	0.0001	0.00
Size farm	−2.558	1.084	0.03			
Size farm (sq)	0.655	0.552	0.24			
Extension service	0.716	0.383	0.07	0.854	0.443	0.06
Constant	8.443	1.721	0.00	8.992	2.006	0.00
Number of observations: 40						
Adj. R-squared: .47				0.266		

Source: Authors' calculations, based on ENMV for 2001.

and medium farmers and 14.7 hectares for big farmers.[11] To capture mainly commercial producers, we select those producers who obtain more than 33 percent of their income from coffee sales; this yields a sample of forty families.

We estimate two variants of the model—a basic version and one in which we control by farm size—and find that in neither variant is the age or the gender of the head of household an important determinant of productivity (table 9-9). As expected, the use of pesticide per hectare is statistically significant, and there is some indication that smaller farmers are more productive. In both the variants, we find a positive correlation between productivity per hectare and technical assistance received: farmers receiving technical assistance would double their gross income per hectare. Considering that the average gross income from coffee per hectare for the farmers in our data is about $2,249, and assuming that farmers' average production costs are about 70 percent of their total sales, we estimate the average impact of technical assistance to be about $675 per hectare per year—a gain that, for the average small and medium coffee grower, working 2.4 hectares, translates into around $1,590 dollars a year, or about 30 percent of gross annual income.[12]

Income Gains in Market Agriculture

In Nicaragua as elsewhere, subsistence agriculture is often associated with low income levels. The share of income derived from subsistence activities dwindles as a household's overall income grows (figure 9-4).

11. CEPAL (2005).

12. Data on production costs as a percent of total sales are from Dirección General de Política Sectorial Agrícola (2004).

Figure 9-4. *Share of Household Income from Subsistence Production in Nicaragua, by Decile of per Capita Expenditure*
Percent

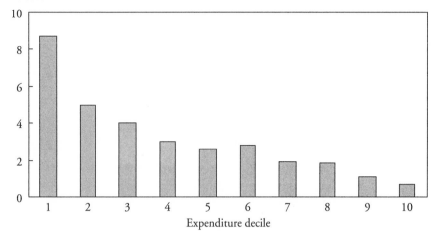

Source: Authors' calculations, based on ENMV for 2001.

In the simulation described below we compare the average monthly wages of those workers employed in market agriculture with the monthly per capita income coming from subsistence production for each working household member in subsistence agriculture. By doing so, we seek to quantify the expected gains for workers from switching out of subsistence activities and into market agriculture. The methodology follows that of Balat and Porto.[13]

We estimate a probit model of participation for individuals who work for a wage in agriculture (table 9-10). We include only those households that derive most of their income from wage income or from subsistence agriculture.[14] The independent variables include demographic and regional characteristics. Using propensity score matching methods, we match laborers in market agriculture with subsistence farmers. We test the balancing property, whose main implication is that both groups can be comparable. The income differential between subsistence farmers and employees in market agriculture is estimated using kernel methods.

The results confirm a big difference in profitability between market and subsistence agriculture (table 9-11). Wage workers in market agriculture would earn an

13. Balat and Porto (2005).
14. This variable is a dummy that takes the value 1 when the household obtains at least a third of its total income from wage employment in agriculture and 0 when the household obtains at least a third of its total income from subsistence agriculture.

Table 9-10. *Probit Estimates for Nicaragua: Selection into Wage Employment in Agriculture*

Constant	0.714
	(22.18)**
Male	−0.469
	(52.01)**
Married	0.011
	(1.82)*
Age	0.022
	(19.43)**
Age sq.	0
	(19.11)**
Household head	
Age 6–12	−1.433
	(59.01)**
Age 13–18	−0.77
	(33.03)**
Age 19–64	−0.86
	(35.53)**
Age 65 or more	0.813
	(18.84)**
Male	1.497
	(87.56)**
Distance to road	−0.005
	(173.88)**
Distance to market	0
	−0.42
Distance to water	−0.131
	(14.87)**
Owner	−0.361
	(62.07)**
Tools	0.112
	(40.16)**
Number of observations: 247	
Treated: 164	
Non-treated: 67	

Source: Authors' calculations, based on ENMV for 2001.
* Significant at 10 percent; ** significant at 5 percent; *** significant at 1 percent.

extra C$1,240 a month (about $93).[15] On average, this amount is nearly half of the imputed per capita income of workers in subsistence production:

ATT	% of expenditure
1239.928	
(116.699)	44

15. This is statistically significant. Standard errors are obtained by bootstrapping.

Table 9-11. *Determinants of Subsistence Production in Nicaragua*

Variables	Impact on subsistence (percentage points)
Head schooling	5.0
Distance to Road (km)	−11.0
Distance to Road*Pacific	2.0
Distance to Road*Atlantic	0.1
Distance to Road*Central	0.4
Road_track	34.0
Road_trocha	75.0
Road_river	78.0

Source: Authors' calculations, based on ENMV for 2001.

These findings confirm that policies that reduce dependence on subsistence agriculture would substantially improve the living standards of the rural poor in Nicaragua.

Determinants of Subsistence Agriculture

A high reliance on subsistence production is usually correlated with remoteness from services, poor physical infrastructure, poor access to credit, and lack of skills.[16] To assess which policy interventions could reduce the degree of dependence on subsistence production, with consequent welfare gains for rural households, we estimate an equation in which the dependent variable is the share of income coming from subsistence activities in the households. As independent variables, we take households' specific characteristics such as household size, household assets, and the household head's gender, age, and schooling level. In addition, we include policy characteristics such as access to credit, distance to roads (in kilometers),[17] road conditions (paved, dirt road, track, waterway), accessibility of the road (passable always, almost always, hardly ever), and a comparison of the road condition today with that in 1998 (better, same, worse).

The results confirm the importance of policies to extend education and, especially, to improve transport infrastructure (table 9-11; see also the appendix to this chapter). One year more of schooling lowers by 5 percentage points the proportion of subsistence activity in household income. For people living in the Pacific region, the share of income supplied by subsistence production increases by 2 percentage points for every additional 10 kilometers of distance from a

16. Nicita (2004). CEPAL (2005) indicates that Nicaragua's production of basic grains, as well as bananas, in 2003–04 was affected by the bad condition of roads, due to the fact that the estates are far from ports.

17. We have included interaction terms of distance with the different regions of the country.

main road. The condition of roads has a strong impact on family income sources: the share of subsistence production in income is 34 percentage points higher for those families who are served by a track than it is for families who are served by a paved road. As road conditions worsen, this proportion rises.

Conclusions

This chapter has assessed the expected impact on Nicaragua of a successful implementation of the Doha Development Agenda and the likely impacts of some potential domestic policies for reducing poverty.

Our results show that, from multilateral trade liberalization in the business-as-usual scenario, Nicaragua could expect an average loss equivalent to 0.6 percent of household per capita spending, with the poorer households losing more. By contrast, the more far-reaching multilateral liberalization in the ambitious Doha scenario would produce an average gain in household purchasing power of 4.6 percent, with the poorest households gaining more. If one allows for changes in Nicaraguan exports to reflect changes in the quantities likely to be produced, then the estimated impacts would be slightly larger, reaching 5 percent on average in the ambitious scenario. Here again, the gains in real income would be larger for poorer households. Simulations also show, for the capital city, Managua, that the expansion in labor demand coming from an increase in exports of manufactured goods would yield a gain of 1.5 percent in average real household income.

Looking at domestic policy options, the chapter has simulated the effects of potential changes in agricultural extension services and improvements in road infrastructure on household welfare. Both these policy interventions are estimated to improve the purchasing power of poorer families—either by increasing the productivity of coffee producers (of whom about 25 percent are in extreme poverty) or by encouraging a switch out of subsistence production and into market agriculture, where the returns to labor are higher. If poor subsistence farmers could switch into the agricultural labor market, they could expect an increase in real income of about 44 percent.

References

Balat, Jorge, and Guido Porto. 2005. "Globalization and Complementary Policies: Poverty Impacts in Rural Zambia." NBER Working Paper 11175. Cambridge, Mass.: National Bureau of Economic Research, March.
CEPAL (Economic Commission for Latin America). 2005. *Istmo centroamericano: Evolución del sector agropecuario, 2003–04.* Mexico City.
Dirección General de Política Sectorial Agrícola. 2004. "Información sobre costos del café." Mimeo. Managua.
MECOVI (Mejoramiento de Encuestas de Condiciones de Vida) and INEC (Instituto Nacional de Estadísticas y Censos). 2001. *Perfil y características de los pobres en Nicaragua.* Managua.

MIFIC (Ministerio de Fomento, Industria, y Comercio). 2004. *Análisis de impactos relevantes, base legal, institucional, programas y proyectos preliminares para implementar el CAFTA.* Managua: Dirección de Políticas Comerciales Externas.

Nicita, Alessandro. 2004. "Who Benefited from Trade Liberalization in Mexico? Measuring the Effects on Household Welfare." World Bank Working Paper 3265. Washington: World Bank.

Winters, L. Alan. 2002. "Trade Liberalization and Poverty: What Are the Links?" *World Economy* 25, no. 9: 1339–67.

Working Group of the Vice Ministers Responsible for Trade and Labor in the Countries of Central America and the Dominican Republic. 2005. "The Labor Dimension in Central America and the Dominican Republic: Building on Progress; Strengthening Compliance and Enhancing Capacity." White Paper, April.

World Bank. 2003. *Nicaragua Poverty Assessment: Raising Welfare and Reducing Vulnerability.* Report 26128-NI. Washington: Central America Department, Latin America and the Caribbean Region.

APPENDIX

Regression Results

Table 9A-1. *Determinants of Subsistence Production*

Share of owncon/income		Share of owncon/income	
Famsize	0.016	Distance to Atlantic	0.113
	(−0.011)		(0.037)***
Head male	0.39	Distance to Central	0.116
	(0.067)***		(0.037)***
Head schooling	−0.047	Extension service	0.519
	(0.009)***		(0.123)***
Head age	0.022	Road_track	0.344
	(0.011)**		(0.081)***
Head age (sq.)	−0.0002	Road_trocha	0.748
	(0.000)**		(0.113)***
Assets	−0.697	Road_river	0.782
	(0.115)***		(0.197)***
Assets (sq.)	0.067	Access_almost always	0.125
	(0.018)***		(−0.076)
Centro	0.521	Access_never	0.026
	(0.124)***		(−0.102)
Pacific	−0.167	Access_other	1.635
	−0.117		(−1.525)
Atlantic	0.761	Same_1998	0.115
	(0.144)***		(−0.087)
Urban	−1.113	Worse_1998	−0.047
	(0.074)***		(−0.105)
Loans	0.16	No information–1998	−0.319
	(0.071)**		(−0.299)
Distance to Road (km)	−0.112	Constant	−5.104
	(0.037)***		(0.302)***
Distance to Road*Pacific	0.131	Observations	2,805
	(0.037)***	Adjusted R-squared	0.432

* Significant at 10 percent; ** significant at 5 percent; *** significant at 1 percent.

PART THREE

Policy Implications

10

Development and Trade Agreements: Beyond Market Access

BERNARD HOEKMAN

The foregoing chapters have assessed the impact of global trade liberalization on world prices and the consequences of relative price changes for
outcomes at the household level, especially for the poor in the poorest countries. This type of analysis complements the much larger literature focusing on
the overall welfare effects of global reforms at the country and cross-country
levels. The main conclusions emerging from the micro, within-country analyses are that deep reforms in trade policy would yield much greater benefits for
poor households than would a more limited approach to trade liberalization
and that complementary actions could greatly increase the potential benefits
for the poor.

Analyses based on global modeling have long motivated calls for deep
reforms of trade policy; the more that is done to remove trade-distorting policies, the greater the aggregate welfare gains for the world as a whole. The new
understanding contributed by the micro analysis is that deeper global trade
reforms will also be pro-poor at the country level: in most of the cases studied,
relatively poor households will benefit more than richer ones. Moreover, the

This chapter draws on the findings of a number of papers prepared for the DFID-supported
Global Trade and Financial Architecture Project. The main conclusions of this project were dis-
seminated as Zedillo and others (2005). The author is grateful to Patrick Messerlin, Susan Prowse,
Sheila Page, and other members of the project for helpful discussions on the subjects discussed in
this chapter.

micro analysis reveals that a business-as-usual approach to liberalization—one that excludes sensitive products and results in more limited reductions in trade barriers—may not help the poor much. Indeed, many poor households may lose from such an approach. An ambitious approach to opening global market access is therefore important.

But whatever the outcome of global efforts to lower trade barriers, a poverty reduction perspective makes clear the need for complementary actions to improve the ability of households in low-income countries to benefit from trade opportunities. Such actions will have the largest impacts if they help households to move out of subsistence production and to improve their productivity. Such actions will generally require resources, motivating the call for additional "aid for trade" for poor countries. Aid for trade is an important complement to trade reforms and is a mechanism through which the international community can promote its espoused goal of greater policy coherence for development in poor countries.

The current approach used in the World Trade Organization (WTO)—and, before it, the General Agreement on Tariffs and Trade (GATT)—to promote development is significantly *incoherent*. Combining multilateral liberalization and discriminatory trade policies, it was introduced in the 1970s following high-income countries' agreement to grant developing economies preferential access to their markets under the Generalized System of Preferences (GSP). Since then, a large body of research has shown that discriminatory trade policies are not efficient at advancing development. Preferential access programs have been of limited use to many developing countries, in that they have not produced the desired export diversification. While a number of countries have benefited from such programs as a result of being granted quota rents on traditional commodities such as sugar and bananas, this arguably has worked against their export diversification. The plethora of preferential access programs has encouraged the proliferation of reciprocal trade agreements, further distorting world trade flows and moving the trading system away from nondiscrimination.[1]

Shifting away from preferential programs and toward a more efficient and effective development instrument—assistance to improve the competitiveness of firms and farmers—would improve policy coherence by marrying greater overall access to markets to an enhanced ability to exploit such access.[2]

Achieving deep global trade reforms would be first best for the world economy and be pro-poor. But to get there implies adjustment costs for industries that have been protected, and the prospect of such costs is a major impediment to liberalization. Negotiators and policymakers need to consider such losses explicitly, so that interest groups that expect to lose do not make liberalization impossible. This

---

1. See, for example, the survey of the literature and the readings in Hoekman and Özden (2007).
2. Hoekman and Prowse (2005a, 2005b).

suggests the need for both a broadly based approach to liberalization—one that spans many areas so as to create new opportunities for workers—and programs to facilitate adjustment: domestic or intranational aid for trade.

The coherence of the trading system with the development objectives and targets laid out in the Millennium Development Goals (MDGs) would be further enhanced if WTO members were also to modify their negotiating approach, recognizing that agreements need to be seen as in the interest of developing countries.

To sum up, new approaches are needed to "special and differential treatment" (SDT) for developing countries. The current approach, which revolves around exceptions from WTO rules, has not been very effective in promoting development. Instead, the focus should be on helping governments to use more effective and less costly instruments to pursue development goals. These ideas are elaborated briefly in this concluding chapter. The first section discusses the political economy barriers to achieving the type of deep multilateral reforms that the previous chapters suggest will maximize the benefits for poor households. The second discusses how complementary reforms could be supported through greater aid for trade and how such aid might be allocated and managed. The third section turns to WTO rules and processes and the need to install new mechanisms to ensure that these do more to support development. A final section concludes.

Achieving Agreement on Liberalization

One reason why the potential gains from trade liberalization are difficult to achieve is that liberalization will generate losses for protected industries and factors of production. For affected producers and workers, there is nothing special about the effects of trade policy reforms: changes in technology and consumer tastes can impose very similar costs (or gains). But because changes in policy entail clear government decisions, the projected costs of adjusting to trade policy reforms can impede the realization of a more liberal and open trade regime. To achieve an ambitious round of trade liberalization that benefits both developing and high-income countries, domestic adjustment costs must be openly recognized and explicitly addressed. In principle, the resources for adjustment can easily be mobilized, given that an ambitious opening of markets will generate global gains that far exceed the losses. But instruments are needed that redistribute part of the gains to groups that will lose.

Compensating losers in the Organization for Economic Cooperation and Development (OECD) countries, which are still the most important markets for developing country exporters, may well be a precondition for achieving an ambitious outcome from the Doha Round. As Verdier notes, there are "pains from trade," and the distributive dimensions of trade integration must be taken into account.[3] Although aggregate gains will exceed losses, so that in principle the winners can compensate the losers while still remaining better off, in practice losers often are not compensated. One reason for this is that compensation is difficult to implement: governments may not have the instruments needed. Verdier notes that trade integration can be expected to affect the redistributive capacity of governments in several ways. From an economic perspective, integration may change the structural parameters of the economy (such as price elasticities and the tax base), rendering domestic redistribution more or less difficult. From a political perspective, it may affect the pattern of political power and coalitions, preventing or promoting compensation through the redistribution of resources inside the economy. Therefore, the capacity and willingness for domestic redistribution and compensation cannot be analyzed separately from the decision to open the country to trade and foreign direct investment.

Verdier's analysis suggests that policymakers may need to provide insurance mechanisms in order to secure national welfare gains. Options include lumpsum, one-off payments and mechanisms that insure against declines in the value of key assets, such as land values that form the basis of local tax revenues in rural communities and educational and training programs that enhance workers' skills.[4] The use of such instruments should not involve manipulation of relative factor and goods prices. Unfortunately, this condition is often violated, reducing the gains from trade liberalization and enhancing the capacity of industries to (re)forge protectionist coalitions. Given that the aggregate gains from freeing trade exceed the aggregate losses, in principle the resources for insurance mechanisms will be generated by the trade reforms. In the case of developing countries, there is an obvious link to be made with development assistance for additional (co)funding of such programs.

Trade Policy Reform: Gradualism, Safeguards, and Reciprocity

The traditional approach in trade agreements to building the needed support for trade reform is to implement liberalization gradually over a number of years, create instruments that industries can use to petition for reimposition of protection, and use issue linkages in the negotiating process so as to enhance the opportunities for creating new jobs in export-oriented or supplying sectors.

Gradualism attenuates the period-by-period adjustment costs for groups that benefit from protection and the potential revenue losses that may accompany deep liberalization. While gradual implementation has a clear rationale, reforms need to be sequenced to ensure that the goal of facilitating adjustment is achieved;

---

3. Verdier (2005). The term "pains from trade" is from Sapir (2000).

4. See Aksoy and Beghin (2005) for discussions of such programs and options in the context of agriculture in OECD countries.

the risk is that the implementation path may create perverse incentives and slow down the needed adjustment rather than encourage it.

An important example is the transition path that was negotiated in the Uruguay Round for eliminating quotas on trade in textiles and clothing. This is analyzed by François and Woertz, who calculate the bilateral ad valorem equivalent export taxes implied by the textile and clothing quotas and evaluate how these implicit taxes changed over the ten-year implementation period (1995–2004).[5] They show that in some importing countries—Canada among them—export tax equivalents fell steadily throughout the period, implying that domestic industry felt steady pressure to adjust. By contrast, in the European Union, about half of the reduction in the tax was left until the end of the period, and in the United States no liberalization at all had occurred with respect to imports from China and India as of 2004; as a result, the adjustment was left to the end, helping to explain the problems observed in 2005 in removing quotas completely.

In addition to gradualism, instruments of contingent protection (safety valves) have historically played an important role in building and maintaining political support for liberalization. The various safeguard mechanisms found in most trade agreements, including Article XIX of GATT, the Agreement on Safeguards, and the Agreement on Antidumping—offer some comfort to import-competing interests and facilitate broader trade liberalization.

It is sometimes argued that contingent protection instruments can be important vehicles for allowing the use of more general trade policy reforms and liberalization and thus that the net effect of their existence and use may be positive.[6] However, this does not mean that these instruments are the most efficient means of supporting a liberalization process. One reason for this is that they do little to encourage adjustment and, in the case of antidumping especially, they create incentives to *avoid* adjustment, thereby imposing an externality on exporters. The use of such instruments has grown significantly in recent years: between 1995 and 2004, WTO members initiated some 2,500 antidumping cases, and the use of safeguard actions, too, has expanded significantly since the WTO was created.

As Bown and McCulloch argue, rather than relying on a multiplicity of safeguards in the WTO (including antidumping measures), a shift should be considered to promote the (temporary) use of subsidies that are conditional on, or promote, adjustment.[7] Possibly such subsidies could be financed from current tariff revenues. Such a shift in approach may require the WTO rules on subsidies to be adjusted accordingly. These recommendations go in the direction of what

5. François and Woertz (2005).

6. See, for example, Nelson (2005) for a review of the literature, and Finger and Nogues (2006) for case study examinations of a number of Latin American countries.

7. Bown and McCulloch (2005).

Richardson calls "opportunity nets"—the adoption of active policies that protect the asset base of workers and communities.[8]

Gradualism and contingent protection are almost universal in the context of
trade agreements and are essentially defensive dimensions of trade policy reform
strategies. The proactive dimension revolves around the creation of new opportunities through the quid pro quo aspects of trade negotiations. Reciprocity,
reflected in cross-issue linkages and package deals, is a key element of the WTO
process. Large rounds of negotiation with a complex agenda are driven by the
need to create a negotiating set that is large enough to offer the prospects of net
gains for all members.

The literature has given much attention to the need for, and benefits of,
reforms in agricultural trade policies and better access to markets for goods.
Agricultural trade policies are an area where OECD countries need to make
concessions, while better market access is key for expanding both North-South
and South-South trade (trade barriers against manufactures are much higher
in developing countries than in developed). Both dimensions of market access
are important, not least because own liberalization by developing countries
will be beneficial to consumers and help to improve the allocation of resources.
The practical question is whether deep reforms can be realized through trade-
offs in these two areas. Arguably the answer is no. This helps to explain the efforts
by the European Union to expand the agenda to issues such as competition,
investment, and procurement policies.

The WTO is driven by mercantilism: the desire by members to improve their
terms of trade through better access to the markets of other members. The focus
is not on the welfare or growth prospects of members or on the identification of
"good" policy; rather it is on the spillovers that national policies impose on others.
Given that most of the developing country markets are small and not that
"interesting" from a mercantilist perspective, these countries have little negotiating leverage in the WTO. This lack of leverage was one factor underpinning the
creation of the system of trade preferences, as it implied that most of the benefits
of membership in the GATT or WTO for small, poor countries would be generated by the most favored nation principle—that is, through extension of what
is negotiated between the larger players to smaller countries.

A major problem with the limited ability to engage in reciprocity is that it
makes agreements less credible, even if countries engage in the process. This is
because, if a developing country is (very) small, there will be weak enforcement
incentives. Given that enforcement is based on affected (foreign) exporters' lob-
bying their governments to bring a case to the WTO, if the market in which a
perceived violation of a commitment occurs is small, the costs of enforcement
may exceed the expected benefits. This, in turn, has implications for the validity

8. Richardson (2005).

of some of the theoretical arguments that have been proposed to motivate the formation of trade agreements (and membership in the WTO). These either stress terms-of-trade arguments, the assumption being that countries negotiate away the negative terms-of-trade externalities that are created by the use of trade policies by the partner country (or countries) or, alternatively, stress the potential for trade agreements to act as lock-in mechanisms or anchors for domestic trade and related policy reforms, thereby making them more credible. The latter rationale is much more relevant for small or poor countries given the limited scope for such countries to affect their terms of trade. However, if agreements are unlikely to be enforced in practice because they do not create adequate incentives for foreign exporters to invest in enforcement, the political economy explanation for cooperation breaks down, and commitments will not be credible. This insight suggests that trade agreements can be useful focal points for reforms, but that domestic "ownership" will be particularly important in their sustained implementation. Insofar as the traditional mechanisms of reciprocal exchange and international enforcement through WTO dispute settlement mechanisms are ineffective, greater weight and attention need to be given to other ways of holding governments accountable for implementation of commitments.[9] This could include more effective transparency mechanisms.

Importance of Reforming Trade in Services

Particularly important from the perspective of the complementary agenda identified in the foregoing chapters is liberalization in the service sector. Services such as finance, telecommunications, and transport are major inputs into the production of goods—agricultural as well as manufactured—and other services. The costs of these inputs can make up a substantial share of the total cost of production, thus affecting the competitiveness of firms and farmers. Services are also important determinants of the productivity of workers in all sectors: education, training, and health services make key contributions to the formation and maintenance of human capital. Thus actions to enhance the efficiency of the service sector, through improving quality and lowering costs, can do much to enhance the ability of households and firms to exploit trade opportunities and to increase economic growth.

Recent research has found evidence for the role of services and services policy reforms as a determinant of growth performance in developing and transition economies. Mattoo and others find a statistically significant relationship, for a large cross-section of countries, between economic growth and reforms in finance and telecommunications that open markets to foreign competition.[10] Eschenbach and Hoekman use time-series data on services policy reforms by

9. Bown and Hoekman (2007).
10. Mattoo, Rathindran, and Subramanian (2006).

transition countries over the period 1990–2004 and find that policy reforms in financial and infrastructure services, including telecommunications, power, and transport, are highly correlated with inward flows of foreign direct investment.[11] Controlling for regressors commonly used in the growth literature, these authors find that measures of services policy reform are statistically significant explanatory variables for the post-1990 economic performance of transition economies.

Some services are the vehicle through which goods and other services are transported and delivered to consumers. Recent research has stressed the importance of transport costs and the links between such costs and the geography of production and trade. François and Wooton examine the interaction between trade in goods and the degree of market power exercised by the domestic trade and distribution sectors, which they call "margin" sectors.[12] They note that an imperfectly competitive domestic service sector can effectively discourage imports, so that the benefits of liberalization of trade in goods may not accrue to consumers but instead be captured in higher profits for distributors. Econometric analysis of the import patterns of twenty-two OECD countries vis-à-vis sixty-nine trading partners supports this prediction: François and Wooton find a statistically significant link between effective market access for goods and the structure of the service sector. They also find that competition in margin sectors matters more for poorer and small exporters.[13]

The findings of the papers just mentioned suggest that a comprehensive "behind-the-border" policy reform agenda that focuses on enhancing competition in service industries can help to boost goods trade and attract much-needed investment, both domestic and foreign. The Doha Round offers an immediate opportunity to pursue further liberalization of the service sector. This is especially important for countries that have no prospect of accession to a major North-South preferential trade agreement that includes services.

Eschenbach and Hoekman reveal that even far-reaching commitments on services in the WTO are not a panacea; what matters is implementation.[14] They find no robust empirical relationship between the extent and depth of commitments made by transition countries in the General Agreement on Trade in Services (GATS) and the actual services policies that these countries pursue. Some of the countries that have made the deepest commitments in the GATS score the lowest on various indicators of services policy reform.

11. Eschenbach and Hoekman (2006b).
12. François and Wooton (2005).
13. This is consistent with the conclusions of research that investigates the incidence of the rents created by preferential market access programs. Thus Özden and Sharma (2006) and Olarreaga and Özden (2005) find that small, poor countries obtain a smaller share of the rents created by preferential access than do larger, richer developing countries.
14. Eschenbach and Hoekman (2006a).

This conclusion again points to the fact that liberalization commitments in the WTO may not be sufficient to assure greater participation by foreign providers of services in domestic markets. One reason for this is the relative weakness of the WTO's monitoring of policies, combined with the fact that many of the markets concerned are so small that foreign providers would not find it worthwhile to use dispute settlement procedures in cases of noncompliance. Another reason may be that services and service markets are often affected by asymmetric information or high fixed costs and associated barriers to entry, so that effective regulation and regulatory supervision of both domestic and foreign operators are needed to ensure that markets are, in fact, contestable. Liberalization programs for trade in services therefore need to be accompanied by domestic policy efforts to install the needed complementary regulatory framework as well as by international assistance to support such efforts.

Development and Trade Agreements: Aid for Trade

As discussed in previous chapters, although there are certainly gains to be had from further trade liberalization, the main need in many developing countries is to bolster trade capacity and enhance competitiveness. This agenda spans many possible areas. A large number of these are services related, such as efforts to lower the cost of, and increase access to, energy, transport, finance, communications, and so on. This, in turn, requires a mix of policy reforms such as greater competition in service markets, along with investments in infrastructure, training, and institutional development.

The G-8 heads of government took an important first step in 2005 toward mobilizing additional resources to address such needs and bolster trade capacity, when they committed themselves to increase aid to build the capacity of developing countries to trade.[15] A few months later, at the September 2005 International Monetary Fund (IMF) and World Bank annual meetings, ministers agreed on the need to expand aid for trade. Prospects for mobilizing the needed assistance increased with the support expressed for allocating additional aid to support trade capacity at the 2005 Hong Kong ministerial meeting of the WTO. That meeting called for establishing a task force on aid for trade to recommend how to operationalize this agenda. In its report, the task force calls for actions to better define demand and ensure a greater supply of assistance as well as for regular monitoring of the development assistance in the trade area that members provide to developing countries.[16]

15. See G-8 Gleneagles 2005, Africa text: para. 22(a), available at www.fco.gov.uk/Files/kfile/PostG8_Gleneagles_Africa,0.pdf [February 2006].
16. WTO (2006).

Many questions will need to be addressed in operationalizing additional assistance, including how such resources should be managed and allocated and what the role of the WTO should be. The basic principles that should be satisfied by an aid-for-trade integration mechanism are simple: support should take the form of grants, be credible and predictable, cover more countries than just the least developed, be based on a process of identification of needs for trade capacity that is truly country driven and country owned, and have its processes and outcomes independently monitored.[17]

Particularly important is the credibility and predictability of funding. Experience shows the need for a mechanism that is dedicated to identifying and addressing the constraints on a nation's trade competitiveness, augmenting the gains from global trade reforms, and helping to offset the adjustment costs of reform.[18]

The elements of such a mechanism have been created recently in the form of the Integrated Framework for Trade-Related Technical Assistance for least developed countries (box 10-1). The Integrated Framework is based on a diagnostic assessment of a country's trade-related constraints and priorities, which in most cases is discussed at the consultative group meetings and roundtables associated with the poverty reduction strategy paper process. While the Integrated Framework reduces the duplication and proliferation of trade initiatives and helps to ensure that assistance is provided according to the needs identified by the country, it does not guarantee that trade needs will be financed.

Various options can be considered for moving forward on aid for trade. One that was agreed in 2006 is to bolster the capacity of the Integrated Framework to engage on trade issues at the national level and to follow up on the action plans that emerge from countries' diagnostic trade integration studies. A task force report on enhancing the Integrated Framework proposed to augment the mechanism with a dedicated fund of some $400 million to help achieve this. These additional resources would assist the least developed countries to develop and implement trade and competitiveness strategies. They would also help to ensure better follow-up by aid donors in providing assistance to countries to implement their strategies. However, there would be no guarantee that, once projects and priorities have been identified, the financial resources needed for larger trade-related investments would be made available. This will depend on the relative priority of the trade agenda in a country's overall development strategy.

One way to reduce the perceived uncertainty of obtaining financing once countries have identified trade projects and programs as priorities is to establish

17. Zedillo and others (2005). Prowse (2006) provides an in-depth discussion on aid-for-trade options and issues.
18. Prowse (2006).

Box 10-1. *The Integrated Framework for Trade-Related Technical Assistance*

The Integrated Framework brings together six multilateral agencies—the IMF, the International Trade Center (ITC), UNCTAD, United Nations Development Program (UNDP), the WTO, and the World Bank. It has two basic purposes: to help least developed countries define a trade agenda by identifying and prioritizing a set of trade-related adjustment and capacity-building needs and associated complementary reforms and to provide support to embed the resulting trade agenda into a country's overall development strategy (usually the poverty reduction strategy) so as to assist the country concerned with obtaining financing for needed investments from donors and international institutions.

The majority of least developed countries (more than forty) have applied for assistance under the scheme. As of 2006, there were seventeen bilateral donors, including Canada, the European Union, Japan, and the United States. A small trust fund finances the national trade assessments (diagnostics) and provides for small-scale technical assistance arising from the action matrixes identified in the assessments. Currently, a small secretariat located at the WTO handles paper flow, and UNDP manages the trust fund.

The first step is for the country to conduct a diagnostic trade integration study, usually in partnership with the IMF, the World Bank, and UNDP. Such a study looks at a range of issues, including the link between trade reform and poverty, the need for additional fiscal measures, likely social adjustment costs, and other complementary behind-the-border policy reforms. It also identifies a prioritized list of trade-related capacity-building needs—many of which concern trade-related infrastructure, trade facilitation, standards, and social costs—that are linked to the country's overall development strategy.

In most cases, the prioritized trade capacity-building plans are presented at the consultative group meetings and roundtables associated with the poverty reduction strategy paper process, where donors make pledges.

Source: Prowse (2006). See also www.integratedframework.org (February 2007).

---

a mechanism under which donors set aside an amount of resources to support trade-related public investments. This could take the form of a multilateral aid-for-trade fund or be provided through bilateral arrangements. A dedicated fund for adjustment assistance and infrastructure related to trade was proposed as an option during a Geneva-based consultation process held in mid-2005.[19] Such proposals are controversial, in that earmarking of funds can be inconsistent with achieving aid-effectiveness objectives insofar as the activities for which funding is earmarked may not be a priority in individual countries. However, the creation of a mechanism that earmarks an overall amount for trade does not imply that countries must identify trade as a priority; it simply provides greater assurance

---

19. See the annex to IMF and World Bank (2005).

to countries that, if they decide that trade projects are a priority, development assistance will be available.

Several proposals have suggested earmarking funds for specific trade-related purposes. For example, the IMF and World Bank argue that existing mechanisms to address regional cooperation are inadequate, resulting in the underprovision of financing and assistance for multicountry trade-related projects.[20] Existing support mechanisms, including the Integrated Framework, center on countries. For many developing countries (not only the least developed), regional cooperation is an important matter. Such integration is also high on the agenda of the European Union and the United States, which are increasingly negotiating reciprocal free trade agreements with developing countries. The European Union sees these agreements as instruments to encourage the formation of economic integration arrangements among subsets of African, Caribbean, and Pacific countries.

Other motivations for mobilizing dedicated funding mechanisms include addressing preference erosion, lowering the adjustment costs of trade reforms, and advancing the trade facilitation agenda.[21] Such needs can, in principle, be met through existing instruments such as the European Development Fund, the Integrated Framework, and the existing facilities of international agencies.[22] However, many developing countries argue that, in practice, existing mechanisms may not be able to address these issues as a result of the way they are designed and the types of instruments that they use.

While it is important that possible aid-for-trade mechanisms not involve replication of the types of governance and oversight processes that have already been established by the governing bodies of the IMF and the World Bank, insofar as specific funding for trade is seen to be important for the WTO to make progress on market access and rule making, there is a case for dedicated funding to help deliver on the global trade liberalization agenda.[23] This need not be a long-term measure, and it need not apply to all donor countries. At the time of writing, it seems unlikely that a stand-alone aid-for-trade mechanism will be created. However, arguably of greater importance is the willingness of donor countries to provide such aid and the recognition that this is needed to comple-

20. IMF and World Bank (2006).
21. Page and Kleen (2005); Grynberg and Silva (2004).
22. For African, Caribbean, and Pacific countries, the Ninth European Development Fund was to provide a total of €20 billion through 2007. While this is intended for all types of development programs, the European Development Fund offers a potential vehicle through which to address specific trade-capacity concerns. Thus it could be an appropriate vehicle through which to address preference erosion, especially as such erosion will in large part be the direct consequence of policy reforms undertaken by the European Union (François, Hoekman, and Manchin 2006).
23. Zedillo and others (2005).

ment trade liberalization commitments and help poor countries to benefit more from trade opportunities.[24]

WTO Rules, Transparency, and Multilateral Monitoring

Much of what is discussed in the WTO under the heading of special and differential treatment and problems related to the implementation of negotiated commitments revolves around perceptions that the existing rules are not fully supportive of development. There is a case for proactive policies to address market failures, and trade policies are unlikely to be effective or appropriate for this purpose. But more efficient policy solutions may be subject to existing (or proposed) WTO disciplines, or national constraints may preclude their use (an example would be a government's limited financial ability to use subsidy instruments to address market failures). It may also be unclear what the appropriate policy is in a specific situation. All these considerations suggest a potential rationale for greater flexibility in the application of WTO disciplines and a need for greater efforts to monitor the use and effects of policy.

Policy Flexibility

In addition to trade preferences through the GSP, the traditional approach of the United Nations Conference on Trade and Development (UNCTAD), GATT, and WTO to special and differential treatment comprises limited reciprocity in trade negotiations and (temporary) exemptions from certain rules, conditional on a country's level of development. Whether such exemptions and limited reciprocity will be beneficial can only be determined by countries themselves, on the basis of country-specific analysis. What types of domestic policies might be most appropriate and effective may not be obvious, suggesting a case for flexibility in the application of rules to allow for experimentation and learning.[25]

There is a large literature on these issues, much of which is surveyed in Pack and Saggi.[26] These authors conclude that, given the intensifying world competition and the growing importance of extensive and complex supply networks, it is critical that policy not discriminate against foreign firms. Governments should seek to reduce transactions and operating costs, and seek to

---

24. Instead of explicit earmarking of funds for a "trade capacity fund," donors are making unilateral commitments to provide funding for trade needs. The proposal by the WTO aid-for-trade task force (WTO 2006) for multilateral monitoring of donor "performance"—the delivery of resources to fund the priority trade projects identified by developing countries—is then particularly important to provide information on activities at the country level.

25. Rodrik (2004).

26. Pack and Saggi (2006).

use domestic regulation and taxes or subsidies to encourage local learning and the use of appropriate technologies, as opposed to firm- or sector-specific interventions.

Pack and Saggi also stress that the case for using trade policy to compensate for market failures is very weak. Economic theory argues that, in the case of market failures, policy interventions should directly target the source of the failure. Trade policy will rarely do this. If trade policies are used, there is a clear efficiency ranking of trade policy instruments, with quotas and quota-like instruments being particularly costly. WTO rules that impose discipline on the use of such instruments will benefit consumers and exporters in developing countries and enhance global welfare. This implies that a good case can be made that the basic trade policy rules of the WTO make sense for all countries, both developed and developing.

The case is less clear for regulatory disciplines. Increasingly, high-income WTO members are seeking to harmonize their "behind the border" regulatory policies. Such a goal may not be optimal for many developing countries. The efforts made during the Doha Round to launch negotiations on the so-called Singapore issues—transparency in procurement, competition policy, investment policy, and trade facilitation—revealed how difficult it is to obtain a consensus on what and how to negotiate on such regulatory matters.

Various approaches can be envisaged to deal with differences in interests and uncertainty with respect to the expected payoffs of alternative regulatory disciplines. One is to build on the status quo—essentially, to allow for (and facilitate) opt-outs by developing countries. This has been the traditional approach toward "development" in the GATT and WTO, as reflected in special and differential treatment provisions and the Enabling Clause, which provided a variety of "holes and loopholes" for developing countries, implying less pressure to reciprocate in negotiations and more opportunities to (continue to) use trade policy instruments and discriminate among countries. These instruments can be complemented by requests for waivers on disciplines that are not covered by the provisions of special and differential treatment. The waiver mechanism has, in fact, been used—for example, for customs valuation—and may be an effective approach to implementation problems, although its outcomes are not certain and it involves negotiating costs.

A variant of the status quo espoused by Sutherland and others entails bolstering the "development dimension" of the trading system by moving toward greater use of multilateral agreements or positive list scheduling of the type used in the GATS to allow for differentiation across countries.[27] Another approach is to allow for opt-outs on the basis of explicit criteria (such as size) that determine the applicability of rules, rather than leave decisions to case-by-case negotiations.

27. Sutherland and others (2004).

Currently, the decision whether or not to self-declare as a developing country is left to individual WTO members, and developed country members then bargain as to whether to accept this designation and provide special and differential treatment. A major advantage of simple country criteria allowing more differentiation—if they could be agreed—is that they would do away with the need for such negotiation. The disadvantage is that criteria are inherently arbitrary and to date have been resisted by many WTO members.

None of these approaches does much to engage governments and help them to identify better policies or areas where complementary actions or investments are needed. Instead, the focus is purely legalistic (understandable given that the WTO is a legal instrument). The intent is to identify a mechanism that allows countries not to undertake investments or implement rules they do not wish to, while avoiding being threatened by dispute settlement proceedings and retaliation for noncompliance.

Core Disciplines

An alternative is to define (by negotiation) a set of "core" disciplines and to make these binding (directly enforceable). Hoekman argues that, from an economic perspective, these basic or core rules would span the most favored nation rule, the ban on quantitative restrictions, commitment to ceiling bindings for tariffs, engagement in the process of reciprocal trade liberalization, and transparency of policy.[28] Currently under the WTO, none of these core rules applies equally to all members. This is partly because of SDT provisions and the enabling clause, which calls for reciprocity in negotiating rounds by developing countries to be limited to what is "consistent with development needs," and more generally because everything is negotiated, so that for every rule there are exceptions.[29]

Given agreement on a set of core principles, countries would be permitted not to implement non-core WTO rules on development grounds. In effect, they would be able to invoke a "development defense" if dispute settlement cases were brought, through agreement that there would be a "circuit breaker" in such instances, involving multilateral consultations with representatives of the trade (WTO) and development (donors, financial institutions) communities on the effectiveness and impacts of the policies concerned. The focus of these interactions would be to help governments to achieve their goals through the use of instruments, including development assistance, that are more efficient than trade policy, if these can be identified.

This more active approach does not imply ceasing to negotiate binding disciplines. In cases where there are significant negative spillovers on another

---

28. Hoekman (2005a, 2005b).

29. These exceptions extend to industrial countries as well (for example, in agriculture, where members have been permitted to impose high tariffs and apply special safeguards).

developing country, for example, these should be identified, and recourse to the dispute settlement mechanism should be allowed. Focusing on a country's identification and pursuit of a national trade agenda and priorities and linking this to the proposed aid-for-trade integration program could help to reduce a government's perceived need to use costly trade policy tools. The monitoring mechanisms would also help to place the implementation of WTO disciplines in a national context and increase information on the effects of the applied trade and related policies.

The idea here is not to make the WTO a development organization. That would not be a desirable goal. Instead, the goal is to put in place a mechanism to support greater integration of developing countries into the WTO and to increase the coherence and transparency of policies that are pursued by developing countries. WTO membership is a binding contract. This gives the WTO its value—traders have greater certainty regarding policy, and governments know what is entailed when they make commitments. Allowing for policy flexibility will increase uncertainty and could reduce the willingness of major trading countries to make commitments in the first place. But agreement that a core set of WTO disciplines would be binding on *all* members should help to address this concern.

The proposed core WTO principles are based on economic principles—they are desirable from an efficiency perspective and would benefit all countries no matter what the level of development. This implies a tension with the current approach in WTO, which is a legal treaty. It is important to note that currently there are no general, unconditionally binding rules in the GATT and WTO; that is, there is no core set of agreed rules; rather, as mentioned, for every rule there is a (negotiated) exception or set of exceptions. Thus SDT is a "normal" aspect of the rules-based trading system, one that supplements the option to rewrite (renegotiate) the rules. Even from the perspective that the WTO is a rules-based system, the proposed policy flexibility mechanism is therefore not inconsistent with the modus operandi of the WTO.

As discussed at greater length in Hoekman, the advantages of the proposed approach are that it would:[30]

—Bolster the engagement with developing country governments on their policies, complementing the WTO trade policy review mechanism (which is arguably underused, in part because the WTO Secretariat is constrained in forming judgments regarding the consistency of observed policies with the WTO or their impacts within and across countries),

—Generate assessments of whether instruments are achieving development objectives,

—Allow discussion or identification of less trade-distorting instruments,

---

30. Hoekman (2005a, 2005b).

—Permit inputs from development institutions that have the experience, local presence, and capacity to provide both policy advice and financial resources (the WTO should not move into project design and financing) and help to improve communication between the development and trade communities, identifying where development organizations should help and where WTO disciplines may be inappropriate.

The proposed approach would also allow countries to consider explicitly and use proactive policies, including "industrial policies," while helping to prevent the downsides of such policies (capture and rent seeking). As discussed in Pack and Saggi, experience shows that it is very difficult in practice to identify the market failures that could justify intervention.[31] This makes the surveillance and monitoring mechanisms particularly important and a valuable element of multilateral cooperation.

The proposed approach complements the one that has greatest support in the current negotiations: an agreement-specific approach involving the ex ante setting of specific criteria to determine whether countries could opt out of the application of negotiated disciplines. Thus negotiators' primary concern is with the details of opt-outs from rules and exemptions from specific agreements. An example is the Doha Round proposal that developing countries be permitted to designate special products and use special safeguard procedures for agricultural products. This approach requires poor countries to determine on an issue-by-issue basis the specific provisions that would be beneficial. What these provisions are may not be clear, and the ability to get agreement from developed countries on such proposals is constrained by the mercantilist calculus—the perceived cost to them of a proposal—rather than by whether the proposal makes development sense. Nonetheless, clearly the agreement- or rule-specific approach also has significant potential to enhance the development relevance of the WTO.

To sum up, focusing on a country's identification and pursuit of a national trade agenda and priorities and linking this to the proposed aid-for-trade integration program could help to reduce a government's perceived need to use costly trade policy tools. The monitoring mechanisms would also help to place the implementation of WTO disciplines in a national context and make information available on the effects of the applied trade and related policies.

Transparency and Analysis of Policies

Improved transparency and analysis of policies and their impacts are key inputs into a better, more developmentally relevant, trading system. Monitoring and constructive engagement under the policy flexibility heading require data. The same is true if developing countries are to enforce their rights through dispute settlement. This suggests that any significant expansion of aid for trade should,

31. Pack and Saggi (2006).

in part, be allocated toward the public good of information. Relevant information is grossly underprovided by the multilateral trading system. This is a major weakness that substantially reduces the system's value from a development perspective.

Despite the existence of the WTO and numerous international organizations that analyze trade flows and policies, very large data gaps remain on the policy barriers to international integration. Even in the area where the information is best—barriers to goods trade—the focus of data collection (and thus analysis) is mostly on statutory most favored nation tariffs and explicit quantitative restrictions on imports or exports. Data and measures of the types of nontariff policy barriers that are increasingly used, such as antidumping and safeguard actions and excessively burdensome product standards, are not collected on a comprehensive and regular basis by the WTO or other organizations. Data gaps are much worse when it comes to policies affecting services trade, foreign investment, and the movement of people. Services now account for more than 40 percent of international transactions, although data limitations imply that there is substantial uncertainty on the real size of the flow. Even less is known about the origins and destinations of services trade and investment flows and the policies that affect them.

Lack of data has made it difficult to examine the relationship between policies and performance and to identify priorities for domestic reform and international cooperation in key areas such as services. Better data on underlying policies are a precondition for better policy advice and understanding of the process of globalization. Better data are also needed for the more pedestrian, but critically important, task of policy monitoring. This is especially relevant in light of the global commitment to take action to attain the Millennium Development Goals. Monitoring of progress and documentation of government policies in both North and South in the pursuit of the MDGs must include trade-related policies. The large gaps in our information on policies affecting international integration impede comparisons of country performance and assessments of the direction and magnitude of policy changes on an annual basis.

An effort to remedy these gaps is urgently needed. Commissioning a group of experts to develop a practical methodology (index) for descriptive and monitoring purposes and to define what specific types of data are needed for the methodology would be a first concrete step to move forward on this agenda. The goal of this first step would be to improve quantification of the impact of policies and to identify what the set of inputs should look like, what policies to focus on, and how to feed information on the existence and enforcement of these policies into the quantitative methodology.

To result in a durable policy-tracking mechanism, this effort will need to be anchored in an organization with a clear mandate for its success and a willingness to provide funding for it and be accountable for results. Given the importance of local information, independence, and objectivity, the recurring effort to update regularly the initial database needs to rely on local expertise. But the central organization should ensure timely delivery of data, quality control, and administration (including provision of funds and exercise of due diligence).

The WTO Secretariat is an obvious candidate to take on the task of compiling comprehensive data on trade policies—going beyond applied and bound tariffs to include bilateral preferences; nontariff measures (antidumping, subsidies, standards, rules of origin); services and investment policies; and data on bilateral flows of services trade, foreign direct investment, and sales by foreign affiliates. However, two critical preconditions need to be satisfied, both of which will require WTO members to have political will and high-level commitment. First, members must grant the secretariat the full independence—as well as the resources—needed to do the job. Second, the data must be made completely public, meaning accessible free of charge on the Internet in a format that is both informative and lends itself to analysis. The experience to date in this regard is not very good. WTO members historically have made their trade-related data accessible only to governments. While much has been done to improve access and transparency through the Internet, notifications are often not user friendly, and internal efforts by the secretariat to collate data into usable formats have not been made public.

Concluding Remarks

While arguments over the direction of causality continue, most observers agree that economic growth (development) and trade expansion (imports and exports) are strongly associated. The WTO promotes trade and, in that sense, is pro-development. However, despite the boom in world trade that has occurred in recent decades, in part under the stewardship of the GATT and WTO, the institution has become a focal point for controversy. Concerns about the WTO vary, with some critics in OECD countries being concerned about loss of sovereignty and others worried that the trade system has become "too legalistic." But the largest group of critics are worried about the impact of the WTO on the economic development prospects of poor countries.[32]

From a development perspective—the one taken in this volume—deep global trade policy reforms will be beneficial, especially if complemented by domestic actions to reduce transactions and operating costs, and these actions are supported with development assistance: aid for trade. The challenge for small or poor countries is how to get the large players that impose the most serious global distortions to remove their detrimental policies (that is, how to achieve an ambitious outcome from the Doha Round), to agree to multilateral rules and procedures that will promote development, and to deliver additional aid for trade.

32. See, for example, Rodrik (2001); Oxfam (2002).

Any solution to this challenge arguably calls for involving a wider set of actors in the WTO. Trade negotiators represent export interests, and on their own these interests are unlikely to generate the political support needed for outcomes that have the best impact on development. One desirable addition might be representatives of the development community, broadly defined. Given that aid is a mechanism through which the international community can enhance the overall coherence of policy interventions and that aid resources are not under the direct control of trade negotiators, more active engagement by development interests in the trade agenda and closer integration of the trade and aid agendas could help to ensure that national trade priorities are addressed and that proposed and actual trade rules help rather than hinder economic growth prospects.

References

Aksoy, Ataman, and John Beghin, eds. 2005. *Global Agricultural Trade and Developing Countries.* Washington: World Bank.

Bown, Chad P., and Bernard Hoekman. 2007. "Making Trade Agreements Relevant for Poor Countries: Why Dispute Settlement Is Not Enough." Brookings Institution Working Paper 2007-05. Brookings, February.

Bown, Chad, and Rachel McCulloch. 2005. "Facilitating Adjustment to Trade in the WTO System." Yale University, Yale Center for the Study of Globalization.

Eschenbach, Felix, and Bernard Hoekman. 2006a. "Services Policies in Transition Economies: On the EU and WTO as Commitment Mechanisms." *World Trade Review* 5, no. 3: 415–43.

———. 2006b. "Services Policy Reform and Economic Growth in Transition Economies, 1990–2004." *Review of World Economics* 142, no. 4: 746–64.

Finger, J. Michael, and Julio Nogues, eds. 2006. *Fighting Fire with Fire: Safeguards and Antidumping in Latin American Trade Liberalization.* London: Palgrave Macmillan and World Bank.

François, Joseph, Bernard Hoekman, and Miriam Manchin. 2006. "Quantifying the Magnitude of Preference Erosion due to Multilateral Trade Liberalization." *World Bank Economic Review* 20, no. 2: 197–216.

François, Joseph, and Julia Woertz. 2005. "Rags in the High Rent District: Rhetoric and Reality in the Elimination of Textile and Clothing Quotas." Yale University, Yale Center for the Study of Globalization.

François, Joseph, and Ian Wooton. 2005. "Market Structure in Services and Market Access in Goods." Yale University, Yale Center for the Study of Globalization.

Grynberg, Roman, and Sacha Silva. 2004. "Preference-Dependent Economies and Multilateral Liberalization: Impacts and Options." London: Commonwealth Secretariat.

Hoekman, Bernard. 2005a. "Making the WTO More Supportive of Development." *Finance and Development* (March): 14–18.

———. 2005b. "Operationalizing the Concept of Policy Space in the WTO: Beyond Special and Differential Treatment." *Journal of International Economic Law* 8, no. 2: 405–28.

Hoekman, Bernard, and Caglar Özden, eds. 2007. *Trade Preferences and Differential Treatment of Developing Countries.* Cheltenham: Edward Elgar.

Hoekman, Bernard, and Susan Prowse. 2005a. "Development and the WTO: Beyond Business as Usual." *Bridges* 9, no. 2–3 (February–March).

————. 2005b. "Policy Responses to Preference Erosion: From Trade as Aid to Aid for Trade." Policy Research Paper 3721. Washington: World Bank.

IMF (International Monetary Fund) and World Bank. 2005. "Doha Development Round and Aid for Trade." Washington, September 12 (siteresources.worldbank.org/DEVCOMMINT/Documentation/20651864/DC2005-0016(E)-Trade.pdf [February 2007]).

————. 2006. "Doha Development Report and Aid for Trade." Washington, September 6 (siteresources.worldbank.org/DEVCOMMINT/Documentation/21046511/DC2006-0013(E)-Trade.pdf [February 2007]).

Mattoo, Aaditya, Randeep Rathindran, and Arvind Subramanian. 2006. "Measuring Services Trade Liberalization and Its Impact on Economic Growth: An Illustration." *Journal of Economic Integration* 21, no. 1: 64–98.

Nelson, Douglas R. 2005. "The Political Economy of Antidumping: A Survey." *European Journal of Political Economy* 22, no. 3 (September): 554–90.

Olarreaga, Marcelo, and Caglar Özden. 2005. "AGOA and Apparel: Who Captures the Tariff Rent in the Presence of Preferential Market Access?" *World Economy* 28, no. 1: 63–77.

Oxfam. 2002. *Rigged Rules and Double Standards: Trade, Globalization. and the Fight against Poverty.* Oxford.

Özden, Caglar, and Gunjan Sharma. 2006. "Price Effects of Preferential Market Access: Caribbean Basin Initiative and the Apparel Sector." *World Bank Economic Review* 20, no. 2: 241–60.

Pack, Howard, and Kamal Saggi. 2006. "Is There a Case for Industrial Policy? A Critical Survey." *World Bank Research Observer* 21, no. 2: 267–97.

Page, Sheila, and Peter Kleen. 2005. "Special and Differential Treatment of Developing Countries in the World Trade Organization." Global Development Studies 2. Sweden, Ministry of Foreign Affairs.

Prowse, Susan. 2006. "'Aid for Trade': Increasing Support for Trade Adjustment and Integration; A Proposal." In *Economic Development and Multilateral Cooperation,* edited by Simon Evenett and Bernard Hoekman. New York and Washington: Palgrave-Macmillan and World Bank.

Richardson, J. David. 2005. "Global Forces, American Faces: U.S. Economic Globalization at the Grass Roots." Mimeo. Washington: Institute for International Economics.

Rodrik, Dani. 2001. "The Global Governance of Trade as if Development Really Mattered." New York: United Nations Development Program.

————. 2004. *Industrial Policy for the Twenty-First Century.* CEPR Discussion Paper 4767. London: Centre for Economic Policy Research.

Sapir, Andre. 2000. "Who Is Afraid of Globalization? The Challenge of Domestic Adjustment in Europe and America." CEPR Discussion Paper 2595. London: Centre for Economic Policy Research.

Sutherland, Peter, and others. 2004. "The Future of the WTO: Addressing Institutional Challenges in the New Millennium." Geneva: World Trade Organization.

Verdier, Thierry. 2005. "Socially Responsible Trade Integration: A Political Economy Perspective." In *Are We on Track to Achieve the Millennium Development Goals?* edited by François Bourguignon, Boris Pleskovic, and Andre Sapir. Annual Bank Conference on Development Economics. Washington: World Bank.

WTO (World Trade Organization). 2006. "Recommendations of the Task Force on Aid for Trade." WT/AFT/1. Geneva, July 27.

Zedillo, Ernesto, and others. 2005. "Strengthening the Global Trade Architecture for Economic Development: An Agenda for Action." Yale University, Yale Center for the Study of Globalization.

Contributors

Jorge F. Balat
Yale University

Irene Brambilla
Yale University

Ania I. Gómez
Universidad de las Américas, Puebla

Bernard Hoekman
World Bank

Aylin Işık-Dikmelik
World Bank

Hiau Looi Kee
World Bank

Gabriel Lara
Universidad de las Américas, Puebla

Alessandro Nicita
World Bank

Marcelo Olarreaga
World Bank

Guido G. Porto
World Bank

Isidro Soloaga
Universidad de las Américas, Puebla

Ernesto Zedillo
Yale Center for the Study of Globalization

Index

249